# Economic Cycles: An Analysis of Underlying Causes

# Economic Cycles: An Analysis of Underlying Causes

Nathaniel J. Mass

**Wright-Allen Press, Inc.**
238 Main Street
Cambridge, Massachusetts 02142

Library of Congress catalog card number 75–10485

ISBN 0-914700-03-0

To my parents
Herbert and Cyrille Mass

# Foreword

The problem of economic fluctuation and instability is a matter of pressing public concern and remains the subject of widespread analysis. In the economic literature, the short-term business cycle of approximately four years' duration has been treated at length descriptively, in simple mathematical models, and, more recently, in econometric models of the economy. But such methods have proven inadequate for isolating the role of various elements of economic structure or for showing how management policies and technology generate the various modes of periodic behavior that have been observed. Because the short-term business cycle is more evident than longer-term fluctuations, almost all economic structure and policies have been associated descriptively with the business cycle. No clear distinctions have emerged to associate particular components of structure and policy with different periodicities of economic variation. Consequently, the business cycle has received disproportionate attention at the expense of other possible rhythms of activity such as the Kuznets cycle (a period of about eighteen years), the Kondratieff cycle (a period of some fifty years), or the life cycle of economic growth (extending over several hundred years).

In this book, Nathaniel Mass shows how employment and inventory policies relate to the short-term business cycle and how the acquisition of capital equipment, rather than contributing essentially to the short cycle, is a primary factor in generating longer-term cycles spanning fifteen to twenty years or more. These distinctions are of the greatest importance because successful governmental economic policies depend on a proper association of policy with economic consequence.

The predominant focus in economic research on short-term and equilibrium analysis has, to a large extent, prevented economists from recognizing that well-known policies and technological characteristics of business are capable of producing cyclic and transient behavior persisting over a long time span. This book by Mass should help in shifting attention from static and equilibrium analysis to the rich and diverse dynamics of change in our social and economic systems.

Jay W. Forrester

Massachusetts Institute of Technology
Cambridge, Massachusetts
July 10, 1975

# Preface

This book develops a sequence of system dynamics models to explore the basic factors underlying short-term and long-term cyclic instability in the economy. It overviews existing theories of economic cycles and provides a general framework for evaluating the impact of social and economic factors on economic cycles of various periodicities. The book has several objectives and corresponding audiences. First, it is intended to serve as a basic textbook introduction to business-cycle theory, showing how mathematical model building can be used to synthesize and clarify the diverse hypothesized causes of economic cycles. Toward this end, the book is designed to be self-contained, so that no previous background in social-systems modeling is required of the reader. As a second objective, the book attempts to analyze several substantive questions regarding the causes and the control of economic cycles. In particular, it investigates the prevalent supposition that fixed capital investment policies underlie the short-term business cycle and concludes that the principal causes of the short cycle are labor-acquisition and inventory- and backlog-management policies. Several implications of this result for business-cycle theory and economic stabilization policy are outlined in the text. As a final objective, the book attempts to outline a procedure for testing the importance of a specified variable in generating real-world behavior. This general procedure should be pertinent to social scientists confronted with the broad problem of synthesizing or choosing among alternative theories of the same social phenomena.

The research reported here is a substudy of the System Dynamics National Modeling Project at M.I.T. The broad objective of the National Modeling Project is to construct a large-scale socioeconomic model of the United States as a basis for increasing public understanding of, and designing policies to deal with, major national problems such as inflation, recession, and balance of payments. This book focuses on one area addressed by the National Model — the question of cyclic fluctuations in economic activity and economic stabilization — to present some of the insights in this area derived from the M.I.T. study of the dynamics of the national economy.

This work was originally written in partial fulfillment of the requirements for the degree of Doctor of Philosophy at the Alfred P. Sloan School of Management at the

Massachusetts Institute of Technology. Several people contributed to the progress of this research. First, I am indebted to Professor Jay W. Forrester, who served as chairman of my dissertation committee. Professor Forrester has been a continuous source of guidance and support during the past few years. By encouraging me to challenge fundamental assumptions of economic theory and methodology, he has contributed materially to my understanding of economic and social behavior. I am further indebted to the other members of my thesis committee — Professor Sidney S. Alexander and Professor Peter Lorange — for their advice regarding the substance and presentation of the thesis.

Several members of the M.I.T. System Dynamics Group also merit special thanks. In particular, Dr. Robert E. Sweeney read the entire book and made numerous helpful suggestions regarding the logic and structure of the argument. In addition, Peter M. Senge offered valuable technical and methodological criticisms that helped to synthesize the focus of several chapters. Diane K. Leonard expertly drew the figures for the text. Mark Tangard typed the final draft.

This research was supported under a grant provided by the Rockefeller Brothers Fund.

Nathaniel J. Mass

Massachusetts Institute of Technology
Cambridge, Massachusetts
July 10, 1975

# Contents

# 1
# Introduction

## 1.1 Background

This book develops a series of dynamic simulation models designed to explore and illuminate the economic processes underlying business-cycle behavior. Business cycles are recurring fluctuations in total production, wages, prices, employment, inventories, and capital investment. Such fluctuations have been observed and charted in the United States for over one hundred years. Arthur Burns notes that the average length of business cycles in the United States between 1854 and 1961 was forty-nine months.[1]

Figure 1–1 plots industrial activity between 1899 and 1960. Figure 1–1 A shows cycles in industrial activity of roughly four years' duration occurring around a long-term growth trend in output; Figure 1–1 B plots the same data, corrected for the growth trend, to illustrate the magnitude and periodicity of the cycles.

Historically, economists have devoted considerable attention to studying business-cycle behavior. As a product of their research, numerous business-cycle theories have been advanced, and a large volume of empirical information related to business cycles has accumulated.[2] Interest in business-cycle behavior initially grew out of the manifest inconsistency between the output and employment fluctuations characteristic of business cycles and the full-employment assumptions underlying classical economics, particularly Say's Law of markets.[3] In more recent years, business-cycle research has focused on explaining changes in aggregate production, consumption, and investment and on designing stabilization policies intended to restrain business-cycle contractions and to temper inflationary upswings.[4] A major objective of such policies,

[1]Burns (1969), p. 14. For a discussion of typical business-cycle behavior, see Evans (1969), pp. 416–428, and Gordon (1961), pp. 219–297.

[2]A survey of the principal business-cycle theories appears in Chapter 2.

[3]Sowell (1972) provides an excellent summary of the development of theoretical opposition to the assumptions of Say's Law.

[4]The term business cycles is here used in the broad sense of defining fluctuations in the national output of goods and services relative to potential output (the output of the economy when all factors of production are fully utilized). This definition may apply either to "classical" business cycles, in which output undergoes actual reduction, or to the "growth cycles" more recently experienced in the United States and characterized by alternate acceleration and retardation in the rate of growth of output and employment. For reference, see Gordon (1961), pp. 3–6, and the comment by Paul Samuelson in Zarnowitz (1972), pp. 175–176. Bronfenbrenner (1969) contains a good summary of recent international experiences with business cycles.

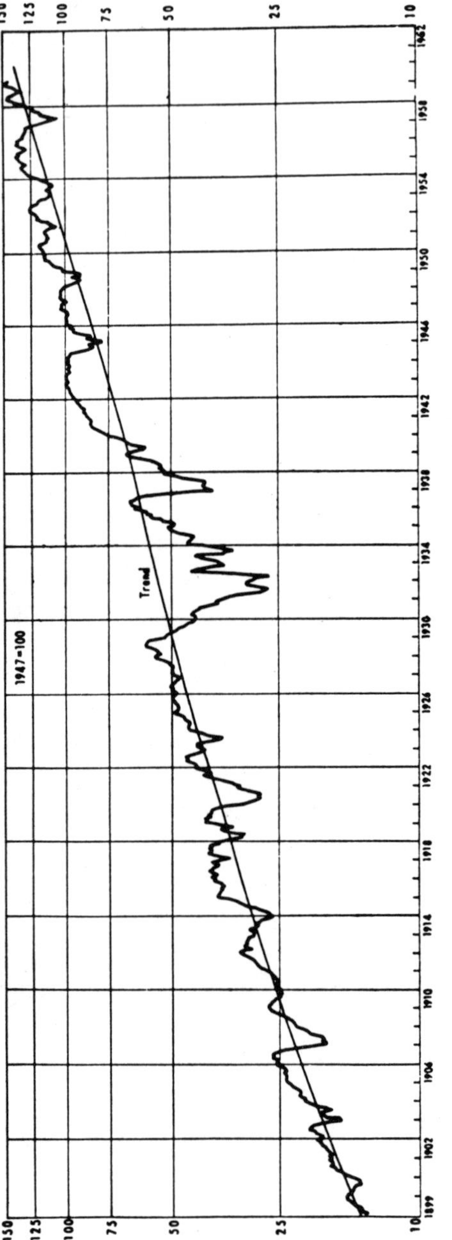


A. Index of industrial activity before correction for trend

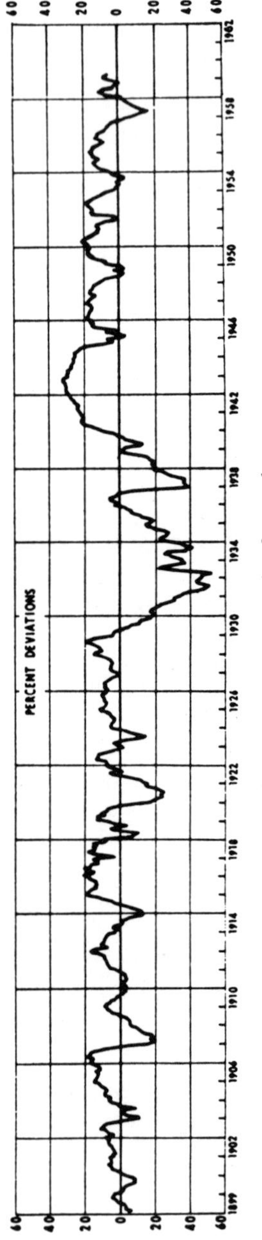


B. Index of industrial activity after correction for trend

**Figure 1-1** Business cycles in the United States, 1899–1960

Source: Gordon (1961), p. 255.

in accordance with the Federal Employment Act of 1946, has been to sustain high employment and reduce the variability of employment and income occasioned by business-cycle fluctuations.[5]

This book develops a general model of the production sector of the economy. The model interrelates inventories, backlogs, and employment and investment decisions to provide a deeper understanding of the factors underlying short-run (four-year) and intermediate-run (fifteen- to twenty-year) economic cycles. A better understanding on the part of decision makers of the causes of cyclic behavior is critical to the formulation of effective stabilization policies. To date, however, the proliferation of business-cycle theories, each emphasizing somewhat different causal factors, handicaps the policy maker or student of economic stabilization policy by cultivating a fragmentary view of the important interactions underlying economic cycles. As Haberler has observed, "the analysis of existing theories of the cycle has furnished a number of hypotheses. Few of these seem to be definitely wrong or a priori impossible. What is unsatisfactory, however, is the exclusiveness with which many writers proclaim one or other of these hypotheses as the only possible solution."[6] One objective of the present work, therefore, was to make a first effort to integrate the existing theories of the business cycle in a unified framework of analysis.

A related objective was to explore the dynamic implications of widely held business-cycle theories. Are the economic decisions embodied in established business-cycle theories actually major determinants of the four-year cycle? Within the basic production sector, it is possible to test the relative importance of specified processes or relationships in generating short-term cycles. An evaluation of business-cycle theories is carried out by isolating the central causal elements of each theory and incorporating those elements into the basic production sector. Through computer simulation of the resulting model, the relative validity and importance of each theory can be gauged. For example, suppose one wishes to test the importance of a particular relationship hypothesized to contribute to cyclic fluctuations. By simulating the sector before and after inclusion of the hypothesized relationship and comparing the simulations, it is possible to determine the *incremental effect* of that relationship on the periodicity and magnitude of production cycles.

To provide a concrete illustration of the theory-testing process, Chapters 3 through 5 analyze the role of labor-adjustment (hiring and termination) policies and capital-investment policies in generating short-term business cycles. As discussed in depth in section 2.2, a large number of business-cycle theories, including those of Paul A. Samuelson, John R. Hicks, and James S. Duesenberry, emphasize fluctuations in fixed capital investment as a cause of overall fluctuations in income and output. Such theories have been widely influential from a theoretical standpoint and have stimulated much subsequent business-cycle research. In addition, widespread acceptance of those theories has led to the formulation of economic stabilization policies designed to regulate investment expenditures. However, Chapters 4 and 5 suggest that economic

[5]Holt and Modigliani (1961) cite a related objective of stabilization policy: they argue that business fluctuations are costly to producers because of increased costs incurred for hiring, layoffs, and overtime.

[6]Haberler (1964), p. 361.

cycles induced by investment in fixed capital tend to be of much longer duration than typical four-year business cycles, given reasonable parameter values for the delays in planning, construction, and depreciation of capital equipment. Moreover, Chapter 3 indicates that business-cycle fluctuations can arise from production and employment policies independent of changes in capital stock. These observations, which suggest that investment in fixed capital cannot be an essential cause of business cycles, call for reassessing the basic economic processes assumed to underlie business fluctuations.

Section 1.2 expands upon the preceding comments and further details the objectives of the research described here. Section 1.3 provides an overview of Chapters 2 through 6.

## 1.2 Objectives and Methodology of the Research

A major objective of the research described in this book was to help isolate the factors involved in generating business cycles and longer-term fluctuations in capital stock and aggregate output. Arthur Burns has noted that most existing theories of the business cycle center on the determinants of fixed capital investment.[7] However, as Moses Abramovitz suggests, fixed capital is a highly durable factor of production characterized by delays of up to several years between the early consideration of an investment project and the subsequent completion of construction. According to Abramovitz, the long delays in capital acquisition and depreciation cast doubt on any role for investment in fixed capital as an integral factor in generating four-year business cycles.[8] On the other hand, he suggests that fluctuations in fixed capital investment may underlie the fifteen- to twenty-year fluctuations in the rate of growth of aggregate output and capital stock observed in many countries.

An investigation of the periodicities associated with different factors of production provides the principal focus of Chapters 2 through 5 of this book. A study of the economic fluctuations induced by different factor inputs is important from a policy standpoint because economic policies have differential effects on the rates of acquisition of the different factors. For example, monetary policies and investment tax credits principally attempt to regulate capital spending; on the other hand, many government expenditure and subsidy policies chiefly aim at direct control of the level of employment within the economy.

In principle, factors of production can be arranged in a continuum according to their longevities and their acquisition delays. However, in this book, labor and fixed capital are chosen as contrasting factors of production; labor is readily acquired and dismissed in countries such as the United States, while fixed capital equipment takes longer to plan and construct and is a durable asset lasting many years.[9]

The present work explores the causes of economic cycles of varying duration by developing a sequence of modifications to the basic production sector. The modifica-

[7] Burns (1969), pp. 10–11.

[8] See Abramovitz (1961).

[9] Other nations, such as Japan and some West European countries, maintain longer-term employer commitments to workers; for example, some nations are characterized by continually tight labor markets that do not permit rapid labor turnover in the form of frequent hiring and dismissal. Chapter 6 briefly discusses the impact of relative labor-market tightness and attitudes toward employment on economic stability.

tions incorporate different factors hypothesized to underlie economic cycles and, in particular, different combinations of factors of production. The subsequent analysis draws upon and provides a survey of major economic theories of the business cycle to illustrate the process of testing alternative economic theories through progressive model refinement and evaluation. Such a process can be applied fruitfully in any discipline when an investigator confronts several alternative explanations of the same phenomena.

Finally, the book illustrates the development of a dynamic theory of economic behavior,[10] which Ragnar Frisch has defined as a theory

> that explains how one situation grows out of the foregoing. In this type of analysis, we consider not only a set of magnitudes in a given point of time and study the interrelations between them, but we consider the magnitudes of certain variables in different points of time and we introduce certain equations which embrace at the same time several of these magnitudes belonging to different instants.[11]

As defined by Frisch, the dynamic theory contrasts with the static-equilibrium theory prevalent in economic literature. According to Haberler, the static theory

> can never explain a movement in time. It can only answer the question: Given certain data at a certain moment, what will be the result at that moment? . . . Usually the assumption is made that, after a change in the data has occurred, a certain period of time must elapse before a new equilibrium emerges. Comparative statics in the strict sense confines itself to describing the two equilibria, the starting-point and the destination of the economic system. Any attempt, on the other hand, at analyzing in detail the process of transition from one equilibrium to the other . . . marks the first step towards a "dynamization" of static theory. For it leads inevitably to the recognition of the fact that, as the result of certain reactions, the process of transition, and hence the final equilibrium, may be different. It also suggests that, after a given change in the data, a stable position will be reached only under special assumptions (stability conditions), which cannot be taken for granted without careful analysis.[12]

The development of a dynamic theory of economic behavior is particularly critical in studying the business cycle, which is inherently a disequilibrium phenomenon characterized by cumulative movement of production in alternating opposite directions. The several dynamic models of the business cycle developed here contain generic structures that describe and interrelate typical production, employment, and investment decisions.[13] These generic structures should be more widely applicable, beyond

[10]Some familiarity with the principles of system dynamics modeling is a requisite background for this analysis. System dynamics is an approach to simulation modeling of social and industrial systems that emphasizes the causal-feedback structure of such systems. To provide a minimum background for readers of this book, Appendixes C and D present some introductory notes on system dynamics. Appendix C discusses the equation structure of system dynamics models and gives an overview of the DYNAMO simulation language. Appendix D describes the representation and properties of information and material delays. Forrester (1961, 1969) and Goodman (1974) provide a more comprehensive introduction to the methodology for readers interested in economic and social-systems modeling.

[11]Frisch (1933), in Gordon and Klein (1965), pp. 155–156.

[12]Haberler (1964), pp. 249–250.

[13]Chapter 2 discusses the elements of a generic business-cycle theory.

business-cycle research, in dynamic economic analysis of both macroeconomic and microeconomic behavior. The collection of generic structures should be particularly useful to students of economics who wish to gain some background in system dynamics modeling or to students of system dynamics who are interested in economic theory.

## 1.3 Organization

Chapter 2 reviews the economic literature on business cycles and suggests a classification of business-cycle theories according to the factor inputs underlying production. The review shows that existing business-cycle theories stress investment in fixed capital as a cause of the business cycle; the majority of these capital-investment theories build upon the framework of Paul Samuelson's 1939 analysis of the multiplier and accelerator principles.[14] However, given the magnitude of lags in fixed capital construction and depreciation, Chapter 2 suggests that fixed capital investment chiefly influences economic cycles of much longer duration than the four-year business cycle.

Chapter 2 also reviews the theoretical and econometric literature on inventory investment. Inventory-investment theories, which focus on shorter-term adjustments in production, intuitively appear to provide a superior explanation of business cycles than capital-investment theories. However, as stated in Chapter 2, existing econometric models typically relate inventory investment to average sales, inventories, and backlogs without relating underlying inventory production to available stocks of labor, capital, and other factor inputs.

Chapter 3 builds upon the prevailing inventory-investment theories to construct a production-sector model interrelating the available stock of factor inputs, production rate, inventories, and unfilled order backlogs. In Chapter 3, the basic production sector, which can represent either the behavior of a single firm or the behavior of the aggregate wholesale-manufacturing sector of the economy, is tested in response to a variety of incoming order patterns. Labor is treated as the only factor of production in Chapter 3. Computer simulations in Chapter 3 show that the basic production sector exhibits approximately four-year fluctuations in employment, production, and inventories in response to random noise, or temporary changes, in incoming orders. The fluctuations are explained in terms of the hiring and production policies of the sector. Sensitivity experiments further indicate that parameter variations within a 50–100 percent range yield cycles of roughly three- to five-year periodicities.

Chapter 3 further refines the basic production sector to include variable labor productivity, price expectations, and endogenous consumption. Advance inventory purchases in expectation of price increases are shown to exert a strong destabilizing effect on production. In contrast, endogenous consumption based on consumer incomes does not strongly affect model behavior. As discussed in section 3.7, the relatively minor influence of consumption is attributable to increasing prices, which partially offset rising nominal incomes during an upswing; moreover, the gradual adjustment of consumption patterns to income changes tends to attenuate variations in

[14]Smith (1970) contains an elementary exposition of the multiplier and accelerator concepts; see especially his chaps. 6 and 9.

consumption relative to fluctuations in income. These results are especially interesting in light of the great emphasis in business-cycle studies on multiplier-accelerator interactions, and the lesser emphasis devoted to expectational factors such as the effects of expected price changes.

Leaving the essential model structure unchanged, Chapter 4 alters the coefficients of the basic production sector to describe fixed capital as a factor of production. Such parameters as the factor delivery delay and average factor lifetime are changed to reflect characteristics of fixed capital equipment rather than labor. The simulations in Chapter 4 exhibit fluctuations of roughly fifteen to twenty years' duration, a period significantly longer than the period observed in Chapter 3 for the basic production sector which incorporates labor as the only factor input. The fluctuations resemble the Kuznets cycle observed in the rate of growth of output and capital stock. These results suggest that the same model of a production sector, adapted to describe different factor inputs, can explain both the business cycle and the longer-term economic fluctuations.

Chapter 5 synthesizes the results of Chapters 3 and 4 by extending the basic production sector to include both labor and fixed capital. The resulting model exhibits a four-year cycle in labor, inventories, and production, which is superimposed on a longer-term cycle in fixed capital. This analysis verifies that the periodicities associated with adjustments in labor and fixed capital differ sufficiently so that the individual cycles remain distinct when labor and capital combine as joint factors of production.

Finally, Chapter 6 summarizes the insights gained from the previous chapters and outlines directions for future related work. As discussed in Chapter 6, the principal policy insight gained from the research concerns the need to evaluate the differential effects of proposed stabilization policies on the acquisition of labor, capital, and other factors of production. Such an examination should illuminate the short-term effectiveness of proposed policies in enhancing economic stability and should also expand the scope of traditional stabilization analyses to longer-term policy impacts on economic growth, unemployment, and inflation.

# 2
# Classification of Business-Cycle Theories

## 2.1 Objectives Underlying General Business-Cycle Theories

Over the past eighty years, economic theorists have advanced a wide variety of explanations for business-cycle behavior. Such explanations may be considered generic insofar as they abstract from the specific characteristics of individual cycles and attempt to identify a set of general processes that contribute to cyclic instability. Any effort, such as in this book, to understand the generic features of the business cycle assumes some regularity of behavior and commonality of structure underlying different cycles. Section 2.1 overviews the justification and objectives for a generic approach to the study of economic cycles.

Chapter 1 noted that business-cycle fluctuations have exhibited an average periodicity of roughly forty-nine months over the past hundred years. Individual cycles have differed widely, however, in their relative intensity (amplitude) and duration. For example, as Figure 2–1 indicates, American business cycles between 1857 and 1957 varied in periodicity from twenty-eight months to ninety-nine months.

The irregularity of business-cycle fluctuations clearly invalidates any explanation of the business cycle as a strictly periodic phenomenon. Nonetheless, the persistence of business cycles and the recurrence of fairly stable phase relationships between such variables as orders for capital equipment, production, and inventories provide evidence for the existence of a basic set of factors underlying business-cycle behavior.[1] As Gottfried Haberler has argued,

> It should be noted that the mere fact that each cycle is an historical individual is not a sufficient argument against a general theory. Are there two men who are in all respects alike? Does this dissimilarity in many respects destroy the possibility and practical usefulness of anatomy, physiology, etc.? That each cycle is unique in many respects does not prevent all cycles from being similar in other respects, over and above those similarities which constitute the fundamental elements of the cycle.
>
> It will be shown that any economy organized on such lines is liable to cumulative, self-reinforcing processes of expansion and contraction. The

[1]Chap. 10 of Gordon (1961) provides a good overview of the behavior and average phase relationships characteristic of American business cycles. Also, see Burns and Mitchell (1946) and Evans (1969).

| Dates of Turning Points | | Duration in Months | | |
|---|---|---|---|---|
| **Peak** | **Trough** | **Expansion** | **Contraction** | **Full Cycle** |
| — | Dec. 1854 | — | — | — |
| June 1857 | Dec. 1858 | 30 | 18 | 48 |
| Oct. 1860 | June 1861 | 22 | 8 | 30 |
| Apr. 1865 | Dec. 1867 | 46 | 32 | 78 |
| June 1869 | Dec. 1870 | 18 | 18 | 36 |
| Oct. 1873 | Mar. 1879 | 34 | 65 | 99 |
| Mar. 1882 | May 1885 | 36 | 38 | 74 |
| Mar. 1887 | April 1888 | 22 | 13 | 35 |
| July 1890 | May 1891 | 27 | 10 | 37 |
| Jan. 1893 | June 1894 | 20 | 17 | 37 |
| Dec. 1895 | June 1897 | 18 | 18 | 36 |
| June 1899 | Dec. 1900 | 24 | 18 | 42 |
| Sept. 1902 | Aug. 1904 | 21 | 23 | 44 |
| May 1907 | June 1908 | 33 | 13 | 46 |
| Jan. 1910 | Jan. 1912 | 19 | 24 | 43 |
| Jan. 1913 | Dec. 1914 | 12 | 23 | 35 |
| Aug. 1918 | Mar. 1919 | 44 | 7 | 51 |
| Jan. 1920 | July 1921 | 10 | 18 | 28 |
| May 1923 | July 1924 | 22 | 14 | 36 |
| Oct. 1926 | Nov. 1927 | 27 | 13 | 40 |
| Aug. 1929 | Mar. 1933 | 21 | 43 | 64 |
| May 1937 | June 1938 | 50 | 13 | 63 |
| Feb. 1945 | Oct. 1945 | 80 | 8 | 88 |
| Nov. 1948 | Oct. 1949 | 37 | 11 | 48 |
| July 1953 | Aug. 1954 | 45 | 13 | 58 |
| July 1957 | April 1958 | 35 | 9 | 44 |

**Figure 2-1** Duration and turning points of business cycles, 1854–1958
Source: Gordon (1961), p. 251.

first thing to prove is that these processes are self-reinforcing—that is to say that, once expansion or contraction has started (for whatever reason), forces are released which make for further expansion or contraction. In other words, certain deviations from the equilibrium are not corrected automatically, but lead the system farther away from equilibrium.

The next step will then be to discuss why these processes of expansion and contraction always come to an end. Must they come to an end? Cannot they go on indefinitely? Why does expansion not lead to stable equilibrium? Are periods of expansion interrupted and reversed by accidental disturbances, or do they necessarily give rise to maladjustments?

We shall see that in these respects various possibilities are open, which do not exclude one another, and that there is no reason to postulate a single solution which must apply to all cases.

The guiding principle of our approach is to proceed cautiously step by step . . . . we start with the most general aspect of the problem . . . and then proceed to less and less general features, where the conclusions depend to an increasing extent on the particular social-economic environment. This procedure has the advantage that it does not close the door to more ambitious theoretical constructions. But it would seem that such constructions cannot be safely undertaken except on the basis of such preparatory analyses.[2]

According to Haberler, a generic theory of the business cycle explains why:

1. given an initial impetus, the economy exhibits cumulative change in one direction;
2. expansion (contraction) terminates, thereby leading to stabilization or reversal of production; and
3. expansion (contraction), in fact, typically gives way to decline (increase) in production.

The survey of business-cycle theories in section 2.3 and the discussion in Chapters 3 through 5 focus on explaining the business cycle in the generic sense just outlined. Such an objective may be contrasted, for example, with attempts in many macroeconometric models to forecast turning points in economic aggregates within a particular business cycle.[3] Rather than focusing on short-term prediction, this book attempts to provide a framework for identifying the range of factors that may underlie short-term (three- to five-year) and medium-term (fifteen- to twenty-year) economic fluctuations. As discussed in Chapters 4 through 6, such a framework is necessary for evaluating the short-term and long-term impacts of proposed economic stabilization policies.

## 2.2 Alternative Classification of Theories

Several categorizations of business-cycle theories are currently available in the economic literature. Figure 2–2, for example, lists the categories developed by Robert A. Gordon, Alvin H. Hansen, Gottfried Haberler, and Wesley C. Mitchell. Both individually and collectively, their categories constitute a fairly comprehensive résumé of existing business-cycle theories.

The research reported here suggests an alternative classification of business-cycle theories that differs substantially in emphasis from the categories listed in Figure 2–2. Essentially, theories are classified here according to their assumed underlying factors of production (for example, capital or labor, or both).[4] Clearly, a new typology of

[2]Haberler (1964), pp. 276–277.

[3]App. K of Forrester (1961) discusses the feasibility of point prediction in social systems. Forrester subjects the same (deterministic) industrial dynamics model to several different random noise sequences in incoming order rate; analyzing the resulting model behavior, he shows that the principal effect of the different noise inputs is to alter the timing of turning points in employment but not the overall periodicity or magnitude of employment fluctuations. Therefore, according to Forrester, "a dynamic model should be used for determining the behavior character of a system but not its specific future state" (p. 436).

[4]The book also discusses a second classification criterion with respect to the factors underlying the business cycle. The second criterion, subsidiary in importance to the question of factors of production, concerns whether business-cycle fluctuations arise fundamentally from the decision-making process of the firm or whether they depend on business-market interactions. Chapter 3 suggests that market changes or multiplier interactions—that is, feedback from consumer incomes to household purchases—are not fundamental in generating business cycles. Chapter 3 shows, for example, that fluctuations in employment, production, and inventories can occur despite a constant incoming order rate. Several of the theories cataloged by Mitchell, for example, under the headings of "uncertainty theories" and "emotional [psychological] factor in business decisions" also emphasize the role of internal business decisions in generating economic cycles. This issue is significant because, if business cycles are generated largely as a result of the internal policies of business firms, then stabilization policies may more profitably focus on means for restructuring internal policies to enhance stability. Such an analysis should be applicable both to the firm and to the national economy.

| Robert A. Gordon | Gottfried Haberler | Alvin H. Hansen | Wesley C. Mitchell |
|---|---|---|---|
| 1. Theories that emphasize changes in price-cost relationships and changes in business expectations ("business-economy" theories) | 1. Purely monetary theory | 1. Aggregate demand theories | 1. Weather |
| 2. Monetary explanations | 2. Overinvestment theories<br>a. Monetary overinvestment theories<br>b. Nonmonetary overinvestment theories<br>c. Accelerator theories | 2. Confidence and credit | 2. Uncertainty |
| 3. Theories emphasizing the role of savings and investment<br>a. shortage-of-capital theories<br>b. investment opportunity theories<br>c. theories emphasizing the dependence of investment on final output | 3. Changes in cost, horizontal maladjustments, and overindebtedness | 3. Overinvestment<br>a. monetary<br>b. nonmonetary | 3. Emotional factor in business decisions |
| 4. Agricultural and meteorological theories | 4. Underconsumption theories | 4. Monetary disequilibrium | 4. Innovations |
| | 5. Psychological theories | 5. Impulse and propagation | 5. Savings and investment |
| | 6. Harvest theories | 6. Agriculture | 6. Construction work |
| | | | 7. Generalized overproduction |
| | | | 8. Banking operations |
| | | | 9. Production and flow of money income |
| | | | 10. Profit making |

**Figure 2-2** Existing classifications of business-cycle theories

Sources: Gordon (1961), Haberler (1964), Hansen (1951), and Mitchell (1927).

business-cycle theories is warranted only if it yields additional insights into economic behavior and policy. Therefore, the remainder of section 2.2 overviews the rationale underlying the proposed classification scheme as a prelude to the analysis in Chapters 3 through 5. Section 2.3 subsequently provides a summary of the major existing theories of the business cycle pertaining to each category in the classification scheme.

Factors of economic production differ along several dimensions: delivery delay, average lifetime within the firm, price, and so on. For purposes of exposition, consider an economy with only two factors of production—capital and labor.[5] Compared with capital equipment, labor is usually more readily acquired and less specialized (it can be reallocated more readily between different production tasks or economic sectors), and

[5]Note that capital, according to this definition, aggregates all fixed capital plant and equipment, while labor subsumes both production workers and managerial personnel.

it generally represents a shorter-term commitment. For example, a long process of planning and organization (including the negotiation of bank credit), in addition to technical construction, necessarily precedes the acquisition of capital equipment. The total delay in acquiring capital may therefore be on the order of two to three years.[6] In contrast, the delay in acquiring labor in the United States is roughly on the order of two to six weeks for production labor and several months for professional or managerial personnel.[7]

The long planning and construction delay for fixed capital is accentuated by the durable nature of capital equipment. Investment decisions that embody a rapid adjustment of capital stock to the desired level of capital pose a relatively large risk of overexpansion. If a firm develops excess capacity, perhaps because of declining sales, the firm will incur high storage and interest costs over the lifetime of the equipment, thereby lowering profits and the firm's unused debt capacity. From a risk standpoint, therefore, fixed capital investment decisions should reflect a fairly gradual adjustment of capital stock in response to market trends.[8] Again in contrast to fixed capital, labor can be discharged fairly rapidly in many firms as an excess internal workforce develops.

The preceding discussion has delineated some of the different characteristics of labor and fixed capital. The differences suggest that production cycles induced by capital investment and labor hiring should, in turn, possess very different characteristics. In particular, Chapters 3 through 5 argue that short-term fluctuations in employment, production, and inventories are primarily caused by inventory-workforce interactions, while longer-term capital-equipment cycles are caused by fluctuations in fixed capital investment.[9] A heuristic argument underlying this position has been well summarized by Abramovitz:

> For a number of reasons, the simpler capital-stock adjustment models with their implied requirements for balanced growth rate take on heightened interest when considered in the context of long swings rather than in that of shorter business cycles. First, insofar as these models treat investment as dependent in part on current or past changes in the demand for finished goods, there has always been justifiable skepticism about their applicability to durable equipment and structures, so long as the theory was supposed to illuminate investment movements in short cycles. Since investment in durables is made for long periods of time it is doubtful whether it would respond

[6]Frisch estimates that the average total delay for completing large units of fixed capital, such as industrial plants or waterpower plants, is approximately three years. See Frisch (1933), in Gordon and Klein (1965), p. 167. For relevant econometric estimates of lagged investment functions, see chap. 4 of Evans (1969).

[7]Estimates of the average duration of vacancies in American manufacturing industries over the business cycle are available in Henize (1974).

[8]App. E of Forrester (1961) discusses the psychological smoothing of information and its relation to delay in system response.

[9]These long-term capital cycles resemble the so-called Kuznets cycle. Kuznets cycles are eighteen- to twenty-year cycles in the rate of growth of capital stock, total output, and employment. Abramovitz (1961) and Hickman (1963) detail the characteristic behavior of Kuznets cycles. As discussed in Chapter 4, long-term movements in capital stock may also underlie the fifty-year Kondratieff cycles observed in some countries. See Kondratieff (1935) for a description of these cycles.

readily to income change over short periods. This difficulty disappears, however, when we consider expansions lasting 8 to 12 years or more.[10]

According to Abramovitz, then, fixed capital investment is unlikely to be an essential factor in generating the short-term cycle, since the delays in capital formation have about the same magnitude as the four-year business cycle, and the delays in capital depreciation run much longer. The viewpoint that fixed capital is not essential in generating the business cycle has two principal dimensions: first, business cycles can occur independently of changes in fixed capital investment; second, fixed capital variations cannot independently generate four-year cycles. For example, Chapter 3 shows that, if fixed capital stock does not vary, short-term production and inventory-management policies governing labor acquisition still generate four-year cycles. Moreover, Chapter 4 indicates that four-year business cycles do not appear in an economy in which fixed capital is the only variable factor of production. These results demonstrate that fixed capital variations cannot be an intrinsic cause of four-year business cycles.

Abramovitz's supposition has been supported by computer simulations of the "ordering function" of the national socioeconomic model under construction by the System Dynamics Group at M.I.T.[11] The ordering function is a generalized structure designed to represent the factor-input ordering decisions characteristic of a business firm or industry. By varying its internal parameters, the ordering function can be used to represent such factor inputs as labor, which is readily acquired and discharged, or capital equipment and buildings, which have a relatively long delivery delay and depreciate over a long lifetime. Computer simulations of the ordering function exhibit a three- to four-year production and inventory cycle when the ordering-function parameters are adapted to describe labor hiring and firing, and an approximately twenty-year cycle when the model parameters are altered to describe fixed capital.

The results and arguments just summarized tend to confirm the importance, from a theoretical standpoint, of classifying business-cycle theories according to their underlying factors of production. The distinction among periodicities of fluctuation induced by different production inputs also has considerable practical policy significance. If, for example, fixed capital investment primarily influences cycles of much longer duration than the short-term business cycle, then monetary or other government policies designed to influence capital spending can have a significant long-term effect on growth in aggregate output in addition to a short-term impact on the demand for capital goods. Over a long time span, the rate of expansion of capital equipment determines the increase of potential output for a given rate of growth in the labor force.[12] Therefore, government policies that influence capital expenditures may exert important long-term impacts on the growth of both productivity and output. These

[10]Abramovitz (1961), in Gordon and Klein (1965), p. 537.

[11]The objectives and overall structure of the national model are summarized in Gilbert W. Low, Nathaniel J. Mass, Peter M. Senge, "The National Socio-economic Model," System Dynamics Group Memorandum D-2006-3 (Cambridge, Mass.: M.I.T., July 1974). See also Forrester (1975). The computer models developed in Chapters 3-5 constitute simplified versions of the ordering function.

[12]See Hickman (1963) for a discussion of the rate of growth of potential output in the United States during the postwar period.

impacts need to be examined in the context of a model that considers both the long-term and the short-term cyclic effects of policy measures. Chapters 4 through 6 expand upon these issues.

## 2.3 Overview of Existing Theories

This section provides a brief survey of theories of the business cycle within the classification scheme proposed in section 2.2. Most business-cycle theories rely upon fluctuations in fixed capital investment to explain business-cycle behavior. Other theories emphasize inventory investment as a source of short-run fluctuations but fail to treat explicitly the mix of factor inputs underlying the production stream. Chapter 4 subsequently shows that capital-investment policies tend to generate cycles of significantly longer periodicity than four-year business cycles; in addition, Chapters 3 and 5 build upon the inventory-investment theories by developing models incorporating explicit factors of production to show that short-term employment and production policies generate approximately four-year cycles.

*Capital-Investment Theories.* John Maynard Keynes's *General Theory of Employment, Interest, and Money* fundamentally reoriented the focus of the macroeconomic theory of income determination toward the three components of aggregate demand: consumption, investment, and government spending. In particular, the *General Theory* popularized the concept of a consumption schedule relating consumer expenditures to aggregate income and described a model of investment based on the marginal efficiency of capital.[13] Probably due to Keynes's influence, post-Keynesian theories of the trade cycle have in turn tended to revolve around the processes of consumption and investment. Keynes himself writes:

> But I suggest that the essential character of the Trade Cycle and, especially, the regularity of time-sequence and of duration which justifies us in calling it a cycle, is mainly due to the way in which the marginal efficiency of capital fluctuates. The Trade Cycle is best regarded, I think, as being occasioned by a cyclical change of the marginal efficiency of capital, though complicated and often aggravated by associated changes in the other significant short-period variables of the economic system. . . . This brings me to my point. The explanation of the time-element in the trade cycle, of the fact that an interval of time of a particular order of magnitude must elapse before recovery begins, is to be sought in the influences which govern the recovery of the marginal efficiency of capital.[14]

Building upon the income-expenditure approach developed in the *General Theory*, Samuelson attempted in his classic 1939 paper to explain business-cycle behavior by means of a simple model of the multiplier and accelerator. Samuelson's contribution has been described by Evans as follows:

> [Samuelson's] article marked the first step to integrate Keynesian theory with older business cycle theory, particularly the accelerator. In doing so,

[13]Keynes (1936), pp. 111–112 and 135–136, summarizes Keynes's definition of the marginal efficiency of capital.
[14]Ibid., pp. 313, 317.

Samuelson supplied the critical missing link, an endogenous explanation of how movements of the economy during one cycle could generate further cycles. As we have seen, all previous nonmonetary theories of the cycle were forced to rely on primarily exogenous elements to explain the lower turning point.[15]

The basic Samuelson model consists of three discrete difference equations:[16]

$$C_t = cY_{t-1} \quad (2.1)$$
$$I_t = v(Y_{t-1} - Y_{t-2}) \quad (2.2)$$
$$C_t + I_t + G_t = Y_t \quad (2.3)$$

Equation 2.1 states that consumption C at time t equals the income of the previous period, $Y_{t-1}$, multiplied by a constant marginal propensity to consume. Equation 2.2 states that investment in fixed capital is proportional to the difference between the incomes of the two previous periods. Underlying equation 2.2 is the assumption of a constant desired capital-output ratio v in the economy. This assumption can be seen as follows. Suppose that producers desire to hold v units of capital for each unit of sales.[17] Also assume that producers adjust their capital stock to the desired value in one time period. Then, desired capital at time t equals $(v)(Y_{t-1})$; that is the desired capital-output ratio multiplied by the sales of the previous period. By the previous assumption of a one-period lag in capital adjustment, actual capital stock at time (t−1) equals desired capital at time (t−2), or $(v)(Y_{t-2})$. Fixed capital investment, $I_t$, therefore equals $[(v)(Y_{t-1}) - (v)(Y_{t-2})] = v(Y_{t-1} - Y_{t-2})$, as indicated by equation 2.2. Finally, equation 2.3 represents an equilibrium condition; it states that aggregate production equals the sum of consumption, investment, and government expenditures.

Without exploring in detail the assumptions underlying Samuelson's model, several general points can be made. Chiefly, in terms of the classification scheme of section 2.2, the Samuelson model relies upon capital-investment behavior as an explanation of business-cycle fluctuations.[18] However, as suggested in section 2.2 and elaborated in Chapters 4 and 5, fixed capital investment appears unlikely to be an essential causal factor in fluctuations of less than twelve to fifteen years' duration. The multiplier and accelerator principles have been elaborated widely in the economic literature over the last thirty-five years. For example, Nicholas Kaldor (1940) extended the principles to embody nonlinear consumption and investment schedules, and R. M. Goodwin (1948, 1951, 1955) developed a nonlinear investment function broadly resembling Kaldor's investment function. The Goodwin model explicitly introduces lags

[15]Evans (1969), p. 362.

[16]The version of the multiplier-accelerator system presented here is actually attributable to Hicks (1950). However, this version is nearly identical to Samuelson's model, both conceptually and algebraically.

[17]Note that because of the equilibrium assumptions underlying equations (2.1–2.3) in the multiplier-accelerator model, production, income, and sales are considered equal. Consequently, in equation (2.2), for example, investment depends directly on production rather than on sales.

[18]In the preceding equations, note that the output rate is not explicitly related to the capital stock, except through the dependence of desired capital on sales of the previous period. Therefore, the equations must implicitly contain an adjustment of labor or some other factor of production to equate output and sales. Such implicit assumptions arise as a result of the equilibrium character of the multiplier-accelerator theory as developed in the literature.

in production (supply) relative to demand and distinguishes orders for fixed capital equipment from shipments (arrival) of capital. John R. Hicks (1950) and Arthur Smithies (1957) developed models that generate cyclic fluctuations around a long-term growth path. Yet, despite such developments, the analysis in Chapters 4 and 5 suggests that economic cycles induced by investment in fixed capital must have a significantly longer duration than four-year business cycles. Therefore, capital-investment theories seem to be largely inadequate for explaining short-term business-cycle behavior, although they may provide useful insights into causes of medium-term economic cycles.[19]

The accelerator principle provides a second class of theories emphasizing capital investment as a cause of the business cycle. Although obviously closely related to the multiplier-accelerator theories discussed earlier, the accelerator principle provides an explanation of production and inventory fluctuations for a single firm or whole economy subject to a *given demand for final output*. The accelerator theory will therefore be described briefly because it resembles the production model developed in Chapter 4.

Albert Aftalion's theory of the business cycle was a forerunner of the accelerator principle and provides a good illustration of the major elements of the accelerator theory.[20] According to Aftalion, an increase in the demand for consumer goods depletes consumer-goods inventories, thereby creating shortages, and leads to an increased demand for capital goods in order to expand production. However, the construction of capital goods takes years, so that shortages endure and prices and profit margins remain high for a long period of time.[21] The delay in manufacturing new capital equipment thus provides a growing stimulus for capital production and eventually leads to overexpansion of capacity. As overexpansion occurs, inventories of capital goods rise above the level of desired inventories. To reduce inventories, the production of capital goods must be contracted sharply, leading to a decline in aggregate income and employment.

Aftalion compared the time required for the manufacture of capital goods to the time that elapses between the moment of lighting a furnace and the time the furnace begins to emanate heat:

> If one rekindles the fire in the hearth in order to warm up a room, one has to wait a while before one has the desired temperature. As the cold continues, and the thermometer continues to record it, one might be led, if one has not the lessons of experience, to throw more coal on the fire. One would con-

[19]Gordon (1961), p. 252, hypothesizes that fluctuation in long-term investment opportunities may underlie a "major" cycle of six to eleven years' duration, as distinguished from the "minor" cycle resulting from "changes in short-term business expectations and . . . minor maladjustments." Hansen (1951) also emphasizes the distinction between major and minor cycles. The results in Chapters 4 and 5 suggest that fixed capital investment induces a fifteen- to twenty-year or longer cycle. In terms of periodicities, this cycle seems to resemble more closely the Kuznets cycle or the long-term Kondratieff cycle than the major cycle. See Chapters 4 and 5 for further discussion.

[20]See Aftalion (1909, 1927); also J. M. Clark (1917). Econometric tests of the accelerator model are summarized in Goodwin (1951), Chenery (1952), and Kuh and Meyer (1955).

[21]Aftalion was criticized by Bouniatian (1924) for ignoring changes in the utilization of capital that lower the overall lag of adjustment of supply to demand. Variations in capacity utilization are explicitly considered in the models described in Chapters 4 and 5 of this book.

tinue to throw coal, even though the quantity already in the grate is such as will give off an intolerable heat, when once it is all alight. To allow oneself to be guided by the present sense of cold and the indications of the thermometer to that effect is fatally to overheat the room.[22]

Aftalion attributed the period of the business cycle to the length of the delay in capital production. Similar hypotheses advanced by A. C. Pigou and D. H. Robertson center on the gestation period of capital goods.[23] The effects of delays in acquiring capital are explored further in Chapter 4, which provides a model that exhibits a long-term capital cycle in response to a noisy incoming order stream or a temporary change in incoming orders.

A third class of capital-investment theory, the monetary overinvestment theory originated principally by Knut Wicksell and F. A. Hayek, emphasizes the impact of rising credit demands (resulting from increased financing of inventories and capital equipment) on interest rates, and the subsequent depressive effect of high interest rates on the rate of fixed capital investment.[24] Reductions in excess bank reserves caused by a high demand for loans also force an eventual contraction of credit. The principal feedback loops underlying the monetary overinvestment theory are shown in Figure 2–3. An increase in investment demand raises the demand for loans, thereby increasing bank lending to business while forcing up the interest rate. A high interest rate, in turn, is assumed to depress investment demand. At the same time, bank lending to business depletes available excess reserves, thereby accentuating the rise in interest rates. Moreover, declining excess reserves force a reduction in bank lending to business. Thus both declining credit availability (measured by the lower level of excess reserves) and rising interest rates act to reverse the initial increase in bank lending.

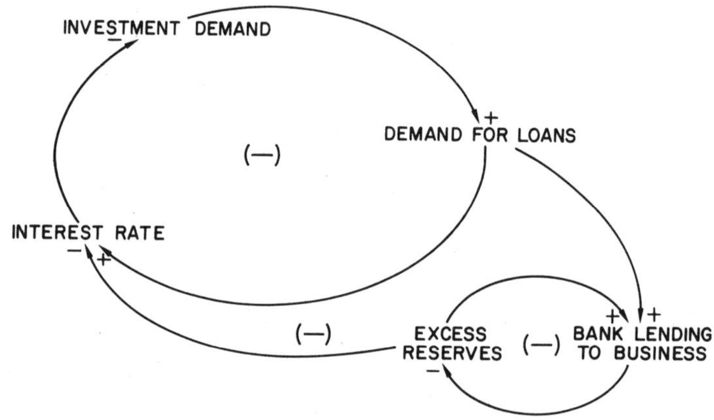


**Figure 2-3** Major feedback loops underlying the monetary overinvestment theory

[22]Quoted from Haberler (1964), pp. 135–136.
[23]See Pigou (1927) and Robertson (1915) for reference.
[24]See Wicksell (1907, 1935) and Hayek (1935).

In general, a consideration of the monetary overinvestment theories falls outside the scope of this work. However, two points should be noted. First, as stated by Michael K. Evans and others, the monetary overinvestment theories inherently incorporate the supposition that business-cycle expansions could continue indefinitely if the credit supply were continually expanded.[25] Second, as noted by Gordon, the monetary overinvestment theories emphasize the impact of interest rates on investment but ignore the influence of product demand.[26] For both these reasons, the development of an adequate model of the ''real'' sector of the economy—interrelating production rate, inventories, and unfilled order backlog—is a necessary prelude to an adequate monetary explanation of the business cycle. Chapters 3 through 5 of this book attempt to develop such a framework.

*Inventory-Investment Theories.* Section 2.2 proposed a classification of business-cycle theories according to underlying factors of production. Although numerous capital-investment theories have been developed in the literature, very few complete theories dealing explicitly with labor as a factor of production have been advanced. In recent years, however, the analysis of business-cycle fluctuations has increasingly tended to distinguish between investment in inventories (working capital) and investment in fixed plant and equipment. Since inventory investment represents a shorter-term adjustment than fixed capital investment, inventory-investment theories, which treat short-term investment policies, appear to offer an explanation of the short-run cycle that is superior to theories focusing on fixed capital investment. The discussion below analyzes prevalent inventory-investment theories of the business cycle. It should be emphasized, however, that the inventory-investment theories do not correspond directly with the classification proposed in section 2.2, which deals with labor as the single factor of production. As will be shown, the majority of quantitative inventory theories focus on demand-side variables, such as sales and inventories, and do not explicitly consider the combination of factor inputs underlying production. Therefore, Chapters 3 through 5 subsequently build upon the existing inventory-investment models to incorporate explicit factors of production; these chapters show that supply variables such as labor and capital adjustments exert a critical impact on the periodicity of economic fluctuations.

The recognition of the importance of inventory investment in business-cycle behavior stems from Abramovitz's observation that inventory changes accounted for 23 percent of the total change in output during business-cycle expansions and for 47 percent of the change in output during contractions before World War II.[27] Analyzing more recent data, Thomas M. Stanback, Jr., found that changes in manufacturers' inventories accounted for 79, 56, and 25 percent, respectively, of the change in gross national product during the recessions of 1948/49, 1953/54, and 1957/58.[28] Finally, Lawrence R. Klein and Joel Popkin argue that the business cycle could be virtually

[25]Evans (1969), p. 332. Chapter 3 shows that production fluctuations would occur even if credit availability does not serve as a restraint on business expansion.

[26]Gordon (1961), p. 360.

[27]Abramovitz (1950), p. 7.

[28]Stanback (1961), p. 12.

eliminated if inventory fluctuations were reduced by 75 percent, although they do not suggest any policies to accomplish such a reduction.[29]

Some recognition of the role of inventory investment in generating typical business-cycle fluctuations is also reflected in the classical economic literature. For example, it was noted earlier that Keynes, in his *General Theory,* attributed business-cycle behavior to fluctuations in the marginal efficiency of capital. However, at the conclusion of a chapter entitled ''Notes on the Trade Cycle,'' Keynes asserts:

> Recent American experience has also afforded good examples of the part played by fluctuations in the stock of finished and unfinished goods—''inventories'' as it is becoming usual to call them—in causing the minor oscillations within the main movement of the Trade Cycle. Manufacturers, setting industry in motion to provide for a scale of consumption which is expected to prevail some months later, are apt to make minor miscalculations, generally in the direction of running a little ahead of the facts. When they discover their mistake they have to contract for a short time to a level below that of current consumption so as to allow for the absorption of the excess inventories; and the difference of pace between running a little ahead and dropping back again has proved sufficient in its effect on the current rate of investment to display itself quite clearly against the background of the excellently complete statistics now available in the United States.[30]

In a similar vein, Joseph Schumpeter originally attributed the short-term trade cycle to fluctuations in innovations and fixed capital investment, but he later suggested the possible role of inventory behavior.[31]

In a series of papers published in the 1940s, Lloyd A. Metzler attempted to analyze inventory behavior within the framework of the multiplier and accelerator principles.[32] According to Maurice W. Lee, ''Metzler developed a special application for dynamic analysis which provides us with a valuable bridge to the area covered by present-day cycle model constructions.''[33] The basic elements of Metzler's theory are captured by the following three equations:[34]

$$y(t) = u(t) + s(t) + V_o \tag{2.4}$$
$$u(t) = \beta y(t-1) \tag{2.5}$$
$$s(t) = \beta y(t-1) - \beta y(t-2) \tag{2.6}$$

Equation 2.4 states that production at time t, y(t), equals the production of consumer goods for sale, u(t), plus the production for inventories, s(t), plus noninduced net investment, $V_o$.[35] Equation 2.5 states that the production of consumer

[29]Klein and Popkin (1961), p. 76.

[30]Keynes (1936), p. 332.

[31]See Gordon (1961), p. 367.

[32]See Metzler (1941, 1946, 1947). For a useful elaboration of Metzler's theory, see Nurkse (1952, 1954).

[33]Lee (1963), p. 403.

[34]Metzler (1941).

[35]Metzler therefore assumes that fixed capital investment is held constant while inventory investment is allowed to vary.

goods for sale, u(t), equals the consumption of the previous period. It assumes that consumers in each period spend a constant fraction, $\beta$, of the income received during that period; it further assumes that there is no lag between the receipt and expenditure of income.[36] Finally, equation 2.6 states that inventory production equals the difference between the consumption of the two previous periods. In this simplified model Metzler assumes that producers wish to maintain some constant inventory stock, $S_o$, and that they attempt to adjust stocks to their desired value over one period. Equation 2.6 is explained by Metzler as follows:

> . . . s(t) may be either positive or negative. If stocks exceed the normal level, $S_o$, which business wishes to maintain, businessmen will produce fewer consumer's goods than they expect to sell in the hope that by so doing they can reduce inventories. In this case s(t) is negative. On the other hand, if stocks are lower than the normal level, $S_o$, an attempt will be made to replenish inventories so that s(t) will be positive. Whether positive or negative, however, production for inventories in period t will equal the difference between the normal level, $S_o$, and the actual level of stocks at the close of period t−1. But in period t−1, entrepreneurs intended to produce enough so that stocks at the close of that period would equal the normal level, $S_o$, i.e., they produced an amount sufficient to cover expected sales plus whatever was needed (positive or negative) to make stocks equal $S_o$ . . . . the difference between the normal level, $S_o$, and the actual level at the close of period t−1 is simply the difference between actual and anticipated sales of that period [that is, $\beta y(t-1) - \beta y(t-2)$].[37]

Metzler's model is very similar to Samuelson's multiplier-accelerator model. Just as Samuelson's model popularized the multiplier-accelerator theory of fixed capital investment, the Metzler model provided a major impetus to the theory of inventory behavior. Gordon describes the behavior of Metzler's model as follows:

> Let an expansion in demand occur for any reason. Since production responds to an increase in demand only with a lag, the initial effect is an unplanned reduction in inventories. Seeking to maintain a constant ratio of inventories to sales, producers attempt to increase inventories. This expands output, income and demand still further, so that inventories do not rise by as much as planned. But with a marginal propensity to consume of less than one, demand increases more slowly than does output. Hence, inventories begin slowly to accumulate, though less rapidly than businessmen desire. Eventually, producers reestablish the desired ratio of inventories to sales, and no further expansion of inventories is planned. This is equivalent to a decline in (inventory) investment; as a result, output and incomes fall, and the downswing begins. During the decline, the attempts of producers to reduce inventories as sales decline lead to further contraction of output, incomes, and sales. Eventually, however, since consumption does not decline as rapidly as incomes, inventories are reduced to the desired level. Once disin-

[36]Metzler (1941), in Gordon and Klein (1965), pp. 102–103.

[37]Ibid., p. 107. In the same paper, Metzler later extends his model to encompass a level of desired inventory that depends on average sales.

vestment in inventories stops, output rises to satisfy current and expected sales. This increase in production expands income and sales, and a new cycle begins.[38]

With regard to the classification scheme described in section 2.2, Metzler fails to identify the factor inputs giving rise to production; he states that the production decision depends on past sales and on actual and desired inventory holdings, without specifying how production capacity adjusts to the desired level. As shown later, by omitting explicit factors of production, Metzler ignores a critical influence on the periodicity of inventory cycles.

In recent years, Metzler's theory has been elaborated to deal with such factors as order backlogs and price expectations. For example, Lawrence Klein (1950) extended the Metzler model to incorporate a gradual adjustment of inventories to desired inventories (in contrast to the "one-period" adjustment assumed by Metzler) and considered changes in the timing of inventory purchases induced by price changes. Paul G. Darling (1959) and Gary Fromm (1961) modified the inventory-investment model to subsume the effects of order backlogs on desired production rates. Michael C. Lovell (1961) disaggregated inventories to separate purchased goods and goods in process from inventories of finished goods. However, these writers all fail to consider explicitly the determinants of the inventory output rate. Their studies usefully elaborate the determinants of inventory demand and the lag structures underlying inventory purchases; however, they neglect the effects of factor-input levels on the rate of net inventory production and on the timing of inventory adjustments. As a result, the models may be useful for short-run forecasting, as long as underlying supply conditions are fairly stable; but they seem to be broadly unsuited for longer-term forecasting or for analyzing policies that alter relative supply conditions or the optimal factor mix. Therefore, Chapters 3 through 5 of this book expand upon existing inventory models to study the effects of the acquisition of different factor inputs on inventory and production behavior.

[38]Gordon (1961), pp. 351–352.

# 3 Inventory-Workforce Interactions

## 3.1 Summary and Organization

Chapter 3 develops a general model of the production sector of the economy, interrelating inventory-production policies and labor-hiring and labor-termination decisions. To focus on the behavior modes induced by labor adjustments, labor is the only factor of production represented in Chapter 3. Section 3.2 provides a general overview of the major feedback loops connecting employment, inventories, production, and unfilled order backlogs. Section 3.3 develops the equations for the basic production sector. The computer simulations in section 3.4 show that labor-acquisition policies can cause a production, inventory, and employment cycle of roughly four years' duration. The sensitivity experiments presented in section 3.4 indicate that when model parameters are changed within a 50–100 percent range, model-generated cycles remain between approximately three and five years' duration.

Sections 3.5 through 3.7 extend the basic production sector to encompass issues described in the economic literature on business cycles. Section 3.5 adds two new elements to the production sector to allow for variations in labor productivity caused by prevailing pressures for expansion and by the length of the work week. Section 3.5 demonstrates, as suggested previously by Wesley Mitchell, that production and inventory swings are accentuated by the tendency for labor efficiency to decline during periods of peak production because of shortages of materials, the allocation of managerial time to expediting and placating customers, and worker fatigue from extended overtime.[1] Section 3.6 illustrates how increased inventory purchases in expectation of material shortages and rising prices contribute to instability. Finally, section 3.7 develops a simple endogenous consumption sector, along the lines of the consumption function contained in Lloyd Metzler's inventory model, to study the effects of multiplier-accelerator interactions on inventory behavior. The results of section 3.7 suggest that the multiplier theory, according to which rising incomes and employment generate increased consumer expenditures, may be a far less important explanation of

[1]Actually, as noted by Gordon (1961) and Hultgren (1960), output per man-hour has tended to rise during both business-cycle upswings and business-cycle downswings. However, a reduction in the growth of labor productivity relative to the long-term growth rate does appear to characterize most upswings.

production amplification than inventory- and backlog-management policies endogenous to the firm. While extending the range of issues encompassed in the basic production sector, the modifications developed in sections 3.5 through 3.7 do not exert a significant impact on the periodicity of the inventory-labor-production cycle. The conclusions of Chapter 3 lend broad support to the contention that short-term employment and inventory-management policies underlie typical four-year business cycles.

## 3.2 Overview of the Inventory-Workforce Structure

Chapter 3 develops a model interrelating inventories, order backlogs, employment, and production. The model is designed to show how production and hiring policies within a firm, industry, or national economy can interact to create fluctuations in employment and demand that are characteristic of a business cycle.

*Amplification of Production.* Business cycles are characterized by amplification of demand in successive stages of production. For example, as shown in Figure 3–1, employment and production in producer-goods industries typically fluctuate more widely than in consumer-goods industries.[2] More generally, the magnitude of fluctua-

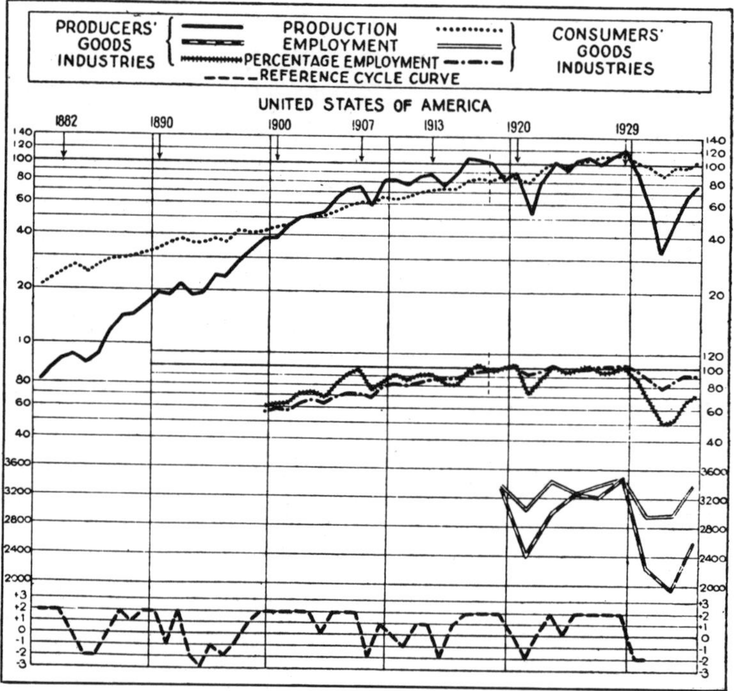


**Figure 3-1** The relative magnitude of fluctuations in producer- and consumer-goods industries

Source: Haberler (1964), p. 280.

[2]Kuznets (1926) provided much of the original empirical evidence to support the existence of relatively greater fluctuations in producer-goods industries. The theoretical explanation of this observed behavior pattern was first developed by Dennison (1922), Frank (1923), and T. W. Mitchell (1923).

tions in sales and production increases progressively in moving from the retail level to wholesale and manufacturing industries and, finally, to raw material suppliers (see Figure 3–2). As noted by Haberler, fluctuations in producer-goods industries are "much more regular, and conform much more closely with these business cycles in general, than the fluctuations in the consumers' goods industries."[3]

To represent fully the growing amplification of production through the chains of a typical production-distribution system, a model would need to represent three or four stages similar to those shown in Figure 3–3.[4] As a simplification, the wholesale and manufacturing sectors of Figure 3–3 can be aggregated together. The response of the simplified system to incoming orders emanating from the consumer and retail sectors can then be studied. Sections 3.3 through 3.6 follow such an approach. The corres-

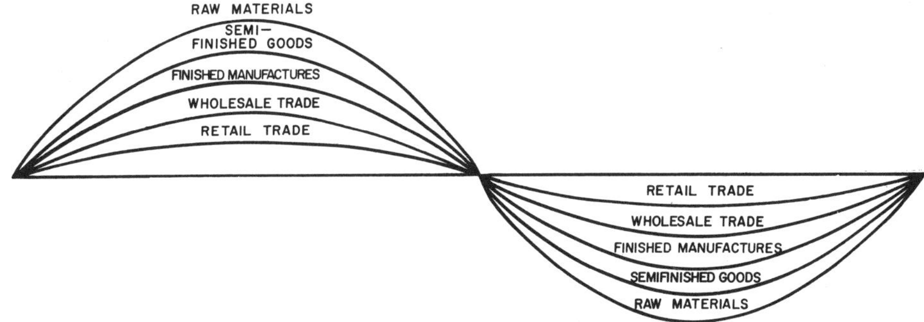


**Figure 3-2** The relative magnitude of production fluctuations in a typical production-distribution chain

Source: Hansen (1951), p. 187.

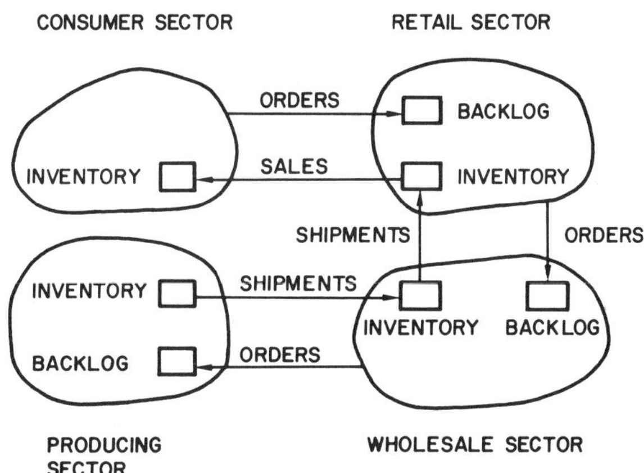


**Figure 3-3** A four-tier production-distribution system

[3]Haberler (1964), p. 282.

[4]Chap. 15 of Forrester (1961) develops the equations for a three-tier production-distribution system.

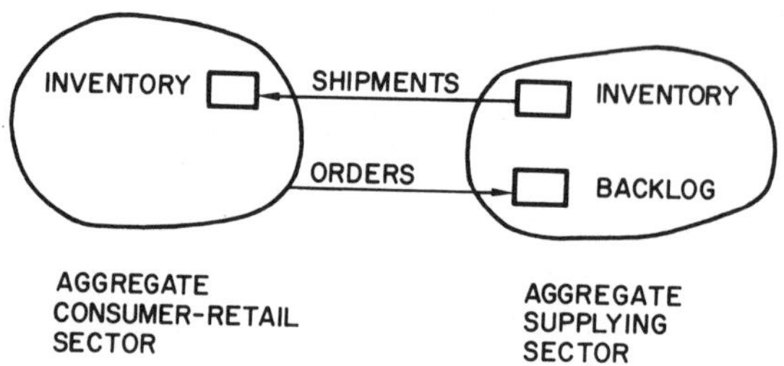


**Figure 3-4** A simplified two-tier production-distribution system

ponding system boundary is shown in Figure 3–4. Section 3.7 expands the system boundary to include endogenous consumption based on wage incomes.

*Determinants of the Production Rate.* This section overviews the factors that can induce production within a particular sector of the economy to fluctuate by more than incoming orders.[5] The analysis applies in modified form to the behavior of a single firm or industry or, as suggested previously, to the aggregate wholesale-manufacturing sector of the economy.

Figure 3–5 shows, in simplified form, the determinants of net labor acquisition, which is assumed to depend on the discrepancy between available labor and desired labor. Labor is acquired when desired labor exceeds actual labor, and it is discharged when desired labor is less than actual labor.

In Figure 3–5, desired labor is first assumed to depend on desired production.[6] For example, assuming a constant productivity of labor, p, then desired labor would be (desired production)/p. Figure 3–5 also exhibits a second influence on desired labor hiring, namely, the expected growth rate of production. If, for example, labor productivity is constant while demand for the sector's output is growing at a rate of 3 percent per year, then the stock of labor would also need to expand at 3 percent per year. In Figure 3–5, the expected growth rate of demand is expressed in terms of an expected growth rate of production; the latter, in turn, is calculated on the basis of past growth in production. This relationship, which is justified further in section 3.3, reflects both an extrapolation of past growth in desired production and the propagation of relative optimism or pessimism throughout the sector. As Pigou has stated,

> once optimism has been generated, it tends to spread and grow, as a result of reactions between different parts of the business community. This comes about through two principal influences. First, experience suggests that, apart altogether from the financial ties by which different business men are bound together, there exists among them a certain measure of psychological interdependence. A change of tone in one part of the business world diffuses itself

[5]The justification of the precise model formulations is deferred to section 3.3.

[6]As shown in Figure 3–5 and discussed later, the desired production rate is calculated on the basis of unfilled order backlogs and inventory adequacy. The acquisition of factor inputs based on expected growth in demand is computed separately for each factor input, since the planning horizon for different production factors can differ widely.

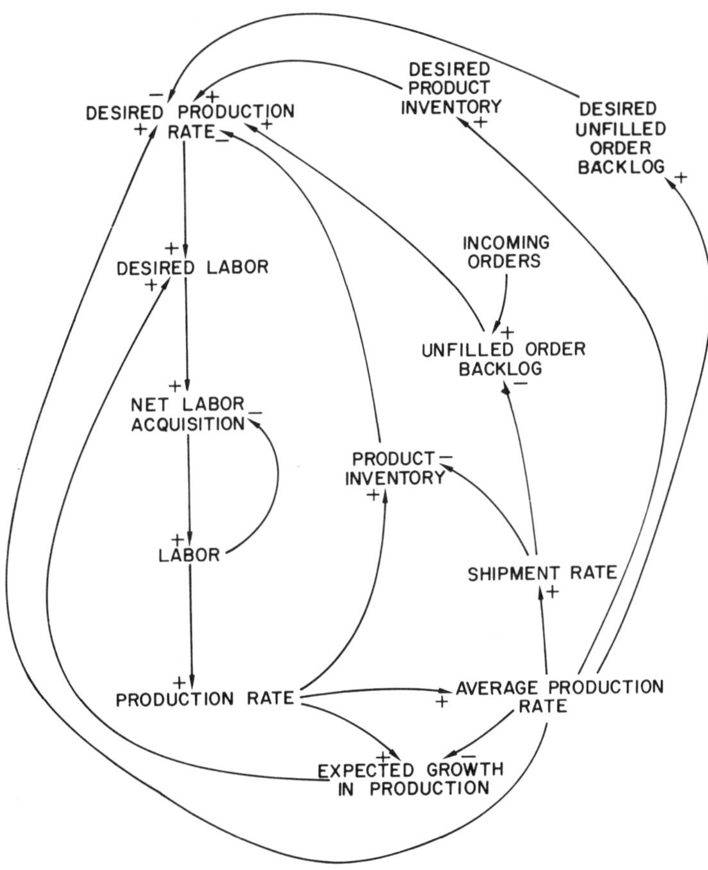


**Figure 3-5** Overview of the determinants of labor hiring

> over other and wholly disconnected parts. . . . Secondly . . . optimism on the part of one group of business men itself creates a justification for some improved expectation on the part of other groups.[7]

The extrapolation of trends in aggregate demand tends to amplify the changes in desired labor caused by changing desired production.

The sector's desired production rate, shown in Figure 3–5, is assumed to depend on three factors: the average production rate, the discrepancy between the sector's actual and desired unfilled order backlog, and the discrepancy between actual and desired product inventory. The formulation assumes that the sector will maintain its past average rate of production if inventory and unfilled order backlog are normal. Discrepancies in inventory or in unfilled order backlog create incentives to raise or lower production.

As noted, desired production in Figure 3–5 is assumed to depend partly on the difference between actual and desired unfilled order backlogs for the sector's output. If

[7]Quoted from W. C. Mitchell (1927), p. 18.

the sector attempts to maintain a given delivery delay for its product, then the desired unfilled order backlog will equal the product of the production rate and the desired delivery delay. An unfilled order backlog greater than this desired value would yield a longer delivery delay than desired, whereas a smaller backlog would bring about a shorter delivery delay than desired.

The following simple example illustrates the effect of order backlogs on desired production. Suppose the sector experiences an increase in incoming orders. Increased orders raise the unfilled order backlog over its desired value. As a result, desired production increases by an amount equal to (unfilled order backlog − desired unfilled order backlog)/backlog adjustment time. Eventually, as production capacity (labor) expands, the shipment rate rises, thereby lowering the unfilled order backlog. Moreover, the increase in production capacity raises the desired unfilled order backlog. Both the declining unfilled order backlog and the increasing desired unfilled order backlog reduce the backlog discrepancy. Over time, however, as the backlog discrepancy is eliminated, desired production drops according to the formula just given. Therefore, production gradually exceeds desired production, and the initial shortage of production capacity is converted to an excess. Continuing analogously, we can see that backlog adjustments cause successive overbuilding and underbuilding of production capacity.

Desired production in Figure 3–5 also depends on the difference between the desired and the actual product inventory. For example, if the sector wishes to expand its product inventory, the production rate must be increased. In Figure 3–5, the desired product inventory is assumed to depend on the average production rate within the sector; the relationship implies an increased need for in-process and final-goods inventories in the presence of an increase in demand as a protection against production disruptions and inventory stock-outs.[8]

The dependence of desired product inventory levels on a firm's average sales or production is one factor producing amplification of incoming order streams. Suppose, for example, that sales are 1,000 units per year and that the firm normally holds a quarter-year's worth of inventories to ensure efficient production and distribution operations. Also, suppose that the firm attempts to correct inventory discrepancies over half a year. If the firm's sales then increase from 1,000 to 1,100 units per year, production orders of 100 units per year will be placed to offset the increase in demand. At the same time, the higher level of sales will produce an increase in desired inventory from 250 to 275 units. The resulting inventory discrepancy of 25 units will generate production orders of (25/0.5), or 50, units per year, to increase stocks to the higher desired level. Therefore, as a result of the 100-unit per year increase in sales, production orders temporarily rise by 150 units per year. If, instead of producing for itself, the sector places orders for 150 units with a supplier and the supplier also holds a quarter-year's worth of inventory, then the supplier's desired production rate will rise by 150 + ((0.25(150)/0.5)) = 225 units per year. In this way an expansion in sales can induce an expansion of production greater than twice the initial increase.

[8]Section 3.3 further discusses the motives for holding inventories.

The amplification caused by inventory ordering can exceed even the figures cited above as a result of (1) rising prices and (2) lengthening delivery delays that accompany an expansion of demand. For example, if merchants order further ahead from their suppliers in anticipation of rising prices, orders will temporarily increase, thereby placing an additional upward pressure on price. The expansion of orders may continue until sufficient inventories and production capacity build up to generate a downward pressure on price. Once the rate of growth of price declines, however, advance orders for inventory are reduced, thereby leading to excess capacity in the supplying sector. Such magnification of orders in response to price changes is discussed in detail in section 3.6.

The amplification of orders due to lengthening or contracting delivery delays is analogous to the price-expectation effect described earlier. The nature of this effect was described in an early article by Thomas W. Mitchell. He hypothesized an initial situation in which retailers, caught short of inventories, increased their orders for goods. As goods are shipped, manufacturers' inventories are depleted, thereby creating shortages and raising the delivery delay for goods. At this point, according to Mitchell,

> Retailers find that there is a shortage of merchandise at their sources of supply. Manufacturers inform them that it is with regret that they are able to fill their orders only to the extent of 80 per cent; there has been an unaccountable shortage of materials that has prevented them from producing to their full capacity. They hope to be able to give full service next season, by which time, no doubt, these unexplainable conditions will have been remedied. However, retailers, having been disappointed in deliveries and lost 20 per cent or more of their possible profits thereby, are not going to be caught that way again. During the season they have tried with little success to obtain supplies from other sources. But next season, if they want 90 units of an article, they order 100, so as to be sure, each, of getting the 90 in the pro rata share delivered. Probably they are disappointed a second time. Hence they increase the margins of their orders over what they desire, in order that their pro rata shares shall be for each the full 100 per cent that he really wants. Furthermore, to make doubly sure, each merchant spreads his orders over more sources of supply.
>
> Herein originates a large false demand upon manufacturers, and herein lies a great defect of our system of competitive private initiative in industry . . . . the false demand is passed back, stage by stage, along the channels of production. . . . What, in turn, is the natural result of this situation? Eventually the streams of production are not only enlarged but overenlarged. There comes a time when the ultimate sources of supply fill nearly all the orders of their customers. The latter are surprised to find their orders filled promptly and fully, and that they are receiving more than a plentiful supply of materials. There is no longer a shortage. Instead, owing to their previous overordering, there is a surplus. Their rate of ordering slows up a little, and the ultimate sources of supply find business not quite so brisk. The producers in the second stages also fill their orders promptly and fully, thus surprising their customers in turn. Result, orders upon the second stages in the production process slow up a little. And so on down to the retailers. The rivers of

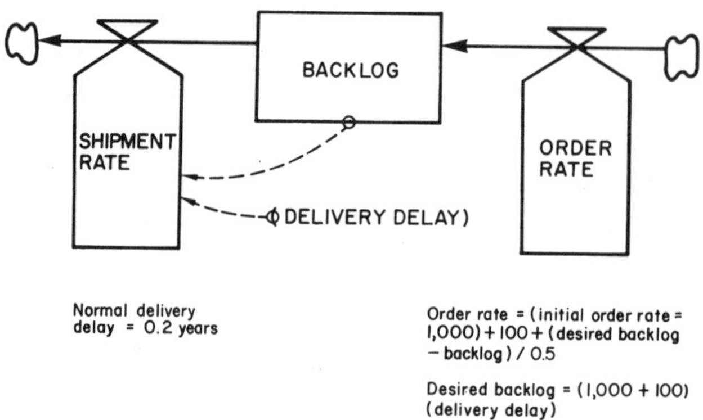


**Figure 3-6** Flow diagram of the effect of desired backlogs on customer orders

production have swollen so that the volume of flow is no longer insufficient to fill the apparent capacity of the market as evidenced in orders. Indeed, production has come to exceed the real demand, and the capacity of production organizations . . . .[9]

A simple numerical example can illustrate the possible magnitude of changes in orders and production induced by backlog-management policies and by rising delivery delays. Suppose, as before, that a firm holds inventory equal to a quarter-year's worth of sales and that sales increase from 1,000 to 1,100 units per year. As shown before, 150 extra units per year of production orders would be generated if the firm attempted to eliminate its inventory discrepancy over a period of half a year.

Suppose now that the normal delay in obtaining inventories from suppliers is 0.2 year (2.4 months) as shown in Figure 3–6. To obtain an additional 100 units per year from suppliers, the firm must add a total of (100)(0.2), or 20, orders to the order backlog level shown in Figure 3–6. If this adjustment is accomplished over half a year, then an additional order rate of (20/0.5), or 40, units per year is created. However, if all firms within the industry simultaneously experience rising demand, increased orders for goods will tend to cause the suppliers' delivery delay to increase. If the delivery delay rises from 0.2 to 0.25 year, the firm's order backlog with suppliers will have to increase to (1,100)(0.25), or 275, units, compared with an initial backlog of (1,000)(0.2), or 200, units. Again assuming a backlog adjustment time for the firm of one-half year, the order rate indicated for backlog correction will be 150 units per year = ((275 − 200)/0.5). Thus the firm's total order rate will be increased by 150 + 150 = 300 units per year, yielding a 200 percent amplification of incoming orders through a single stage of production. Section 3.6 further discusses the amplification of production deriving from price increases and lengthening delivery delays.

## 3.3 A General Model of the Production Sector

Section 3.3 develops the equations for the production sector described verbally in section 3.2. The computer simulations that follow in section 3.4 show the behavior of

[9] T. W. Mitchell (1923), pp. 645–647.

the production-sector model. The basic production sector computes desired inventories of factor inputs on the basis of the sector's desired production rate and growth expectations. The generic sector model provides a framework for interrelating production rates, product inventories, and unfilled order backlogs. Once developed, the basic sector is extended to include changes in labor efficiency (section 3.5), prices (section 3.6), and endogenous consumption (section 3.7). These extensions, drawn from the economic literature on business cycles, encompass possible modifications of the production sector and permit an analysis of several classes of forces contributing to economic instability. The extensions also illustrate the process of constructing or extending a system dynamics model based upon descriptive literature and theory.

In the basic production sector, equation 1 computes the level of inventory of the product INV. Inventory is a level variable that is increased by the production rate PR and depleted through the shipment rate SR.[10] Inventory is initialized in equation 1.1 to equal desired inventory DINV. Figure 3–7 shows a flow diagram of the determinants of the production and shipment rates.

```
INV.K=INV.J+(DT)(PR.JK-SR.J)                                1, L
INV=DINV                                                    1.1, N
    INV     - INVENTORY   (UNITS)
    PR      - PRODUCTION RATE   (UNITS/YEAR)
    SR      - SHIPMENT RATE   (UNITS/YEAR)
    DINV    - DESIRED INVENTORY   (UNITS)
```

The production-sector model utilizes a modified form of the Cobb-Douglas production function prevalent in economic literature.[11] According to the standard Cobb-Douglas formulation,

$$\text{production rate} = A \cdot K^{\alpha} \cdot L^{1-\alpha},$$

where

$$A = \text{constant}$$
$$K = \text{capital stock}$$
$$L = \text{labor}$$

The production function described in equation 2 differs from the standard formulation principally by considering variations in the utilization of capital and labor.[12] As described later, labor utilization in the form of overtime or undertime production is included in the equation for effective labor EL. Analogously, capital utilization in the form of increased work shifts or the utilization of a larger fraction of the existing capital stock is reflected in the formulation of effective capital ECAP.

[10]In the DYNAMO documentor output, an L equation denotes a level variable; N denotes an initial-value equation; C denotes a constant; R a rate equation; and A an auxiliary equation. See Appendix C for a further discussion.

[11]The Cobb-Douglas production function was originally described by Cobb and Douglas (1928) and Douglas (1948). A good summary of the properties of the Cobb-Douglas function appears in Evans (1969), chap. 10.

[12]Okun's Law illustrates the importance of including variable utilization rates in a macroeconomic model. Okun found empirically that a 1 percent reduction in unemployment yielded approximately a 3 percent increase in output. One factor underlying the more than proportionate increase in output is an increase in hours worked during periods of expanding production. Other factors underlying Okun's Law, such as variable labor-force participation rates and variable labor efficiency, generally lie beyond the scope of this book. See Okun (1962).

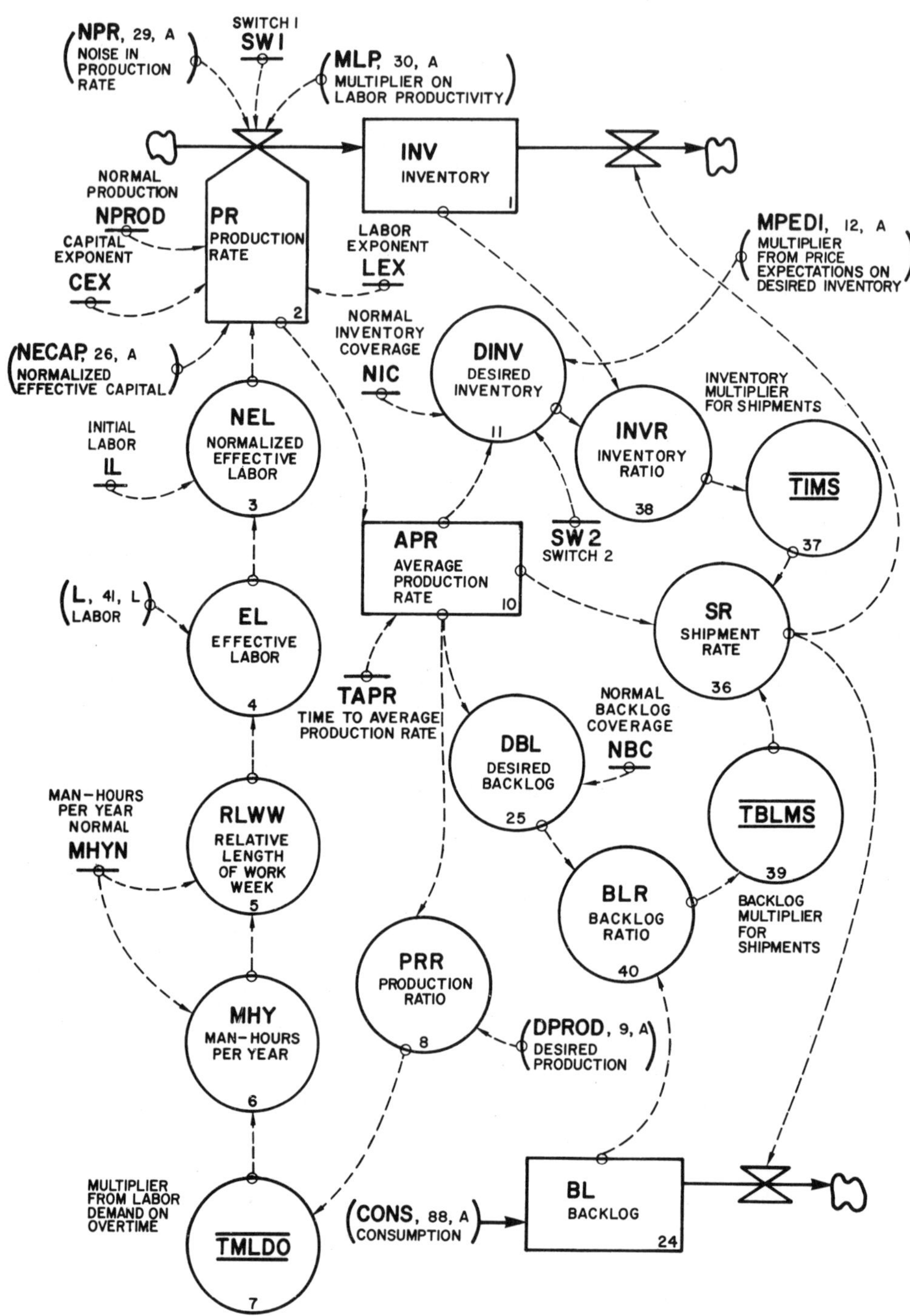


**Figure 3-7** Flow diagram of the influence of labor on the production rate

```
PR.KL=(NPROD)(EXP(LEX*LOGN(NEL.K)))(EXP(CEX*           2, R
  LOGN(NECAP.K)))(NPR.K)(CLIP(MLP.K,1,SW1,1))
NPROD=3E6                                              2.2, C
LEX=1                                                  2.3, C
CEX=1-LEX                                              2.4, N
SW1=0                                                  2.5, C
    PR      - PRODUCTION RATE  (UNITS/YEAR)
    NPROD   - NORMAL PRODUCTION (UNITS/YEAR)
    LEX     - LABOR EXPONENT   (DIMENSIONLESS)
    NEL     - NORMALIZED EFFECTIVE LABOR (DIMENSIONLESS)
    CEX     - CAPITAL EXPONENT   (DIMENSIONLESS)
    NECAP   - NORMALIZED EFFECTIVE CAPITAL
                (DIMENSIONLESS)
    NPR     - NOISE IN PRODUCTION RATE   (DIMENSIONLESS)
    MLP     - MULTIPLIER ON LABOR PRODUCTIVITY
                (DIMENSIONLESS)
    SW1     - SWITCH 1   (DIMENSIONLESS)
```

As noted, labor is the only factor of production analyzed in Chapter 3. Therefore, in equation 2.3, the labor exponent LEX is set equal to unity. With LEX equal to one, the first three terms of equation 2 appear as follows:[13]

production rate PR = (NPROD)(EXP(LEX*LOGN(NEL)))(EXP(CEX*LOGN (NECAP)))

production rate PR = $(\text{NPROD})(\text{NEL}^{LEX})(\text{NECAP}^{CEX})$

production rate PR = $(\text{NPROD})(\text{NEL}^{1})(\text{NECAP}^{0})$

production rate PR = (NPROD)(NEL)

Therefore, setting the labor exponent LEX equal to one guarantees that the production rate is proportional to labor and that capital exerts no influence on production.

In the production-rate equation (equation 2), noise in production rate NPR is an input, normally set to one, used to test the response of the basic production sector to random variations in production. The final term in equation 2 is a CLIP function that equals one, thereby exerting no impact on the production rate, as switch 1 SW1 is set to zero.[14] This switch is activated in section 3.5 to make the production rate depend upon pressures to expand output and upon labor weariness resulting from sustained overtime work.

Normalized effective labor NEL, defined in equation 3, equals effective labor EL divided by initial labor IL. As shown later, effective labor EL initially equals IL so that normalized effective labor NEL initially equals one, and the production rate simply equals normal production NPROD.

```
NEL.K=EL.K/IL                                          3, A
IL=1500                                                3.1, C
    NEL     - NORMALIZED EFFECTIVE LABOR (DIMENSIONLESS)
    EL      - EFFECTIVE LABOR   (MEN)
    IL      - INITIAL LABOR   (MEN)
```

In equation 4, effective labor EL equals labor L times the relative length of work week RLWW. According to this formulation (with production proportional to EL), production increases proportionately as the average hours worked rise.

[13]In connection with equation 2, note that EXP (a*LOGN(b)) equals $e^{a\,ln(b)} = e^{ln(b^a)} = b^a$.

[14]The CLIP function in DYNAMO has the form:

CLIP(a,b,c,d),

where a,b,c, and d are either constants or model variables. The function assumes the value a if c⩾d, and assumes the value b if c<d. In equation 2, SW1 equals zero, so the CLIP function has a value of one.

```
EL.K=(L.K)(RLWW.K)                                          4, A
    EL       - EFFECTIVE LABOR   (MEN)
    L        - LABOR   (MEN)
    RLWW     - RELATIVE LENGTH OF WORK WEEK
                  (DIMENSIONLESS)
```

The relative length of work week RLWW is a dimensionless index of the average hours worked. RLWW equals man-hours per year MHY divided by man-hours per year normal MHYN. MHYN equals 2,080 hours per man-year, reflecting a normal forty-hour work week for fifty-two weeks per year.

```
RLWW.K=MHY.K/MHYN                                             5, A
MHYN=2080                                                     5.1, C
    RLWW     - RELATIVE LENGTH OF WORK WEEK
                  (DIMENSIONLESS)
    MHY      - MAN-HOURS PER YEAR   (HOURS/MAN-YEAR)
    MHYN     - MAN-HOURS PER YEAR NORMAL   (HOURS/MAN-YEAR)
```

Man-hours per year MHY is defined as man-hours per year normal MHYN, modulated by the multiplier from labor demand on overtime MLDO. The multiplier from labor demand on overtime MLDO represents the effects of relative labor demand on the use of overtime or undertime.

```
MHY.K=(MHYN)(MLDO.K)                                          6, A
MHY=MHYN                                                      6.1, N
    MHY      - MAN-HOURS PER YEAR   (HOURS/MAN-YEAR)
    MHYN     - MAN-HOURS PER YEAR NORMAL   (HOURS/MAN-YEAR)
    MLDO     - MULTIPLIER FROM LABOR DEMAND ON OVERTIME
                  (DIMENSIONLESS)
```

The multiplier from labor demand on overtime MLDO is an increasing function of the production ratio PRR, which, in turn, is defined as the ratio of desired production DPROD to the average production rate APR. MLDO is shown graphically in Figure 3–8. As desired production rises above average production, pressures to expand output cause workers to be placed on overtime, thereby raising average labor productivity per year. Therefore, to the right of Figure 3–8, the average hours worked increase with rising pressures to produce. When desired production exceeds average production by 10 percent, the multiplier has a value of 1.07, which raises both hours worked and production by 7 percent, thereby eliminating 70 percent of the production discrepancy. The function eventually saturates at a value of 1.2, when production falls short of desired production by 40 percent. At this point, overtime production eliminates (20 percent/40 percent), or 50 percent, of the production gap. The saturation at the right of Figure 3–8 reflects the assumption that overtime becomes increasingly costly as its use expands or that labor pressures or union regulations place an upper bound on hours worked.

To the left of Figure 3–8 some labor is assumed to go on undertime, working a reduced week, when desired production falls below average production. The multiplier has a value of 0.85, representing a 15 percent contraction of the average work week, when desired production equals 60 percent of average output. The saturation at the left of the table reflects management reluctance to place workers on undertime and organizational pressures to maintain output, even if production is temporarily excessive. Under circumstances of continued labor excess, however, labor would be gradually reduced through firing or attrition (see equations 64–67). Section 3.4 analyzes the effect of managerial policies toward overtime on the relative stability of employment, inventories, and production.

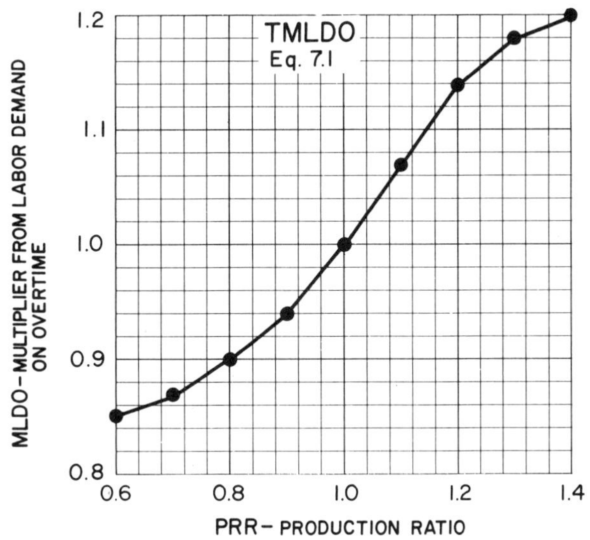


**Figure 3-8** The effect of desired production on overtime

```
MLDO.K=TABHL(TMLDO,PRR.K,.6,1.4,.1)                    7, A
TMLDO=.85/.87/.9/.94/1/1.07/1.14/1.18/1.2              7.1, T
    MLDO    - MULTIPLIER FROM LABOR DEMAND ON OVERTIME
                (DIMENSIONLESS)
    TMLDO   - TABLE FOR MULTIPLIER FROM LABOR DEMAND ON
                OVERTIME
    PRR     - PRODUCTION RATIO  (DIMENSIONLESS)

PRR.K=DPROD.K/APR.K                                    8, A
    PRR     - PRODUCTION RATIO  (DIMENSIONLESS)
    DPROD   - DESIRED PRODUCTION  (UNITS/YEAR)
    APR     - AVERAGE PRODUCTION RATE  (UNITS/YEAR)
```

In equation 9, desired production DPROD equals the average production rate APR plus a correction for inventories and backlogs. When inventories and backlogs equal their desired values, desired production equals average production, thereby indicating that the sector's current output rate is adequate to cover demand. If inventory is above the desired level, or if the backlog becomes excessive, desired production will exceed the average production rate, thereby inducing a net expansion of output. The time to correct inventories and backlogs TCIB is assumed to be 0.8 years, or roughly 10 months.[15] Figure 3–9 contains a flow diagram of the determinants of desired production.

[15]One possible extension of the production sector would incorporate a nonlinear adjustment time, as suggested by Fromm and Modigliani, that embodies a gradual adjustment of small inventory and backlog discrepancies and a more rapid adjustment of large discrepancies. See Fromm (1961), pp. 43–44, for discussion.

```
DPROD.K=APR.K+(DINV.K-INV.K+BL.K-DBL.K)/TCIB          9, A
TCIB=.8                                               9.1, C
    DPROD   - DESIRED PRODUCTION  (UNITS/YEAR)
    APR     - AVERAGE PRODUCTION RATE  (UNITS/YEAR)
    DINV    - DESIRED INVENTORY  (UNITS)
    INV     - INVENTORY  (UNITS)
    BL      - BACKLOG  (UNITS)
    DBL     - DESIRED BACKLOG  (UNITS)
    TCIB    - TIME TO CORRECT INVENTORIES AND BACKLOGS
                (YEARS)
```

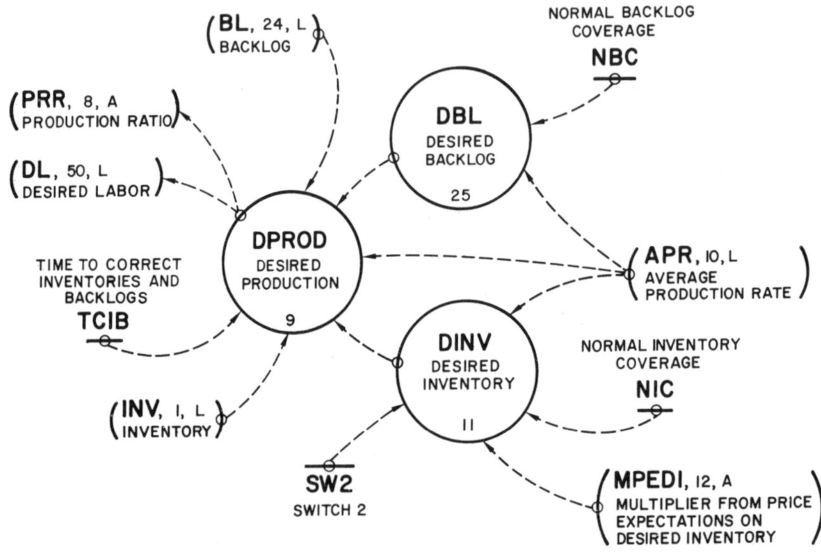


**Figure 3-9** Flow diagram of the determinants of desired production

The inclusion of inventory and backlog correction terms in the equation for desired production appears to be consistent with the results of recent econometric research. For example, Ruth P. Mack (1967) and Gary Fromm (1961) conclude that desired inventories and unfilled orders both exert a significant impact on inventory investment. In addition, Paul Darling (1959) found that inventory investment varies positively with sales and with changes in unfilled orders.[16]

The average production rate APR, computed in equation 10, is an exponentially averaged value of the actual production rate PR.[17] The time to average production rate TAPR is specified as one year.

```
APR.K=APR.J+(DT/TAPR)(PR.JK-APR.K)                    10, L
APR=PR                                                10.1, N
TAPR=1                                                10.2, C
    APR     - AVERAGE PRODUCTION RATE  (UNITS/YEAR)
    TAPR    - TIME TO AVERAGE PRODUCTION RATE  (YEARS)
    PR      - PRODUCTION RATE  (UNITS/YEAR)
```

[16] Also, see Stanback (1961), p. 41, and Zarnowitz (1961), pp. 426, 451.

[17] For a discussion of exponential averaging, see Appendix D to this volume and Forrester (1961), app. E.

The desired inventory DINV equals the average production rate APR multiplied by normal inventory coverage NIC. In addition, the equation embodies a CLIP function, here set to a neutral value of one, that makes desired inventory DINV depend on expected price changes. In the economic literature, desired inventories are typically assumed to depend on production or sales as a reflection of the level of activity of the firm. The motives for holding inventory have been described as follows by Ruth Mack:[18]

1. Bridging the time required for processes (economic transformations) to be performed.
2. Efficient production or purchasing lots.
3. Insurance against losing sales because of fluctuations in demand or other matters.
4. Smoothing operations by provision for more or less foreseeable fluctuations.
5. Grasping the potential advantage (or avoiding the disadvantage) of actual or expected changes in conditions in markets in which purchases or sales are made.
6. Providing elective freedom from the tyranny of planning for uncertain events.

Most of the six motives for holding inventory cited by Mack do not specify clearly whether desired inventory should depend on the production rate or on sales. Certain of the motives, however, appear to favor relating desired inventory to the production rate. For example, desired stocks of purchased materials and goods in process should depend on average production.[19] In addition, it should be noted that inventory ordering in most corporations is conducted by those directly involved in production. Therefore, desired inventory in equation 11 is based on the average production rate. This formulation may be regarded as an approximation to a more complex underlying structure that depends on both average production and sales.

```
DINV.K=(APR.K)(NIC)(CLIP(MPEDI.K,1,SW2,1))                11, A
NIC=.5                                                    11.1, C
SW2=0                                                     11.2, C
    DINV    - DESIRED INVENTORY  (UNITS)
    APR     - AVERAGE PRODUCTION RATE  (UNITS/YEAR)
    NIC     - NORMAL INVENTORY COVERAGE  (YEARS)
    MPEDI   - MULTIPLIER FROM PRICE EXPECTATIONS ON
                DESIRED INVENTORY (DIMENSIONLESS)
    SW2     - SWITCH 2  (DIMENSIONLESS)
```

The order backlog BL for sector output is a level variable that increases through incoming orders and diminishes through shipments. The incoming order, or consumption, stream CONS is subsequently defined in equations 88 and 89 as an exogenous input for purposes of testing sector behavior. Backlog is initialized in equation 24.1 to equal desired backlog DBL.

```
BL.K=BL.J+(DT)(CONS.J-SR.J)                               24, L
BL=DBL                                                    24.1, N
    BL      - BACKLOG  (UNITS)
    CONS    - CONSUMPTION  (UNITS/YEAR)
    SR      - SHIPMENT RATE  (UNITS/YEAR)
    DBL     - DESIRED BACKLOG  (UNITS)
```

[18]Mack (1967), p. 27.

[19]For example, Lovell (1961) bases desired stocks of purchased materials and goods in process on production rate in an econometric model of inventory investment.

Desired backlog DBL is calculated in equation 25 as the product of the average production rate APR and a constant normal backlog coverage NBC of 0.2 years. NBC represents the sector's desired delivery delay for its product; an order backlog equal to DBL would result in a delivery delay of NBC years if shipments equaled the average production rate.

```
DBL.K=(APR.K)(NBC)                                         25, A
NBC=.2                                                     25.1, C
    DBL     - DESIRED BACKLOG   (UNITS)
    APR     - AVERAGE PRODUCTION RATE   (UNITS/YEAR)
    NBC     - NORMAL BACKLOG COVERAGE   (YEARS)
```

Noise in production rate NPR is a test input used to represent random fluctuations in production.[20] The standard deviation of noise in production rate SDNPR is initially set to zero, so that the production stream is noise-free.

```
NPR.K=NPR.J+(DT/TSNPR)(NORMRN(1,SDNPR)-NPR.J)              29, L
NPR=1                                                      29.1, N
TSNPR=1                                                    29.2, C
SDNPR=0                                                    29.3, C
    NPR     - NOISE IN PRODUCTION RATE  (DIMENSIONLESS)
    TSNPR   - TIME TO SMOOTH NOISE IN PRODUCTION RATE
                (YEARS)
    SDNPR   - STANDARD DEVIATION OF NOISE IN PRODUCTION
                RATE (DIMENSIONLESS)
```

The shipment rate SR equals the average production rate APR times an inventory multiplier and a backlog multiplier. A decline in inventory relative to desired inventory or a decline in backlog relative to desired backlog lowers the shipment rate. Conversely, an increase in inventory or backlog raises the shipment rate.

```
SR.K=(APR.K)(IMS.K)(BLMS.K)                                36, A
    SR      - SHIPMENT RATE   (UNITS/YEAR)
    APR     - AVERAGE PRODUCTION RATE   (UNITS/YEAR)
    IMS     - INVENTORY MULTIPLIER FOR SHIPMENTS
                (DIMENSIONLESS)
    BLMS    - BACKLOG MULTIPLIER FOR SHIPMENTS
                (DIMENSIONLESS)
```

The inventory multiplier for shipments IMS raises or lowers the shipment rate SR according to the inventory ratio INVR (defined as the ratio of inventory INV to desired inventory DINV). Given abundant inventories, the sector's delivery delay will be relatively short, and shipments will therefore increase for a given order backlog. With low inventories, the reduced availability of goods will limit shipments. At the extreme, if inventories fall to zero, no shipments can occur.[21] Rather than have a sharp break at the point of zero inventory availability, the inventory multiplier shown in Figure 3–10 is drawn as a continuous curve that reflects the aggregation of diverse product lines,

[20]NPR is modeled as an exponentially averaged value of normally distributed random noise. This formulation approximates a constant-power-per-octave noise input. Forrester (1961), app. F, discusses the characteristics of noise in social systems.

[21]For a discussion of the effects of inventories on delivery delay, see Forrester (1961), pp. 147–149. Also see T. W. Mitchell (1923) and W. C. Mitchell (1927), pp. 5–18.

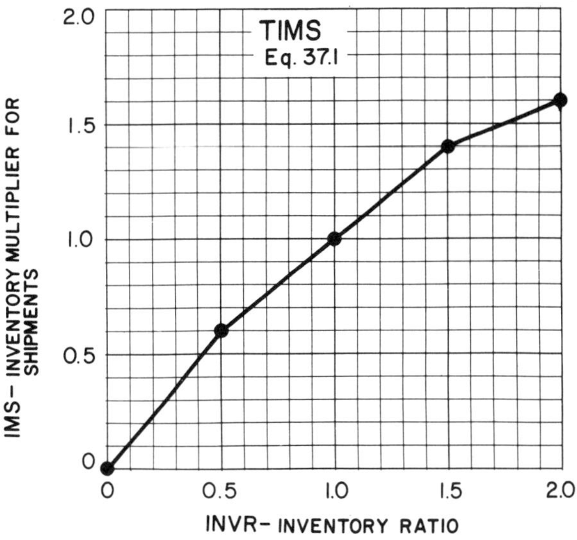


**Figure 3-10** The effect of inventory availability on shipments

and perhaps firms or industries, into a single production unit. As aggregate inventories become low, shortages of particular products, or shortages arising in particular firms, will gradually depress aggregate shipments. Therefore, the aggregation of diverse products and firms causes the delivery delay and the shipment rate to vary smoothly, rather than change abruptly, in response to changing inventory availability.

```
IMS.K=TABHL(TIMS,INVR.K,0,2,.5)                              37, A
TIMS=0/.6/1/1.4/1.6                                          37.1, T
IMS=1                                                        37.2, N
    IMS     - INVENTORY MULTIPLIER FOR SHIPMENTS
                (DIMENSIONLESS)
    TIMS    - TABLE FOR INVENTORY MULTIPLIER FOR
                SHIPMENTS
    INVR    - INVENTORY RATIO   (DIMENSIONLESS)

INVR.K=INV.K/DINV.K                                          38, A
    INVR    - INVENTORY RATIO   (DIMENSIONLESS)
    INV     - INVENTORY   (UNITS)
    DINV    - DESIRED INVENTORY   (UNITS)
```

The backlog multiplier for shipments BLMS (equation 39) is similar to the inventory multiplier IMS. As shown in Figure 3–11, a high order backlog is assumed to create pressures to expand shipments, while shipments fall off as backlog declines. At the extreme, no shipments can be sent if the unfilled order backlog within the sector falls to zero.

```
BLMS.K=TABHL(TBLMS,BLR.K,0,2,.5)                             39, A
TBLMS=0/.6/1/1.4/1.6                                         39.1, T
    BLMS    - BACKLOG MULTIPLIER FOR SHIPMENTS
                (DIMENSIONLESS)
    BLR     - BACKLOG RATIO   (DIMENSIONLESS)
```

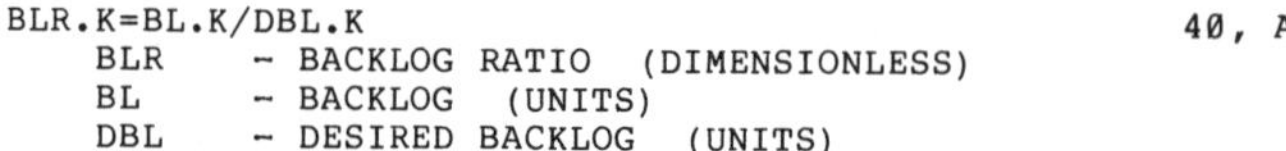

```
BLR.K=BL.K/DBL.K                                          40, A
    BLR    - BACKLOG RATIO  (DIMENSIONLESS)
    BL     - BACKLOG  (UNITS)
    DBL    - DESIRED BACKLOG  (UNITS)
```

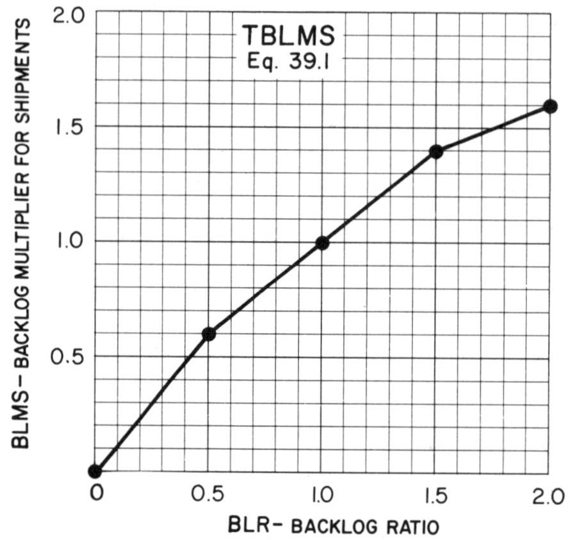


**Figure 3-11** Backlog multiplier for shipments

Labor L, defined in equation 41, is a level variable that is increased by the hiring rate HR (measured in men per year) and reduced by the termination rate TR. The initial value of labor is set arbitrarily at 1,500. Figure 3–12 shows the determinants of the hiring and termination rates.

```
L.K=L.J+(DT)(HR.J-TR.JK)                                  41, L
L=IL                                                      41.1, N
    L      - LABOR  (MEN)
    HR     - HIRING RATE  (MEN/YEAR)
    TR     - TERMINATION RATE  (MEN/YEAR)
    IL     - INITIAL LABOR  (MEN)
```

The hiring rate HR is computed as the level of vacancies VAC divided by a constant delay in filling vacancies DFV. The value of one-quarter year (three months) for DFV is a compromise between the two to six weeks typically required to hire production labor and the several months required to recruit managerial personnel.[22]

```
HR.K=VAC.K/DFV                                            42, A
DFV=.25                                                   42.1, C
    HR     - HIRING RATE  (MEN/YEAR)
    VAC    - VACANCIES  (MEN)
    DFV    - DELAY IN FILLING VACANCIES  (YEARS)
```

[22]DFV might also include a short training delay for labor to become effective. Such a delay could be represented explicitly in the model by inserting a level of labor in training between the hiring rate and a rate of workers becoming effective.

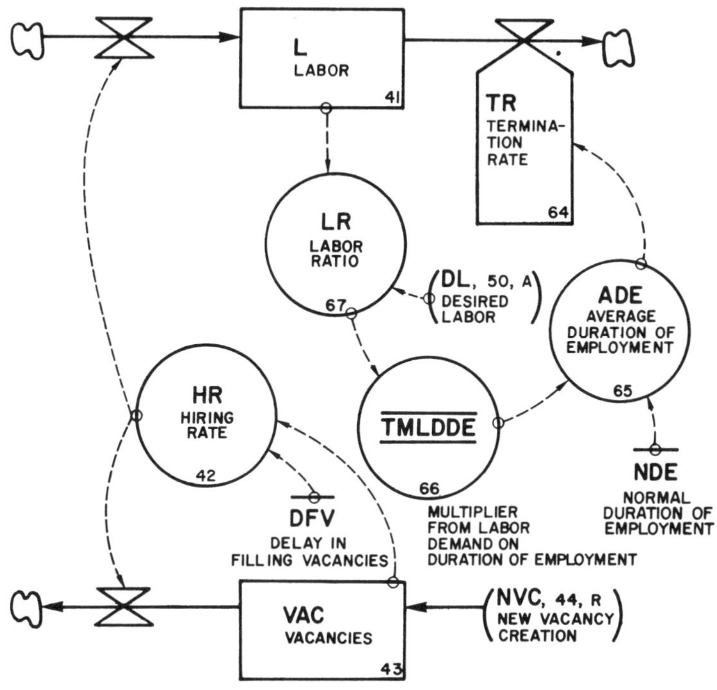


**Figure 3-12** Flow diagram of the determinants of the hiring rate and the termination rate

The level of vacancies VAC (equation 43) increases through new vacancy creation NVC and decreases through the hiring rate HR. The initial level of vacancies is set so that the hiring rate just offsets terminations. This can be seen as follows. According to equation 42, the hiring rate HR equals vacancies VAC divided by the delay in filling vacancies DFV. Therefore, at time zero, HR will equal

$$(L/NDE)(DFV)/DFV = L/NDE,$$

where NDE is the normal duration of employment.

```
VAC.K=VAC.J+(DT)(NVC.JK-HR.J)                              43, L
VAC=(L/NDE)(DFV)                                           43.1, N
    VAC    - VACANCIES  (MEN)
    NVC    - NEW VACANCY CREATION  (MEN/YEAR)
    HR     - HIRING RATE  (MEN/YEAR)
    L      - LABOR  (MEN)
    NDE    - NORMAL DURATION OF EMPLOYMENT  (YEARS)
    DFV    - DELAY IN FILLING VACANCIES  (YEARS)
```

In equation 44, new vacancy creation NVC equals the average new vacancy creation ANVC times the multiplier from labor demand on orders for labor MLDOL. According to the formulation, new vacancy creation simply equals average new vacancy creation ANVC when the supply of labor within the sector is adequate. MLDOL will exceed one, indicating a net expansion of recruitment and hiring efforts, when the labor supply is insufficient. Alternatively, MLDOL will be below one, indicating reduced hiring, when labor is in excess. Figure 3–13 summarizes the influences on new vacancy creation.

```
NVC.KL=(ANVC.K)(MLDOL.K)                                    44, R
    NVC     - NEW VACANCY CREATION   (MEN/YEAR)
    ANVC    - AVERAGE NEW VACANCY CREATION   (MEN/YEAR)
    MLDOL   - MULTIPLIER FROM LABOR DEMAND ON ORDERS FOR
                LABOR (DIMENSIONLESS)
```

Average new vacancy creation ANVC (equation 45) is defined as an exponentially averaged value of new vacancy creation NVC. The dependence of new hiring

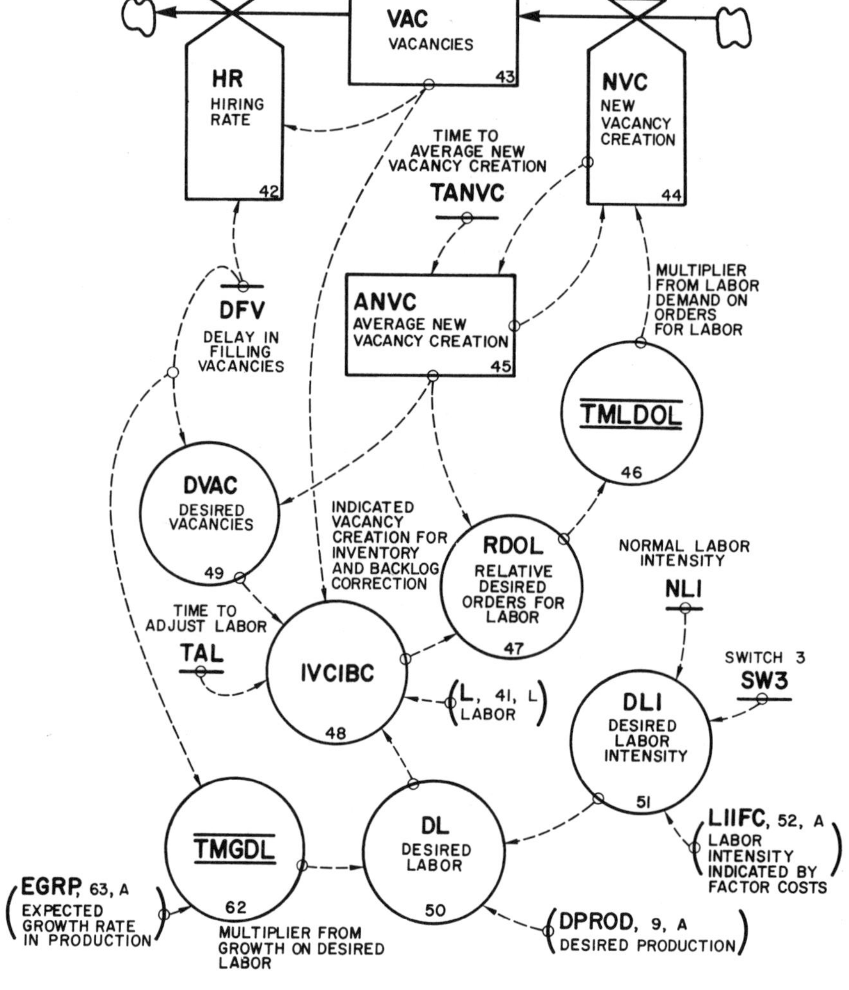


**Figure 3-13** Flow diagram of the influences on new vacancy creation

decisions on ANVC reflects the momentum, inherent in recruiting policies, that arises from reluctance to curtail recruitment activities during temporary business slowdowns and from other factors. ANVC is initialized to equal labor L divided by the normal duration of employment NDE.

```
ANVC.K=ANVC.J+(DT/TANVC)(NVC.JK-ANVC.J)                  45, L
ANVC=L/NDE                                               45.1, N
TANVC=.5                                                 45.2, C
    ANVC    - AVERAGE NEW VACANCY CREATION   (MEN/YEAR)
    TANVC   - TIME TO AVERAGE NEW VACANCY CREATION
                (YEARS)
    NVC     - NEW VACANCY CREATION   (MEN/YEAR)
    L       - LABOR   (MEN)
    NDE     - NORMAL DURATION OF EMPLOYMENT   (YEARS)
```

The multiplier from labor demand on orders for labor MLDOL (equation 46) is an increasing function of the relative desired orders for labor RDOL. As noted, MLDOL raises new vacancy creation NVC above average new vacancy creation ANVC when labor demand is high and lowers new vacancy creation when labor exceeds desired labor.

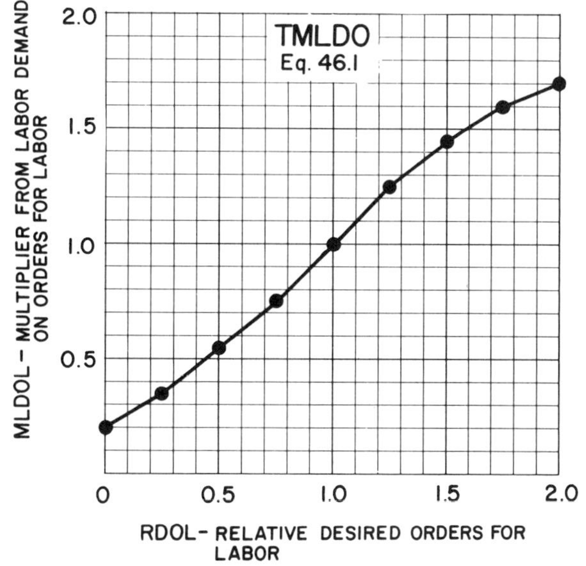


**Figure 3-14** Multiplier from labor demand on orders for labor

```
MLDOL.K=TABLE(TMLDOL,RDOL.K,0,2,.25)                     46, A
TMLDOL=.2/.35/.55/.75/1/1.25/1.45/1.6/1.7                46.1, T
    MLDOL   - MULTIPLIER FROM LABOR DEMAND ON ORDERS FOR
                LABOR (DIMENSIONLESS)
    TMLDOL  - TABLE FOR MULTIPLIER FROM LABOR DEMAND ON
                ORDERS FOR LABOR
    RDOL    - RELATIVE DESIRED ORDERS FOR LABOR
                (DIMENSIONLESS)
```

In equation 47, the relative desired orders for labor RDOL equals the average new vacancy creation ANVC plus the indicated vacancy creation for inventory and backlog correction IVCIBC, the sum divided by ANVC. This expression is equivalent algebraically to [1 + (IVCIBC/ANVC)]. Therefore, RDOL will exceed one when IVCIBC is positive, indicating excess labor demand, and will be below one when IVCIBC is negative, indicating excess labor supply.

```
RDOL.K=(ANVC.K+IVCIBC.K)/ANVC.K                          47, A
    RDOL   - RELATIVE DESIRED ORDERS FOR LABOR
               (DIMENSIONLESS)
    ANVC   - AVERAGE NEW VACANCY CREATION  (MEN/YEAR)
    IVCIBC - INDICATED VACANCY CREATION FOR INVENTORY
               AND BACKLOG CORRECTION (MEN/YEAR)
```

The indicated vacancy creation for inventory and backlog correction IVCIBC (equation 48) equals the difference between desired and actual vacancies, plus the difference between desired and actual labor, divided by the time to adjust labor TAL.

```
IVCIBC.K=(DVAC.K-VAC.K+DL.K-L.K)/TAL                     48, A
TAL=.5                                                   48.1, C
    IVCIBC - INDICATED VACANCY CREATION FOR INVENTORY
               AND BACKLOG CORRECTION (MEN/YEAR)
    DVAC   - DESIRED VACANCIES  (MEN)
    VAC    - VACANCIES  (MEN)
    DL     - DESIRED LABOR  (MEN)
    L      - LABOR  (MEN)
    TAL    - TIME TO ADJUST LABOR  (YEARS)
```

Desired vacancies DVAC (equation 49) represents the number of vacancies required to maintain a hiring rate that equals the average new vacancy creation ANVC.

```
DVAC.K=(ANVC.K)(DFV)                                     49, A
    DVAC   - DESIRED VACANCIES  (MEN)
    ANVC   - AVERAGE NEW VACANCY CREATION  (MEN/YEAR)
    DFV    - DELAY IN FILLING VACANCIES  (YEARS)
```

Desired labor DL (equation 50) is calculated as the desired production rate DPROD times the desired labor intensity DLI and the multiplier from growth on desired labor MGDL.

```
DL.K=(DPROD.K)(DLI.K)(MGDL.K)                            5Ø, A
    DL     - DESIRED LABOR  (MEN)
    DPROD  - DESIRED PRODUCTION  (UNITS/YEAR)
    DLI    - DESIRED LABOR INTENSITY  (MEN/OUTPUT UNIT/
               YEAR)
    MGDL   - MULTIPLIER FROM GROWTH ON DESIRED LABOR
               (DIMENSIONLESS)
```

Desired labor intensity DLI represents a desired labor-output ratio for the sector. DLI is formulated using a CLIP function. In equation 51, switch 3 SW3 equals zero so that DLI equals normal labor intensity NLI. Since the production sector analyzed in this chapter utilizes labor as the single factor of production, NLI is a constant, equal to normal production NPROD divided by initial labor IL. Switch 3 is activated in Chapter 5, where DLI is set equal to labor intensity indicated by factor costs LIIFC to allow for variable factor proportions in a production function utilizing both capital and labor.

```
DLI.K=CLIP(LIIFC.K,NLI,SW3,1)                              51, A
SW3=0                                                      51.1, C
NLI=IL/NPROD                                               51.2, N
    DLI    - DESIRED LABOR INTENSITY  (MEN/OUTPUT UNIT/
               YEAR)
    LIIFC  - LABOR INTENSITY INDICATED BY FACTOR COSTS
               (MEN/OUTPUT UNIT/YEAR)
    NLI    - NORMAL LABOR INTENSITY  (MEN/OUTPUT UNIT/
               YEAR)
    SW3    - SWITCH 3  (DIMENSIONLESS)
    IL     - INITIAL LABOR  (MEN)
    NPROD  - NORMAL PRODUCTION (UNITS/YEAR)
```

The multiplier from growth on desired labor MGDL represents the expansion or contraction of labor indicated by expectations of growth in demand. As discussed in section 3.2, such expectations reflect (1) an extrapolation of current trends in sales or production, and (2) the propagation of optimism or pessimism that alters growth expectations. The latter influence has been described by Wesley Mitchell as follows:

> Once started, a revival of activity spreads rapidly over a large part, if not all, of the field of business. . . . The diffusion of activity is not confined to these definite lines of interconnection among business enterprises. It proceeds also by engendering an optimistic bias in the calculations of all persons concerned with the active direction of business enterprises and with providing loans.
>
> Virtually all business problems involve elements that are not precisely known, but must be approximately estimated even for the present, and forecast still more roughly for the future. Probabilities take the place of certainties, both among the data upon which reasoning proceeds and among the conclusions at which it arrives. This fact gives hopeful or despondent moods a large share in shaping business decisions. A mathematician's mood exercises no influence upon his solution of an algebraic equation; but it does affect his opinion about the advisability of buying the bonds offered him. . . . Most men find their spirits raised by being in optimistic company. Therefore, when the first beneficiaries of a trade revival develop a cheerful frame of mind about the business outlook, they become centers of infection, and start an epidemic of optimism. Perhaps the buoyancy of a grocer gives a lumber dealer no adequate reason for altering his conservative attitude toward the business projects upon which he must pass. Yet, in despite of logic, he will be the readier to buy if his acquaintances in any line of trade have become aggressively confident of the future. The fundamental conditions affecting his own business may remain the same; but his conduct is altered because he sees the old facts in a new emotional perspective.
>
> As it spreads, the epidemic of optimism helps to produce conditions that both justify and intensify it. The mere fact that a growing number of businessmen are gaining confidence in the outlook becomes a valid reason why each member of the group and outsiders also should feel confident. For the hopeful mood means greater readiness to make new purchases, enter into new contracts, etc.—in fine, means that the incipient revival of activity will be supported and extended. There is the stronger reason for relying upon the feeling in that its growth—like the growth in the volume of goods ordered—is cumulative. As new groups of businessmen become infected

with optimism, their demeanor, talk, and actions confirm the faith of those who converted them. Thus the feeling of confidence becomes stronger as it spreads; that is, it becomes an increasingly powerful factor in supporting the movement out of which it grew, and in justifying itself.[23]

Mitchell's verbal description suggests basing the desired growth in labor on expected growth in production; expected growth is, in turn, an extrapolation of recent past growth in output. Therefore, in equation 62, the multiplier from growth on desired labor MGDL equals one, plus the expected growth rate in production EGRP multiplied by the delay in filling vacancies DFV. EGRP is defined in equation 63 as the average (fractional) annual growth rate in production. In addition, DFV represents the planning horizon over which labor can be acquired. Multiplying EGRP by DFV therefore represents the additional labor that must be recruited over the interval DFV for labor to grow at an annual rate of EGRP. This calculation is shown graphically in Figure 3–15. If production is desired to grow at a rate of EGRP, then, starting from some initial time $t_0$, labor at time ($t_0$ + DFV) must equal labor at time $t_0$, $L_{t0}$, times (1 + EGRP·DFV).

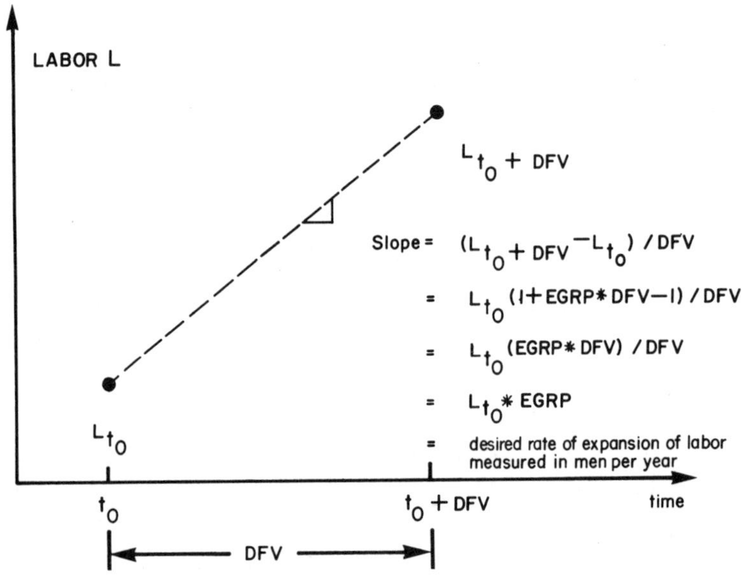


**Figure 3-15** Forward extrapolation of expected growth in production to compute desired labor

```
MGDL.K=1+(EGRP.K)(DFV)                                   62, A
      MGDL    - MULTIPLIER FROM GROWTH ON DESIRED LABOR
                   (DIMENSIONLESS)
      EGRP    - EXPECTED GROWTH RATE IN PRODUCTION
                   (FRACTION/YEAR)
      DFV     - DELAY IN FILLING VACANCIES   (YEARS)
```

[23]W. C. Mitchell (1941), pp. 3–6.

```
EGRP.K=(PR.JK-APR.K)/(APR.K*TAPR)                   63, A
    EGRP    - EXPECTED GROWTH RATE IN PRODUCTION
                (FRACTION/YEAR)
    PR      - PRODUCTION RATE   (UNITS/YEAR)
    APR     - AVERAGE PRODUCTION RATE   (UNITS/YEAR)
    TAPR    - TIME TO AVERAGE PRODUCTION RATE   (YEARS)
```

The termination rate TR in equation 64 equals labor divided by the average duration of employment ADE.

```
TR.KL=L.K/ADE.K                                     64, R
    TR      - TERMINATION RATE   (MEN/YEAR)
    L       - LABOR   (MEN)
    ADE     - AVERAGE DURATION OF EMPLOYMENT   (YEARS)
```

The average duration of employment ADE in equation 65 equals the normal duration of employment NDE times the multiplier from labor demand on duration of employment MLDDE. The normal duration of employment NDE is set at two years. This figure, which is roughly indicative of current conditions in the United States, subsumes the effects of both voluntary departures and involuntary termination of employment.[24] For simplicity, these two processes are not separately represented in the basic production sector. The multiplier from labor demand on duration of employment MLDDE modulates total labor turnover according to the ratio of labor to desired labor.

```
ADE.K=(NDE)(MLDDE.K)                                65, A
NDE=2                                               65.1, C
    ADE     - AVERAGE DURATION OF EMPLOYMENT   (YEARS)
    NDE     - NORMAL DURATION OF EMPLOYMENT   (YEARS)
    MLDDE   - MULTIPLIER FROM LABOR DEMAND ON DURATION OF
                EMPLOYMENT (DIMENSIONLESS)
```

Equations 66 and 67 and Figure 3–16 describe the multiplier from labor demand on duration of employment MLDDE, which is a decreasing function of the ratio of labor to desired labor. The duration of employment declines, through firing, as labor exceeds desired labor, and it increases in times when labor is short. To the right of Figure 3–16, the duration of employment declines to 0.6 years (= 2 × 0.3) as a large excess of labor accumulates.

```
MLDDE.K=TABLE(TMLDDE,LR.K,0,2,.5)                   66, A
TMLDDE=2.5/1.65/1/.5/.3                             66.1, T
    MLDDE   - MULTIPLIER FROM LABOR DEMAND ON DURATION OF
                EMPLOYMENT (DIMENSIONLESS)
    TMLDDE  - TABLE FOR MULTIPLIER FROM LABOR DEMAND ON
                DURATION ON EMPLOYMENT
    LR      - LABOR RATIO   (DIMENSIONLESS)

LR.K=L.K/DL.K                                       67, A
    LR      - LABOR RATIO   (DIMENSIONLESS)
    L       - LABOR   (MEN)
    DL      - DESIRED LABOR   (MEN)
```

Consumption CONS is defined using a CLIP function. Switch 4 SW4 is set to zero in equation 88 so that consumption CONS equals test consumption TCONS.[25] In

[24]*Statistical Abstract of the United States*, 1970, p. 218.

[25]In section 3.7, switch 4 is activated to represent endogenous consumption based on income.

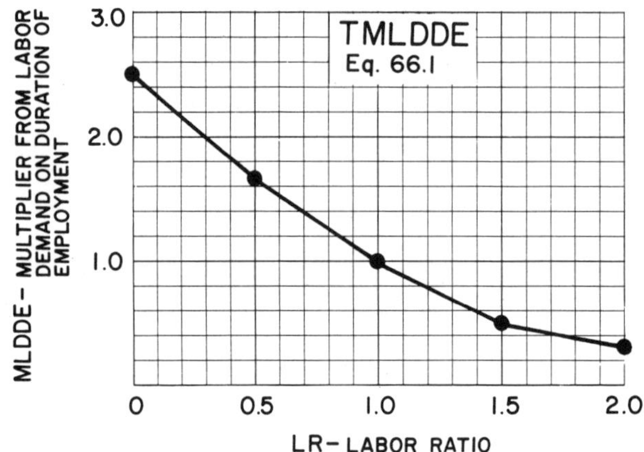


**Figure 3-16** The effect of labor demand on the termination rate

equation 89, in turn, TCONS is defined as a constant consumption rate CCR[26] modified by three test factors—a step function, a noise input, and a ramp function.[27] The test factors can be used to identify the behavior modes characteristic of the production sector. As discussed by Forrester (1961), a test input, such as random noise or a step function, can frequently be used to ''excite'' the oscillatory modes inherent in a system.

```
CONS.K=CLIP(CONSI.K,TCONS.K,SW4,1)                       88, A
SW4=0                                                    88.1, C
    CONS   - CONSUMPTION  (UNITS/YEAR)
    CONSI  - CONSUMPTION FROM INCOME  (UNITS/YEAR)
    TCONS  - TEST CONSUMPTION  (UNITS/YEAR)
    SW4    - SWITCH 4  (DIMENSIONLESS)

TCONS.K=(CCR+STEP(CSH,CST))(NTC.K)+RSW*RAMP(RSLP,        89, A
  RT)
CCR=NPROD                                                89.1, N
CSH=SSC*CCR                                              89.2, N
SSC=0                                                    89.3, C
CST=2                                                    89.4, C
RSW=0                                                    89.5, C
RSLP=20                                                  89.6, C
RT=2                                                     89.7, C
    TCONS  - TEST CONSUMPTION  (UNITS/YEAR)
    CCR    - CONSTANT CONSUMPTION RATE  (UNITS/YEAR)
    CSH    - CONSUMPTION STEP HEIGHT  (UNITS/YEAR)
    CST    - CONSUMPTION STEP TIME  (YEARS)
    NTC    - NOISE IN TEST CONSUMPTION (DIMENSIONLESS)
    RSW    - RAMP SWITCH  (DIMENSIONLESS)
    RSLP   - RAMP SLOPE  (UNITS/YEAR/YEAR)
    RT     - RAMP TIME  (YEARS)
    NPROD  - NORMAL PRODUCTION (UNITS/YEAR)
    SSC    - SWITCH FOR STEP IN CONSUMPTION
               (DIMENSIONLESS)
```

[26]The constant consumption rate CCR equals normal production NPROD, so that incoming orders initially equal the production rate.

[27]A ramp function generates an output that increases or decreases with a specified slope. The function has the form

ramp(a,b),

where a is the RAMP slope, and b indicates the time at which the ramp takes effect. Before time b, the ramp function has a value of zero.

```
NTC.K=NTC.J+(DT/TSNTC)(NORMRN(1,SDNTC)-NTC.J)          90, L
NTC=1                                                  90.1, N
TSNTC=1                                                90.2, C
SDNTC=0                                                90.3, C
    NTC     - NOISE IN TEST CONSUMPTION (DIMENSIONLESS)
    TSNTC   - TIME TO SMOOTH NOISE IN TEST CONSUMPTION
                (DIMENSIONLESS)
    SDNTC   - STANDARD DEVIATION OF NOISE IN TEST
                CONSUMPTION (DIMENSIONLESS)
```

## 3.4 The Behavior of the Production Sector

Section 3.4 discusses the behavior of the basic production sector described in section 3.3. It aims to explore the processes, within a firm or national economy, that cause variations in consumption (incoming orders) to induce variations of greater magnitude in production and the derived demand for labor.

*Procedure for Model Testing.* To facilitate the analysis of sector behavior, the production sector can be excited by a simple test input such as a step change in incoming orders. For two reasons, exciting the model with simple inputs is generally preferable to "driving" the system with exogenous time-series data on the order rate. First, if actual time series are used as input data, changes in the system variables resulting from the internal dynamics of the system may be extremely difficult to separate from changes induced by fluctuations in the input data.[28] Moreover, from a theoretical standpoint, incoming orders to a firm or entire economy are in themselves influenced by such internal variables as wage payments, prices, and delivery delays. For this reason, it appears unsound to input time-series data on orders to a model of the production system and, by letting the model run, attempt to replicate time series for inventories, employment, and other variables.[29]

*Analysis of Model Behavior.* Figure 3–17 illustrates the response of the production sector to a 15 percent step increase in consumption (orders), beginning after one-half year (at time =0.5).[30] Until time =0.5, the system remains in equilibrium, with production equal to the exogenous consumption (incoming order) rate of 3 million units per year. Also, labor, inventory, and backlog equal their desired values.[31] Over time, Figure 3–17 illustrates approximately four-year fluctuations in labor, inventories, and production. The four-year period corresponds quite closely to the average forty-nine-month period cited by Arthur Burns as characteristic of American business cycles.[32]

[28]Forrester (1961), p. 172, discusses the utility of initially testing a model with simple test inputs such as random noise.

[29]The principle that exogenous inputs to a model must not, in actuality, be influenced by internal model variables is discussed in ibid., chap. 12, and Orcutt (1952). For an analysis of the possible erroneous results deriving from violation of this principle, see Forrester, Low, and Mass (1974), pp. 185–187.

[30]The step increase in consumption is implemented in the model by setting the switch for step in consumption to 0.15. A complete model listing, including all commands needed to replicate the computer simulations presented in this book, is contained in Appendix B.

[31]Equation 2, which initializes normal production NPROD at 3 million units per year, and equation 89, which sets the constant consumption rate CCR equal to NPROD, guarantee an initial production and consumption rate of 3 million units per year.

[32]Burns (1969), p. 14.

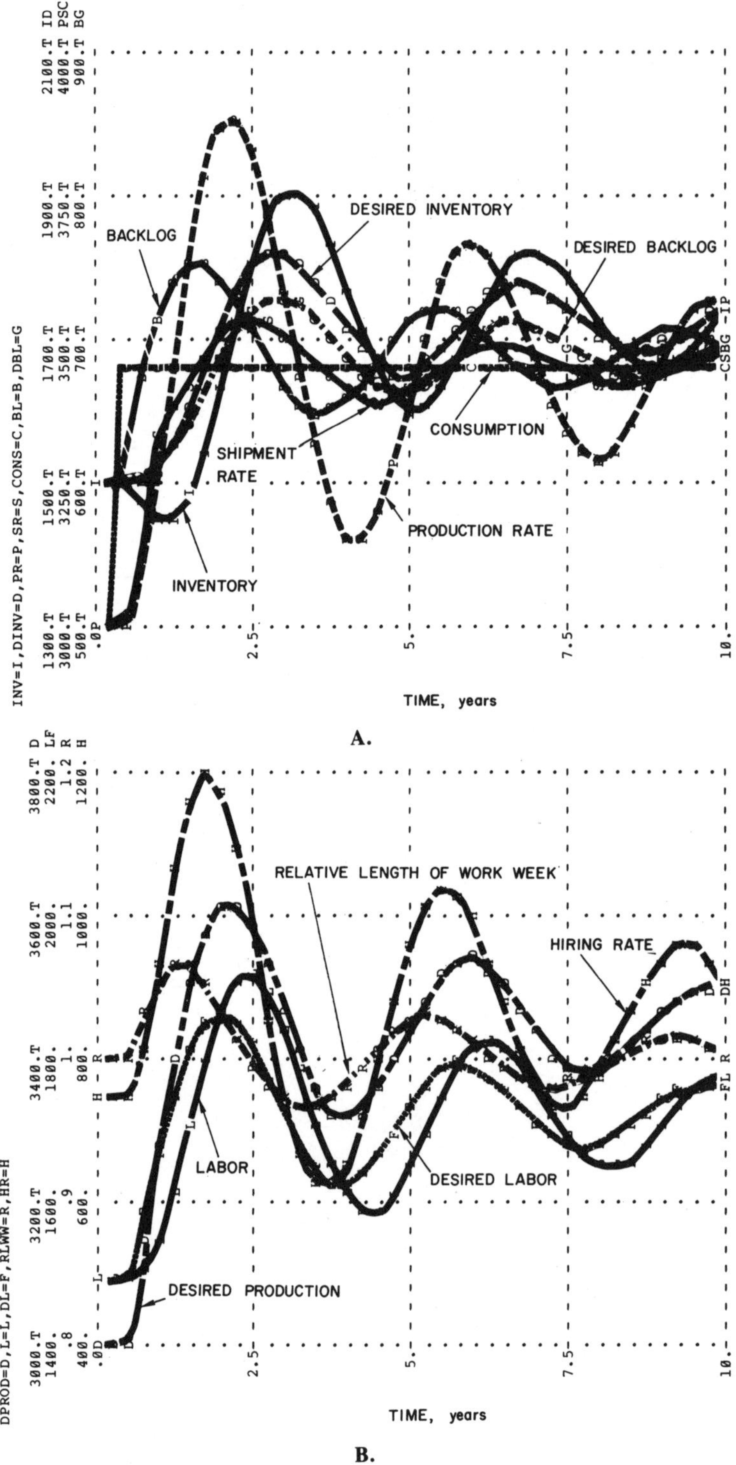


A.

B.

**Figure 3-17** Step response of the basic production sector

In Figure 3–17, as consumption jumps from 3 million to 3.45 million units per year, backlog starts to rise; the increased backlog raises the shipment rate, thereby depleting inventory. Inventory declines from an initial value of 1.5 million units to approximately 1.45 million units at the end of the first year.[33] Over the same time, desired inventory rises to 1.55 million units. Backlog increases from 0.6 million units to about 0.75 million units at year 1.5, while desired backlog rises, over the same interval, from 0.6 million to 0.65 million units. The resulting divergence between actual and desired inventory and between actual and desired backlog causes a rapid expansion in desired production. Figure 3–17B shows desired production rising from 3 million units per year to a peak value of 3.6 million units per year at year 2. The rise in desired production causes a corresponding rise in desired labor, from 1,500 men to approximately 1,850 men at year 2.

In Figure 3–17A, the production rate rises to a maximum value of about 3.9 million units per year in response to the increase in desired production. The increase in the production rate at this point over the initial value of 3 million units per year is 0.9 million units per year, or double the increase in incoming orders. The peak in the production rate lags slightly behind desired production due to the delays in acquiring labor. This lag is somewhat mitigated, however, by using overtime, instead of additional hiring, to expand production. For example, Figure 3–17B shows that the relative length of work week rises to a value of 1.07, implying a 7 percent increase in the average work week, at the start of the second year. The production rate exhibits a four-year period between years 2 and 6. The production cycle is caused by inventory and backlog policies that induce successive overshoot and undershoot of production relative to consumption.

In Figure 3–17A, as long as the production rate is below the consumption and shipment rates, inventory continues to decline, and backlog continues to accumulate. Consequently, inventory reaches a minimum value and backlog approximately attains a maximum value at the point where production rises to just equal consumption.[34] This characteristic behavior of inventory and production in the face of an increase in consumption is displayed in Figure 3–18. That figure shows an expansion of production resulting from an increase in incoming orders occurring at time $t_0$; production rises until it equals the incoming order rate at time $t_1$. However, at time $t_1$, inventory is below, and order backlog above, their desired values. These discrepancies necessitate a continued expansion of production *above the incoming order rate*. In other words, even when production equals incoming orders, expansion must continue in order to eliminate the inventory shortage and large backlog accumulated while production was still less than the incoming order rate. For this reason, the computer output in Figure 3–17B

[33]In DYNAMO computer plots, time is measured on the horizontal scale. To the immediate left of the zero-time axis, the plotting range for each variable is listed alongside its plot symbol. The plot symbols for each variable are listed, in turn, at the left of the plot-range specifications. Thus, for example, in Figure 3–17A, the symbols I and D are plotted on a range of 1.3 million (1,300 thousand) to 2.1 million (2,100 thousand). As noted to the left of the plot range specifications, inventory INV is plotted with the letter I, while desired inventory DINV is plotted with the letter D.

[34]In actuality, Figure 3–17A shows that backlog peaks roughly one-half year after the production rate equals consumption. The slight lag occurs because the shipment rate is constrained by low inventory; therefore, the shipment rate and consumption are equal only at year 1.5.

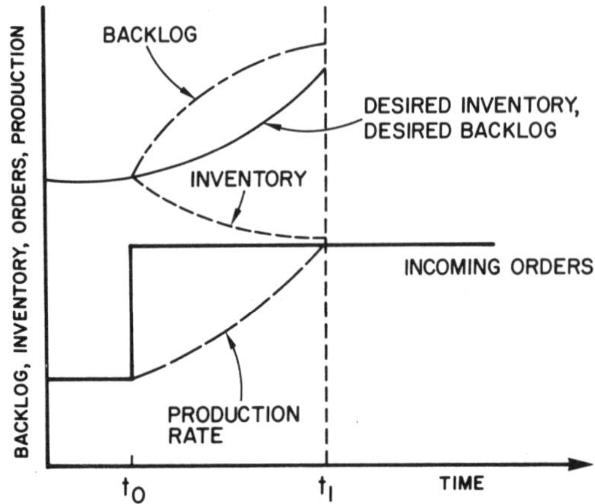


**Figure 3-18** Inventory and backlog discrepancies arising from an increase in incoming orders

shows desired production rising above consumption at the start of the second year and continuing to remain above orders until approximately year 3.[35]

In a firm or in an entire economy, if labor and production continually expand as long as inventories are short, for example, the pattern illustrated in Figure 3–19 will appear. In Figure 3–19, the production rate expands in response to an increase in incoming orders until inventory builds up to equal desired inventory.[36] However, at the point where inventory equals desired inventory, the production rate exceeds incoming orders. Inventory therefore continues to rise above desired inventory. The resulting inventory surplus can be eliminated only if production falls below sales for some period of time. In this way inventory adjustments can lead to production fluctuations around the incoming order rate. Backlogs similarly exert a destabilizing effect on the production rate, thereby accentuating the effect of inventories. Following an increase in orders, output must rise above incoming orders to eliminate the large backlogs accumulated during the initial upsurge in demand. The response of production to backlog behavior could be analyzed in a manner parallel to the response shown in Figure 3–19 for the case of inventories.

The fluctuations in the production rate in Figure 3–17A are convergent over time. Such convergent behavior is reasonable since the consumption rate is perfectly constant after the 15 percent step increase. The damping ratio characterizing production, defined as (1 − the ratio of successive peaks), is approximately 55 percent, indicating that 55 percent of the overshoot in production is eliminated in each successive cycle.[37]

[35]For a detailed verbal and graphical analysis of the causes of inventory fluctuations in a simple second-order inventory-workforce model, see Mass and Senge (1974).

[36]Note that the swings in production would be accentuated if desired inventory was assumed to rise with increasing production or sales.

[37]The production rate peaks at a value of 3.9 million units per year at year 2 and 3.65 million units per year at year 6. The damping ratio, defined relative to the mean point of the oscillation, is therefore

$$1 - \frac{(3.65 - 3.45)}{(3.9 - 3.45)} \cong 0.55.$$

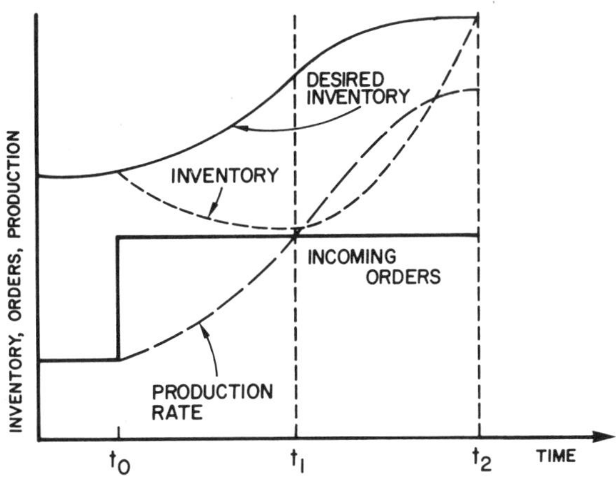


**Figure 3-19** Increase of production above incoming orders

The phase relationships seen in Figure 3–17 appear to correspond closely with available statistical evidence on business cycles. For example, in Figure 3–17A, backlog leads the production rate by approximately one-half year. Backlog peaks before production because backlog begins to decline once the shipment rate exceeds consumption; in contrast, as discussed earlier, production continues to expand beyond consumption in order to build up inventory and reduce backlog to desired values. The one-half year lead of backlog with respect to production conforms closely to evidence presented by Victor Zarnowitz (1961) and Thomas Stanback (1961).

Figure 3–17 also shows a slight lag—roughly one-quarter to one-half year in duration—of labor behind the production rate. The production rate declines even while labor is increasing because use of overtime declines (seen in Figure 3–17B as a declining relative length of work week) as actual production begins to exceed desired production. Therefore, in Figure 3–17B, the hiring rate peaks at year 1.5, but labor continues to expand because the hiring rate still slightly exceeds the termination rate (not plotted). The brief lag of employment behind the reference cycle peaks is discussed by Gordon.[38]

Finally, Figure 3–17A shows a one-year (quarter-cycle) lag of inventory behind the production rate. Since the shipment rate tends to lag behind production slightly, inventory lags behind the shipment rate by about three-quarters of a year—a period very close to the 7–9 month lag cited by Abramovitz for manufacturing industries.[39] Inventory tends to lag behind the production rate because inventory continues to increase, even while production declines, as long as the production rate exceeds the shipment rate. This time pattern of inventory behavior, which is observed in the aggregate economy as well as in many individual industries, has important implications

[38]See Gordon (1961), p. 289. Reference cycles have been analyzed by the National Bureau of Economic Research to identify turning points in general business activity. For a brief description of the approach, see ibid., pp. 265–270.

[39]Abramovitz (1950), p. 119.

for inventory policy. Inventories are commonly thought of as a buffer between production and sales, which are intended to absorb fluctuations in a firm's sales. However, as indicated by Forrester, inventory behavior often exerts a somewhat destabilizing effect on production:

> In [Figure 3–20], inventory, far from helping to smooth production rate, is contributing to the peaks and valleys in production. At time A, inventory is rising during the production peak. This means that when the system is under stress and is producing at its maximum rate, part of this production is going into inventory. Conversely, at the times marked B, inventory is falling during minimum production. This means that part of the customer demand is being filled from inventory. Therefore, the production rate at the times marked B is lower than the rate of sales to customers, while the production rate at A is higher than the rate of sales to customers. Production rate is therefore fluctuating more than sales. To have a neutral effect on production rate, inventory should not be changing at the peaks and valleys of production. To have a favorable effect on suppressing fluctuations in production, the inventory should be falling at the time of the sales peak, and rising at the time of sales valleys. This is almost never found in the usual industrial situation (except where geared to an obvious annual, seasonal demand), since the normal policies followed by most companies tend to create the kind of relationship shown in [Figure 3–20].[40]

As suggested in the preceding quotation, the production fluctuations seen in Figure 3–17 result from inventory- and backlog-management policies governing the sector's behavior. Such fluctuations are independent of major shifts in demand originating outside the sector. The internal generation of production and inventory fluctuations suggests a profitable focus for stabilization policy in designing corporate policies that attenuate, rather than amplify, changes in incoming orders. A further investigation of such policies can be carried out within the framework of the basic production sector presented here.

Figure 3–21 is a second computer simulation of the basic production sector, showing the system response to a noise disturbance in the consumption rate.[41] Like

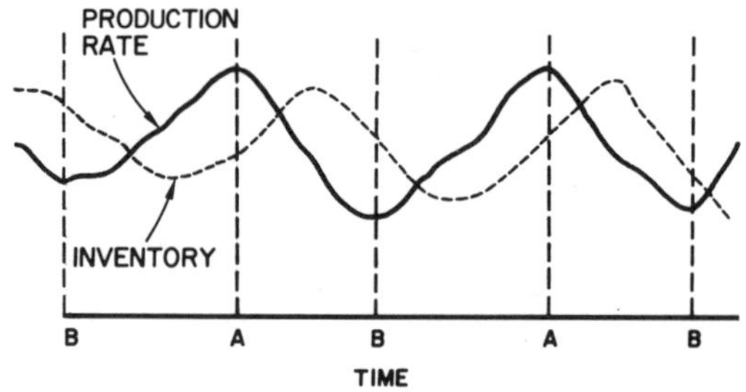


**Figure 3-20** Time phasing of the production rate and inventory

[40]Forrester (1961), p. 209.

[41]Noise in consumption is activated by setting the standard deviation of noise in test consumption SDNTC equal to 0.1. Note that the time scale in Figure 3–21 is extended to twenty years.

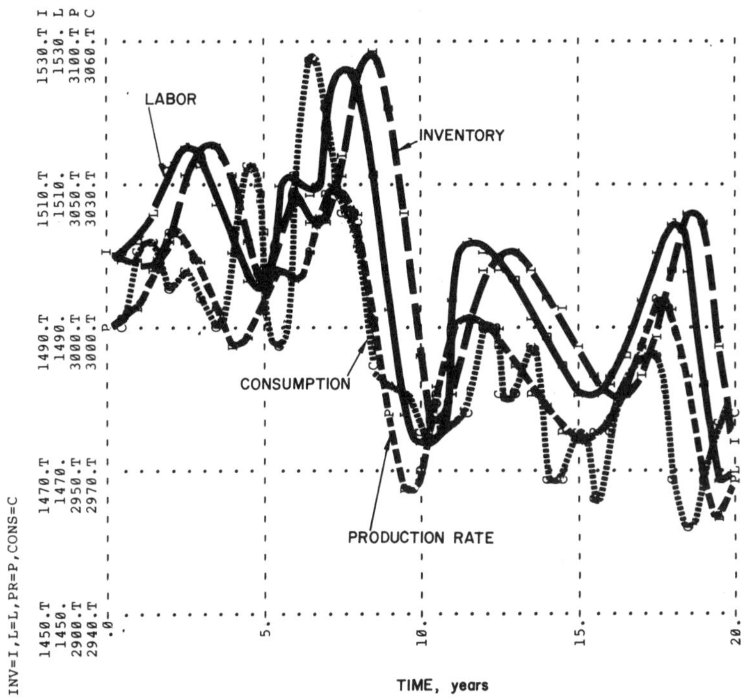


**Figure 3-21** Noise response of the basic production sector

Figure 3–17, Figure 3–21 illustrates a four-year cycle in labor, inventory, and the production rate; the simulation demonstrates how random noise can excite the fluctuations seen previously in response to a step increase in consumption. A detailed explanation of the model behavior in Figure 3–21 would be completely parallel to that given for Figure 3–17, and therefore is not provided here. Nonetheless, the simulation is included for two reasons: first, because random fluctuations in orders are more realistic and are encountered far more commonly than step changes in demand; second, because Figure 3–21 illustrates how any pattern of incoming orders upon which random noise is superimposed may be amplified to yield fluctuations in overall business activity.

*Summary of Analysis.* The preceding discussion has shown how four-year fluctuations in business activity were generated by labor and production adjustments in response to inventory and backlog changes. Such short-term fluctuations closely resemble typical business-cycle behavior, both in terms of overall periodicity and in terms of phase relationships between such variables as order backlog, the production rate, employment, and inventory. The explanation of the model behavior has focused on production overshoot caused by inventory and backlog policies. In periods of expanding demand, desired inventory rises as inventory is depleted and unfilled order backlog rises. To rebuild inventory and lower backlog, production must be raised temporarily above the incoming order rate. However, once inventory and backlog are restored to normal, the production rate still exceeds the order rate, thereby increasing inventory above its desired value. The resulting inventory surpluses can be reduced only by lowering production *below* the order rate. Through this process of adjustment, regular fluctuations are generated in response to any minor changes in demand. These results suggest the potential value of restructuring the policies of the firm to minimize sensitivity to exogenous or random disturbances.

*Sensitivity Analysis.* This section describes several parameter sensitivity tests performed on the basic production sector. The purpose of sensitivity testing is twofold. First, the tests may identify any parameters on whose precise values the system behavior is highly dependent.[42] Such parameters, once identified, may be estimated by using formal statistical methods or other means. Alternatively, the results may identify areas of model structure that need to be altered or expanded. Second, sensitivity experiments may indicate the likely direction of behavior changes induced by policies whose effects can be simulated through parameter changes. For example, simulations described later in this section show how relative conservatism or aggressiveness in inventory management can be related to changes in model parameters.

For each of the sensitivity experiments reported in this section, Figure 3–17 serves as the base, or reference, simulation. Figure 3–17 provides a useful reference because, in evaluating stability, the focus of interest is *relative stability*—that is, the marginal contribution to stability of a particular factor under examination. The sensitivity tests reported in this section cover (1) a reduced use of overtime and (2) a more rapid correction of inventory and backlog discrepancies. The tests indicate that most parameter changes, within a 50–100 percent range, exert little effect on the periodicity or other characteristics of the cycle observed in Figure 3–17.

The results of the first sensitivity test are presented in Figure 3–22. It shows the system response to a 15 percent step increase in consumption when less use is made of overtime and undertime.[43] For any given discrepancy between actual and desired production, the use of overtime equals approximately one-half of its previous value. Such a policy of reduced overtime might be the result, for example, of tight financial controls and concern with overtime costs. Figure 3–23 shows both the new and the old overtime relationships.

Compared with the reference simulation (Figure 3–17), Figure 3–22 exhibits a slight lengthening of the cycle by about one-quarter year and a reduction in system stability. For example, the damping ratio characterizing the production rate is roughly 0.4, compared with its previous value of 0.55. A damping ratio of 0.4 means that the amplitude of each cycle (defined relative to the mean value) equals 60 percent of the amplitude of the previous cycle.

The slight extension of the period of the cycle in Figure 3–22 reflects an increased reliance on new hiring, instead of more overtime use, to eliminate discrepancies be-

[42]A related, and often more important, dimension of parameter sensitivity testing is whether the effectiveness of recommended policies is highly dependent on changes in parameter values. For a discussion of this issue, see Mass (1974b), "Self-Learning Revival Policies in Urban Dynamics."

[43]To facilitate the comparison of different runs, the computer simulations in Chapter 3 describing step response are plotted on identical scales, unless noted otherwise.

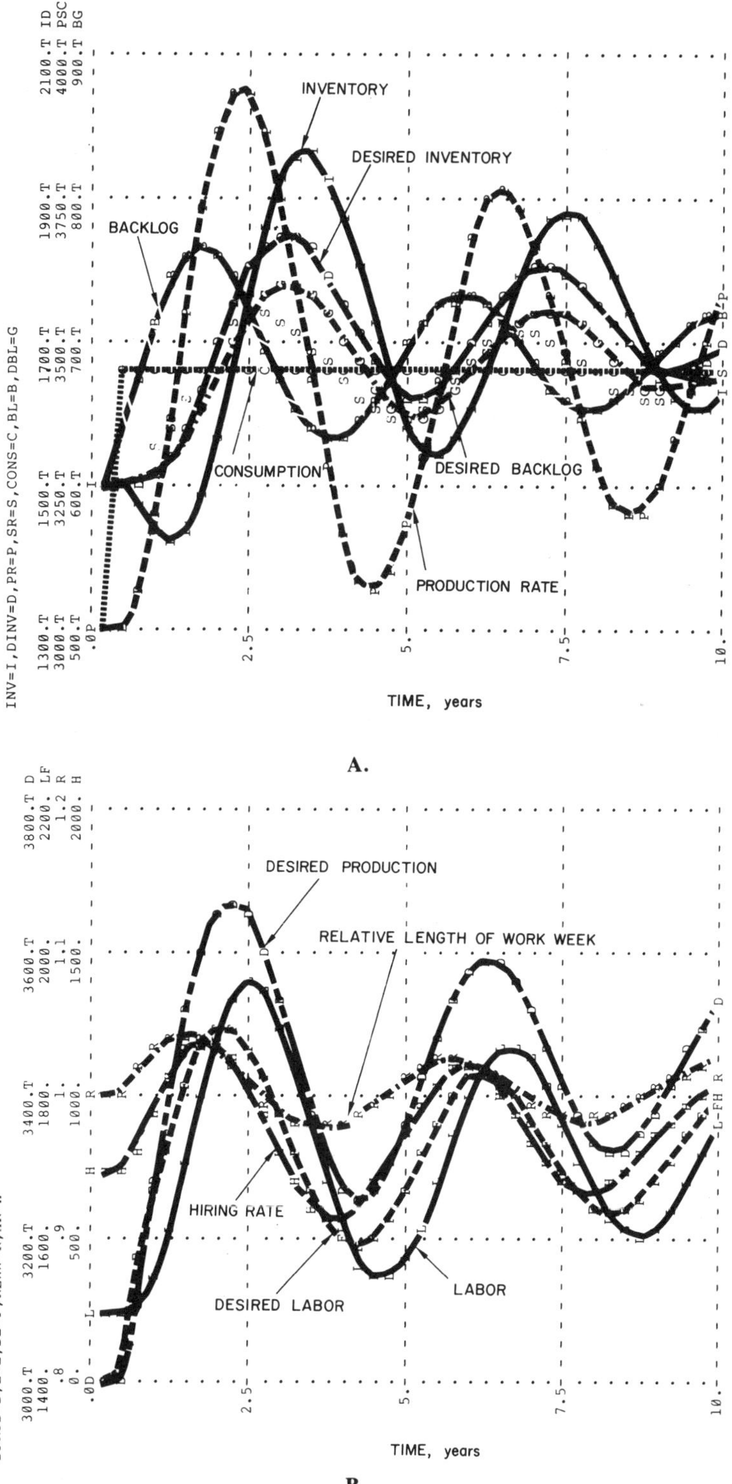


**B.**

**Figure 3-22** Reducing the use of overtime

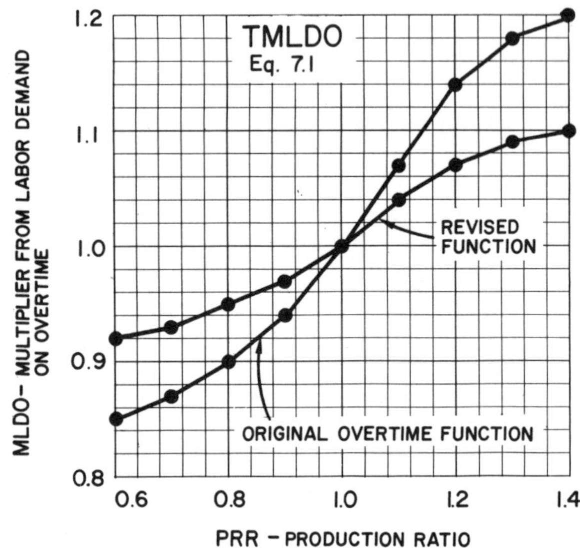


**Figure 3-23** Reduced overtime policy

tween the production rate and desired production. The duration of the cyclic adjustment therefore increases somewhat because of the delays in acquiring and training new labor. The reduced stability also appears to be a consequence of a slower adjustment of the production rate to desired production. In lengthening by about one-quarter year the time required for production to increase to the level of consumption, the policy of reduced overtime both amplifies the severity of the inventory shortage felt at the point of crossing and causes a longer delivery delay (higher unfilled order backlog). As a result, desired production is maintained above its corresponding value in Figure 3–17, thereby accentuating the overshoot and rise in the production rate. This argument can be extended to demonstrate that a lesser reliance on overtime leads to an amplification of changes in the production rate, compared with the reference simulation.

The outcomes in Figure 3–22 are also interesting from the standpoint of corporate policy. The sensitivity test indicates that a reduced use of overtime, motivated by short-term concerns with costs and profitability, can have a deleterious long-run effect through increased hiring, training, layoff, and turnover costs.[44] The results suggest the importance of evaluating the costs of overtime policies both in terms of current costs and in terms of the overall effects on employment stability. For example, the long-run stability derived from increased overtime may frequently offset negative short-term cost considerations. A more detailed analysis of overtime-management policies is warranted along these lines.

The second sensitivity test analyzes the system response to attempting a more rapid correction of inventory and backlog descrepancies, represented by lowering the value of the coefficient time to correct inventories and backlogs TCIB. This coefficient

[44]Holt and Modigliani (1961), p. 4, describe the adverse effects of production fluctuations on business costs.

inherently reflects relative conservatism or aggressiveness on the part of management. A long adjustment time would be associated with a conservative management that adjusts production slowly in response to inventory descrepancies in an effort to avoid overproduction and subsequent inventory surpluses. On the other hand, a short response time would characterize a management that responds quickly to an inventory imbalance. The magnitude of TCIB also reflects technological relationships, such as production lead times and the speed of transportation. Therefore, for example, simulating the production-sector model with a smaller TCIB can be a means for testing Fromm's attribution of milder inventory cycles to faster transportation and shorter lead times.[45]

Figure 3–24 illustrates the system response to a step increase in consumption when the time to correct inventories and backlogs is reduced by 50 percent, from 0.8 years to 0.4 years. Compared with the reference simulation, Figure 3–24 exhibits a reduction in the period of the cycle from four years to approximately three years but little other effect on overall stability or on phase relationships between model variables. For example, the damping ratio characterizing the production rate in Figure 3–24 is roughly 0.55, which is identical to the damping ratio in the reference simulation. Moreover, labor is characterized by roughly the same degree of fluctuation in both simulations. Compared with the reference simulation, Figure 3–24 exhibits somewhat smaller inventory and backlog fluctuations. For example, Figure 3–24A shows a peak inventory of about 1.85 million units, versus a peak value of nearly 2 million units in Figure 3–17A. In addition, backlog rises to about 0.73 million units in Figure 3–24A, compared with a peak value of nearly 0.8 million units in Figure 3–17A. In terms of overall behavior, therefore, more rapid inventory and backlog corrections appear to have only a slight enhancing effect on stability. From a managerial cost-benefit standpoint, moreover, the positive effects deriving from the policy are likely to be outweighed by the costs of achieving a 50 percent more rapid response in production.

The minor impact of changing TCIB, shown in Figure 3–24, can be explained in terms of two offsetting effects of the change. First, on the upswing of production, the production rate is increased more rapidly and therefore intersects the consumption rate at an earlier time than in the reference simulation. In turn, the more rapid increase in the production rate causes inventory to be somewhat higher, and backlog lower, at the point of intersection. In Figure 3–24A, for example, inventory declines only negligibly, compared with Figure 3–17A; also, as noted, backlog only rises to 0.73 million units, which is lower than the 0.8 million units in the reference simulation. Such effects tend to reduce the overshoot of production above consumption (incoming orders) necessary to rebuild inventory and lower backlog to desired values. But the production sector is now attempting to adjust *a given discrepancy* in inventory or backlog twice as quickly. So, although the inventory and backlog discrepancies are roughly one-half as large, the response of production is essentially the same. Due to these offsetting effects, the primary impact of reducing TCIB is to shorten the duration of the cycle, with relatively little impact on the stability of production and employment.

[45]Fromm (1961), p. 48.

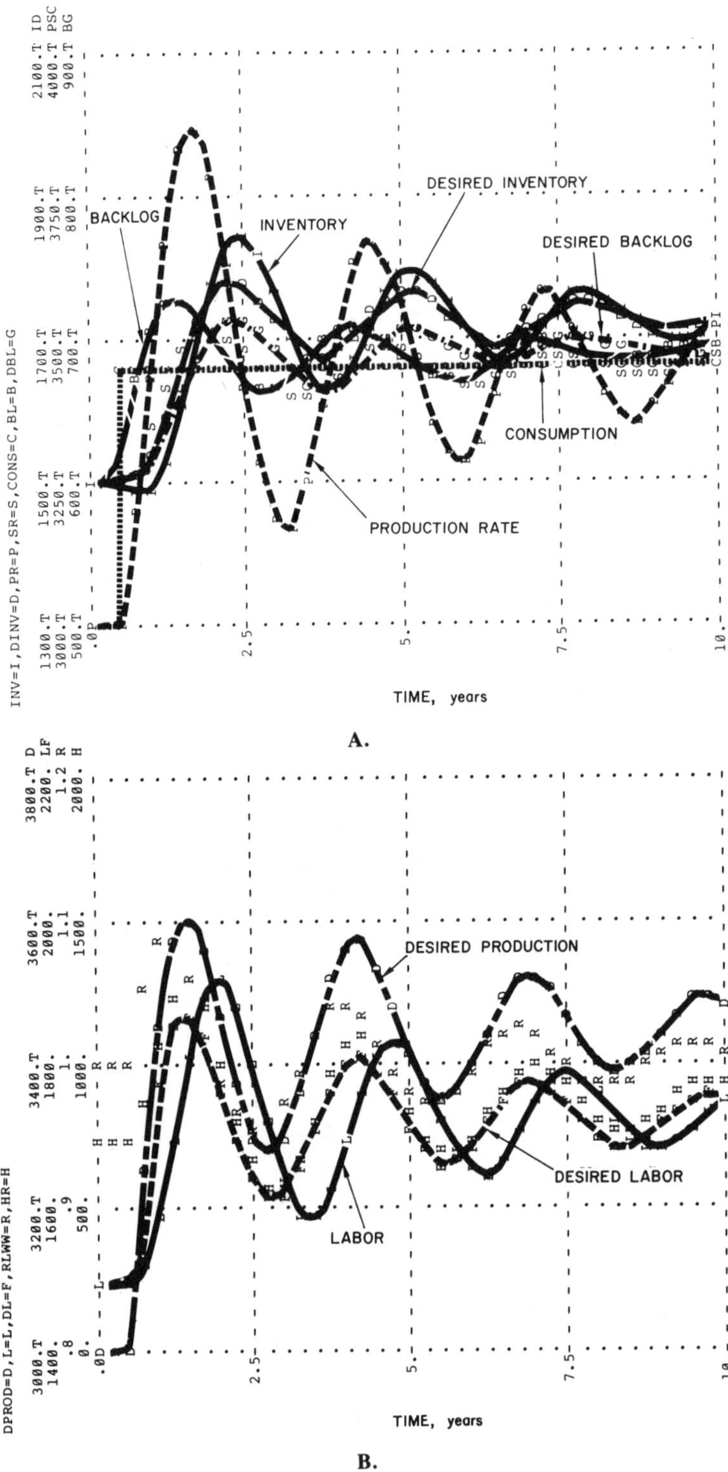


**Figure 3-24** Increased aggressiveness in correcting inventories and backlogs

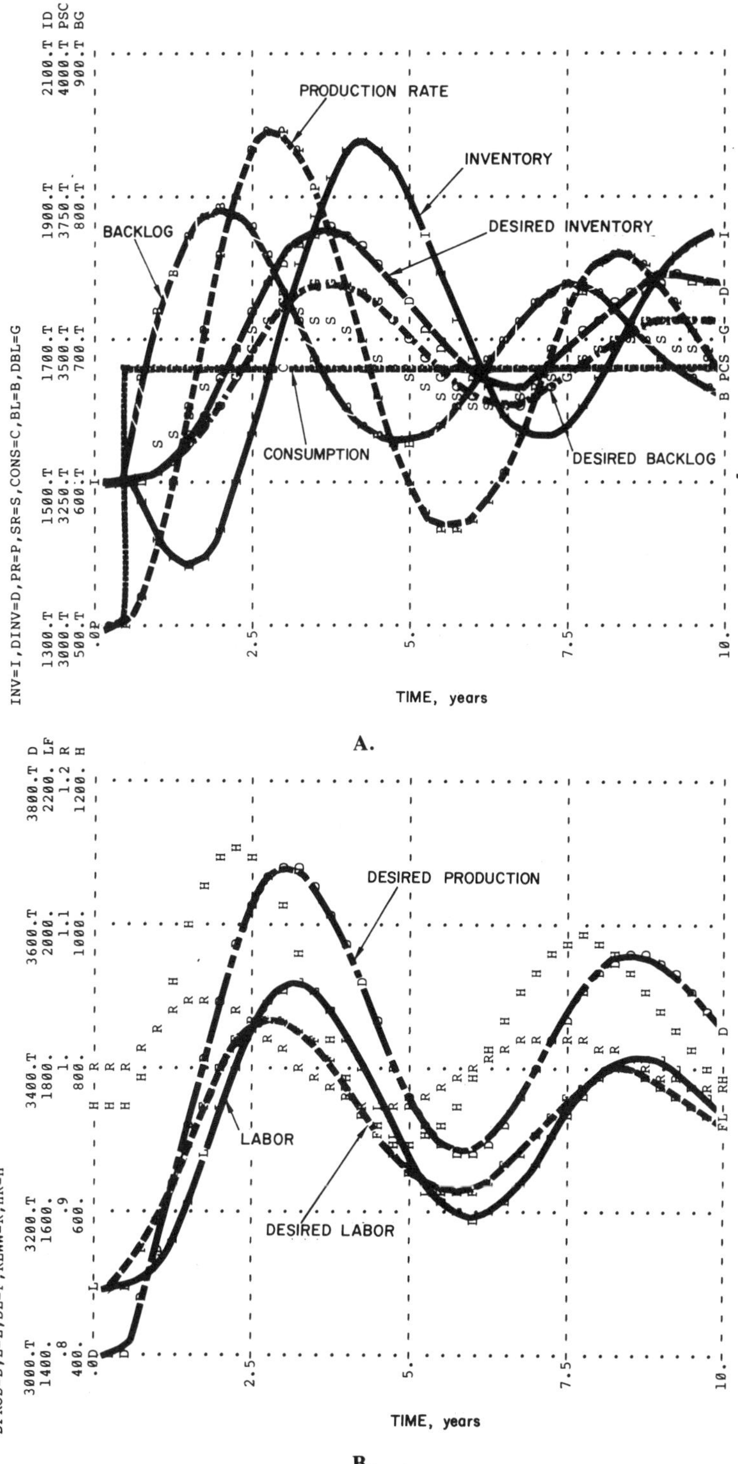


**Figure 3-25** Slower adjustment of inventories and backlogs

Figure 3–25 explores the effects of more gradual correction of inventories and backlogs, the opposite policy to that presented in Figure 3–24. In Figure 3–25, TCIB is increased from 0.8 to 1.6 years, a value that is probably quite long for most firms. As expected from the previous simulation, Figure 3–25 shows a lengthening of the cycle—from four years to five and one-half years—and a very minor reduction in stability. Figure 3–25 is included here, first, to illustrate the minor impact of changes in the parameter TCIB on system stability and, second, to illustrate that variations of TCIB within a reasonable range lead to inventory-labor-production cycles consistently within the 3–5 year periodicity range characteristic of most business cycles.

### 3.5 Variable Labor Efficiency in the Basic Production Sector

Section 3.5 is the first of three sections that extend the range of factors encompassed in the basic production sector. The purpose of these sections is twofold: to gain a deeper understanding of the processes underlying business-cycle fluctuations, and to show how the basic production sector can be elaborated to deal with factors discussed in the descriptive economic literature.

The basic production sector, developed in section 3.3, assumes that the production rate is proportional to labor and to the relative length of the work week. According to this formulation, labor productivity—measured by output per man per year—is assumed to be constant. However, available data show that labor productivity per unit of time varies systematically over the course of the business cycle: productivity tends to rise during the early stages of expansion (relative to a long-term productivity trend), decline in late expansion and early contraction, and finally rise again in the last stages of the downswing.[46] This cyclic variation in productivity has a destabilizing effect on the economy: employment must be expanded rapidly during the business-cycle upswing to offset declining productivity, and it can be reduced sharply during the contraction as productivity once again improves. The discussion that follows provides a verbal description by Wesley Mitchell of the hypothesized causes of variable labor effectiveness over the cycle and translates the verbal description into model equations, which are then added to the basic production sector. The behavior of the resulting system is then analyzed. Finally, the last part of section 3.5 generalizes the findings to identify a class of processes that cause a reduction of output in the face of excess market demand.

*Mitchell's Theory of Cyclic Productivity.* In several of his books, Wesley Mitchell has developed a theory explaining the cyclic behavior of labor productivity.[47] According to Mitchell,

> When revival has ripened into full prosperity . . . employers are constrained to accept any help to be had. They must take on men who are too old, and boys who are too young, men of irregular habits, men prone to malinger, even the chronic "trouble makers." Raw recruits of all sorts must be enlisted and trained in a hurry at the employer's expense. The average efficiency of the working forces is inevitably impaired . . . .

[46]Gordon (1961), pp. 209–292, discusses cyclic variations in productivity, labor costs, and profit margins.
[47]For example, W. C. Mitchell (1927, 1941).

While the relatively inefficient reserve army of labor is thus called into active service, both the standing force and the reserves are kept at work long hours. Now overtime labor is especially expensive to employers not only because it often commands extra rates of wages, but also because it is tired labor. Few manual laborers possess sufficient strength and vitality to stretch out their working day from 8 or 9 to 10, 11, or 12 hours for weeks or even months at a time without loss of efficiency. At first, the closing hours of the long day, after a time, all the hours of every day find the men less alert and less energetic—unable to accomplish as much work per hour as in less busy seasons. Moreover, the quality of the output declines as nerves become fatigued. 'Spoiled work' increases often at an alarming pace, and the resulting loss of materials and time threatens serious encroachments upon profits.

Quite apart from this difficulty of overtime, men cannot be induced to work at so fast a pace when employment is abundant as when it is scarce. Employers complain that in good times their men 'slow down'; employees complain that in dull times they are 'speeded up.' Whatever may be the merits of this chronic dispute about the fairness of the day's work given for a day's pay in either phase of the business cycle, there is abundant testimony from both sides as to the existence of a considerable difference in the energy exerted. Theoretical writers have strangely neglected this point, but the trade journals make much of it. The most trustworthy body of evidence on the subject, however, is contained in the special report by the federal Commissioner of Labor in 1904 upon *Regulation and Restriction of Output*. This evidence is the more convincing because the influence of business conditions upon the efficiency of labor was not a subject of inquiry. Nevertheless, manufacturers and foremen, trade-union officials, and manual workers both within and without the ranks of organized labor called attention time after time to the fact that the pace of work was slower in the flush times of 1900–02 than it had been in the dull times of 1894–96. In different phrases they all gave the same explanation—men are less afraid of discharge when business is good. . . . One final matter may be mentioned: prosperity is unfavorable to economy in business management. When mills are running overtime, when salesmen are sought out by importunate buyers, when premiums are being offered for quick deliveries, when the railways are congested with traffic, then neither the overrushed managers nor their subordinates have the time and the patience to keep waste down to the possible minimum. The pressure that depression applied to attain the fullest utilization of all material and labor is relaxed, and in a hundred little ways the cost of doing business creeps upward. Still less can attention be given to the adoption of improved methods of organization; for changes in habitual routine are always the source of some confusion and delay when they are being introduced, and when an enterprise has all the business it can handle delay is the one thing to be avoided. Even when the feasibility of making an important improvement is demonstrated to the managers of an enterprise, they often defer its introduction to a less busy season. Progress in industrial technique and in business methods would be slower if business communities were always prosperous.[48]

[48]W. C. Mitchell (1941), pp. 32–33, 38–39.

The quotations from Mitchell describe several processes. First, the efficiency of production labor tends to decline during business-cycle expansions due to the hiring of less-suited or less-productive workers, weariness from sustained overtime, and worker slowdowns as a result of reduced fears of dismissal when labor markets are tight. At the same time, management effort is diverted from overseeing production to expediting, placating customers, and similar overhead activities; reduced efficiency, in turn, leads to waste and to increased production costs. As discussed later in section 3.5, the responses described by Mitchell imply a decline in efficiency and output *as a direct consequence of high product demand.*

Mitchell's theory can be readily incorporated into the equations for the basic production sector. Figure 3–26 provides a flow diagram of the necessary additions.

Variable labor productivity is introduced in the basic production sector through the multiplier on labor productivity MLP. Setting switch 1 SW1 to one in the production rate equation (equation 2) makes the production rate equal

(Normal production NPROD)(Normalized effective labor NEL) (Multiplier on labor productivity MLP).[49]

```
PR.KL=(NPROD)(EXP(LEX*LOGN(NEL.K)))(EXP(CEX*          2, R
  LOGN(NECAP.K)))(NPR.K)(CLIP(MLP.K,1,SW1,1))
NPROD=3E6                                              2.2, C
LEX=1                                                  2.3, C
CEX=1-LEX                                              2.4, N
SW1=0                                                  2.5, C
    PR      - PRODUCTION RATE  (UNITS/YEAR)
    NPROD   - NORMAL PRODUCTION (UNITS/YEAR)
    LEX     - LABOR EXPONENT  (DIMENSIONLESS)
    NEL     - NORMALIZED EFFECTIVE LABOR (DIMENSIONLESS)
    CEX     - CAPITAL EXPONENT  (DIMENSIONLESS)
    NECAP   - NORMALIZED EFFECTIVE CAPITAL
                (DIMENSIONLESS)
    NPR     - NOISE IN PRODUCTION RATE  (DIMENSIONLESS)
    MLP     - MULTIPLIER ON LABOR PRODUCTIVITY
                (DIMENSIONLESS)
    SW1     - SWITCH 1  (DIMENSIONLESS)
```

The multiplier on labor productivity MLP is defined in equation 30 as the product of the multiplier from overtime on labor productivity MOLP and the multiplier from production pressure on labor productivity MPPLP; these two new variables are defined in equations 31–35.

```
MLP.K=(MOLP.K)(MPPLP.K)                                30, A
    MLP     - MULTIPLIER ON LABOR PRODUCTIVITY
                (DIMENSIONLESS)
    MOLP    - MULTIPLIER FROM OVERTIME ON LABOR
                PRODUCTIVITY (DIMENSIONLESS)
    MPPLP   - MULTIPLIER FROM PRODUCTION PRESSURE ON
                LABOR PRODUCTIVITY (DIMENSIONLESS)
```

The multiplier from overtime on labor productivity MOLP (equation 31) depends on the average relative length of work week ARLWW, defined as a one-third year exponential average of the relative length of work week RLWW. In the equation for

[49]In equation 2, note that the capital exponent CEX still equals zero, so that production is proportional to normalized effective labor, and capital exerts no impact on the production rate. Switch 1 SW1 equals zero in equation 2, but is set to one in the simulations later in this section to activate the multiplier on labor productivity MLP.

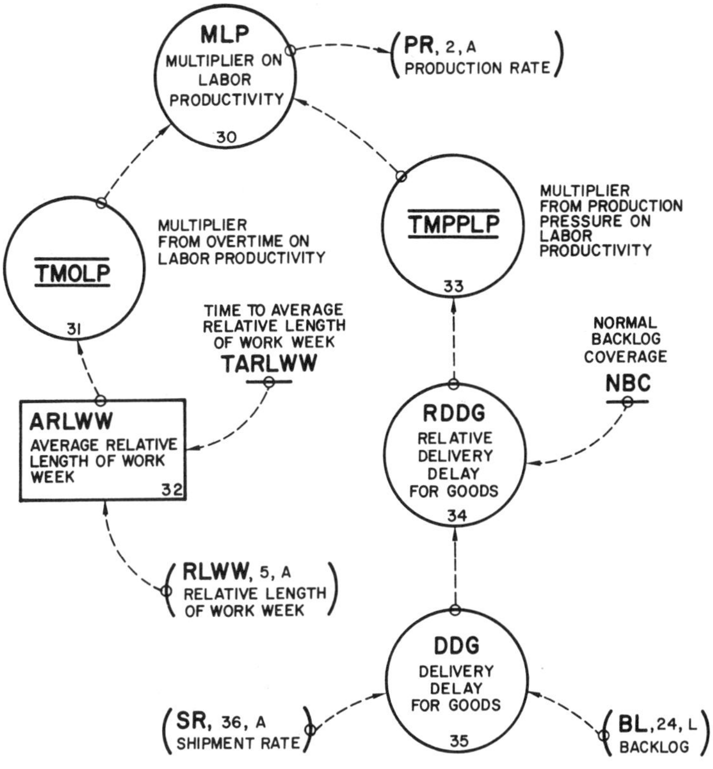


**Figure 3-26** Flow diagram of the effects of overtime and production pressure on labor productivity

MOLP, the average relative length of work week ARLWW is used instead of the actual relative length of work week RLWW because, according to Mitchell, the loss of efficiency from weariness and fatigue is a consequence of overtime sustained over several weeks or months. In other words, the temporary use of overtime may have relatively little adverse impact on efficiency, but its continued use over a longer period leads to a reduction in output per man-hour.

```
MOLP.K=TABLE(TMOLP,ARLWW.K,.8,1.2,.1)                31, A
TMOLP=1.06/1.04/1/.95/.9                             31.1, T
    MOLP    - MULTIPLIER FROM OVERTIME ON LABOR
                PRODUCTIVITY (DIMENSIONLESS)
    TMOLP   - TABLE FOR MULTIPLIER FROM OVERTIME ON LABOR
                PRODUCTIVITY
    ARLWW   - AVERAGE RELATIVE LENGTH OF WORK WEEK
                (DIMENSIONLESS)
```

In equation 32, the average relative length of work week ARLWW, as noted before, is defined as an exponential average of the relative length of work week RLWW. As discussed in Appendix D, an exponential average responds with a lag to a step increase in its input variable. ARLWW responds to a step increase in the input variable RLWW as shown in Figure 3–27. If RLWW increases because of inventory shortages, for example, then ARLWW will initially be below RLWW and will gradually approach RLWW. Since ARLWW is the input variable to the multiplier from overtime on labor productivity MOLP, labor efficiency will remain high at first but will gradually decline as overtime continues.

```
ARLWW.K=ARLWW.K+(DT/TARLWW)(RLWW.J-ARLWW.J)          32, L
ARLWW=1                                              32.1, N
TARLWW=.33                                           32.2, C
    ARLWW   - AVERAGE RELATIVE LENGTH OF WORK WEEK
                (DIMENSIONLESS)
    TARLWW  - TIME TO AVERAGE RELATIVE LENGTH OF WORK
                WEEK  (YEARS)
    RLWW    - RELATIVE LENGTH OF WORK WEEK
                (DIMENSIONLESS)
```

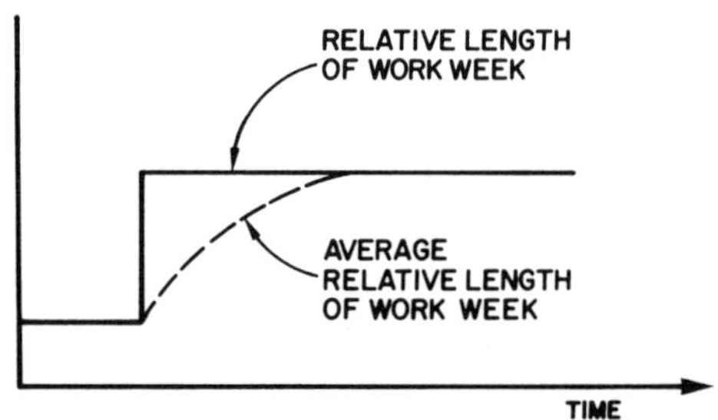


**Figure 3-27** Step response of the average relative length of work week

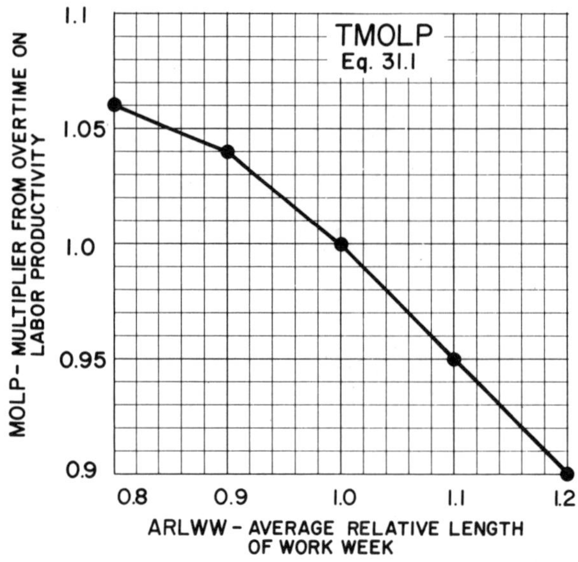


**Figure 3-28** Declining labor efficiency caused by sustained overtime

The values chosen for the table in Figure 3–28 merit some comment. The relative length of work week RLWW enters proportionately into the formulation of the production rate.[50] If labor efficiency were inversely related to RLWW, the use of overtime would yield no additional output. For output to expand with increased overtime, as should be expected within reasonable ranges of hours worked, the multiplier from overtime on labor productivity MOLP must decline less than proportionately to RLWW.[51] For example, if RLWW increases by 10 percent, then labor productivity must decline by less than 10 percent for total production to expand. Figure 3–28 shows a relationship for MOLP that is consistent with this property. Figure 3–29 graphs the overall relationship connecting overtime and output, which is equal to RLWW multiplied by MOLP.[52] Figure 3–29 shows that the production rate continually increases, though at a diminishing rate, with the increased use of overtime.

In equation 33, the multiplier from production pressure on labor productivity MPPLP, shown in Figure 3–30, depends on the relative delivery delay for goods RDDG. The delivery delay is employed as a surrogate for the causes of lowered efficiency described by Mitchell, since, precisely when delivery delays are long, sales effectiveness is lowest and maximum management pressures arise to expedite production, mollify customers, and increase marketing efforts. As a result of such reactions, management effort is diverted from production. Moreover, in the absence of a detailed labor market structure, relative hiring standards regarding labor quality may, to a first approximation, be associated with delivery delay. Long delivery delays are indicative

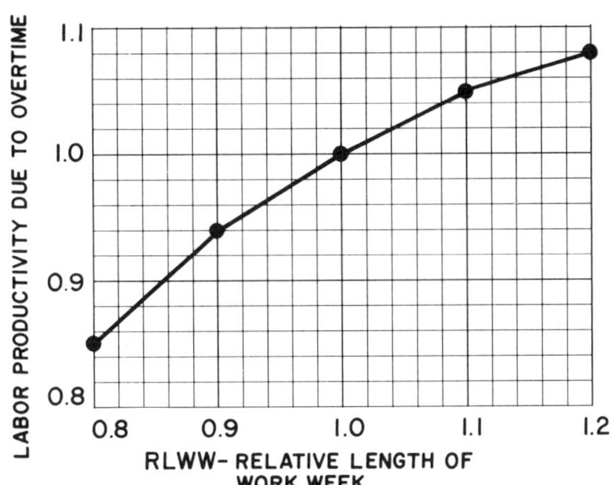


**Figure 3-29** Aggregate impact of overtime on labor productivity

[50]See equation 4, which defines effective labor EL as the product of labor L and the relative length of work week RLWW.

[51]Over still wider ranges than shown in Figures 3–28 and 3–29, output might well fall with increased overtime.

[52]Note that, strictly speaking, the relationship in Figure 3–29 only applies when ARLWW equals RLWW.

of pressures to expand output and employment. Under such conditions, the hiring standards maintained by employers are apt to be fairly lax. In contrast, when delivery delays are short, firms can enjoy greater discretion in setting high standards for labor quality and performance.

```
MPPLP.K=TABLE(TMPPLP,RDDG.K,0,2,.5)                        33, A
TMPPLP=1.1/1.07/1/.8/.7                                    33.1, T
    MPPLP  - MULTIPLIER FROM PRODUCTION PRESSURE ON
               LABOR PRODUCTIVITY (DIMENSIONLESS)
    TMPPLP - TABLE FOR MULTIPLIER FROM PRODUCTION
               PRESSURE ON LABOR PRODUCTIVITY
    RDDG   - RELATIVE DELIVERY DELAY FOR GOODS
               (DIMENSIONLESS)
```

The relative delivery delay for goods RDDG equals the delivery delay for goods DDG divided by normal backlog coverage NBC, as defined in equation 34. In turn, DDG is computed as the ratio of backlog BL to shipment rate SR (equation 35).

```
RDDG.K=DDG.K/NBC                                           34, A
RDDG=1                                                     34.1, N
    RDDG   - RELATIVE DELIVERY DELAY FOR GOODS
               (DIMENSIONLESS)
    DDG    - DELIVERY DELAY FOR GOODS  (YEARS)
    NBC    - NORMAL BACKLOG COVERAGE  (YEARS)

DDG.K=BL.K/SR.K                                            35, A
    DDG    - DELIVERY DELAY FOR GOODS  (YEARS)
    BL     - BACKLOG  (UNITS)
    SR     - SHIPMENT RATE  (UNITS/YEAR)
```

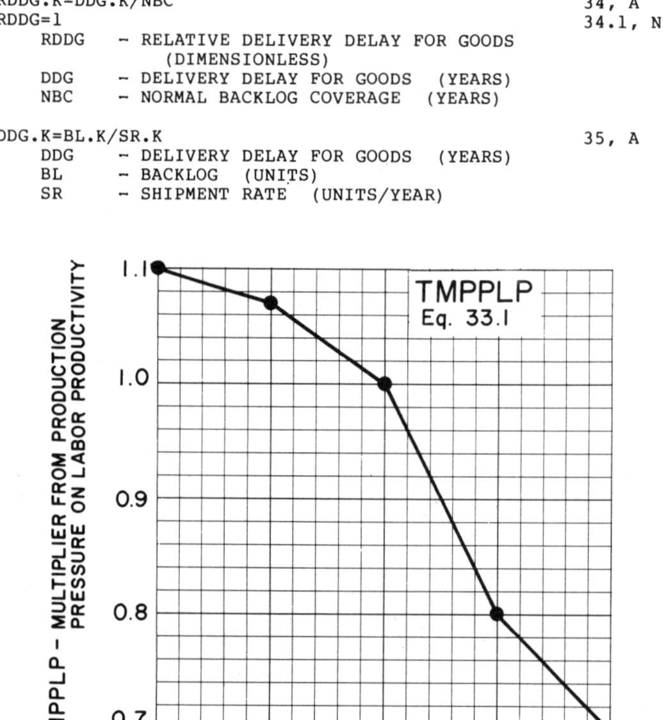


**Figure 3-30** Reduced labor efficiency accompanying large product delivery delays

*Simulations Including Variable Labor Efficiency.* With the basic production sector modified as described in equations 30–35, Figure 3–31 shows the sector's response to a 15 percent step increase in consumption. Compared with the reference simulation (Figure 3–17), Figure 3–31 displays a slightly longer period of oscillation—four and

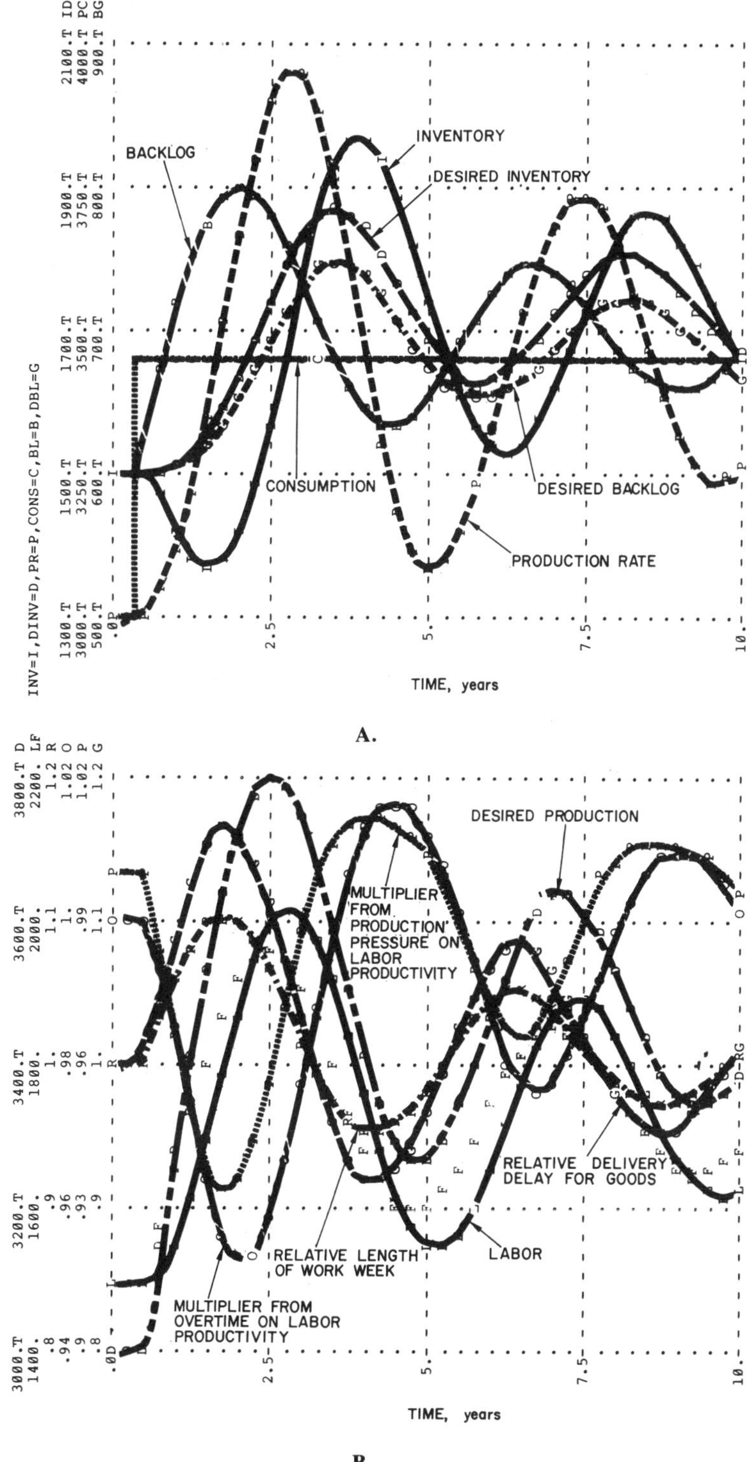


**Figure 3-31** Step response of revised production sector with variable labor productivity

one-half years instead of four years—and somewhat less damping; the damping ratio for production in Figure 3–31 is approximately 0.4, compared with a value of 0.55 in the reference simulation.

In Figure 3–31A, as incoming orders increase, inventory is depleted and backlog rises. As a result, both the relative delivery delay for goods and the desired production increase (Figure 3–31B). Increased desired production results in workers being placed on overtime, manifested in the increase of the relative length of work week to 1.1 at year 2 in Figure 3–31B. Because of sustained overtime and a rising delivery delay, however, average labor productivity is lower than in the reference simulation, thereby slowing the growth of output. The more gradual rise in the production rate can be seen in two ways in Figure 3–31A. First, the production rate intersects consumption at year 1.5, approximately half a year later than in the reference simulation. Second, inventory declines to nearly 1.35 million units, and backlog rises to 0.8 million units, compared with corresponding values of 1.45 million and 7.5 million units in the reference simulation. As a result, desired production is relatively higher in Figure 3–31B at the point where production intersects consumption. The increase in desired production, in turn, causes a greater overshoot of production and contributes to relatively greater fluctuations in production and employment. For example, labor rises to a peak value of about 2,000 in Figure 3–31B, compared with 1,900 in the reference simulation. Moreover, labor continues to rise for an additional one-half year compared with the standard simulation. The sustained rise of labor in Figure 3–31B is a consequence of the need to offset declining productivity through increased labor hiring to keep the production rate in balance with desired production. Similarly, the increased periodicity exhibited in Figure 3–31 is a consequence of lower efficiency and slower growth of production during the upswing.

*Alternative Responses to Excess Demand.* Several general comments bear mention concerning the implications of cyclic labor productivity. The behavior pattern exhibited in Figure 3–31 differs substantially from the classical view of supply and demand conveyed in the economic literature. Classical economic theory assumes that market clearing occurs through price adjustments that induce expanded consumption when output exceeds demand, and induce expanded production when demand exceeds supply. However, the classical theory ignores major effects, including the influences described by Mitchell, that cause reduced output in response to excess market demand. If, for example, management attention is diverted from production to overhead activities as a result of short-term pressures, then short-term production may decrease, as Mitchell explains. As a consequence, the initial excess of demand may be sustained.

The preceding hypotheses may be further developed through an example. Suppose the economy, or a particular industry, is characterized by excess demand over a sustained period. A condition of excess demand might come about through increased consumer spending, lengthened delays in receiving materials or capital equipment, or deliberate policy measures, such as restrictive monetary policies, that impede the financing and acquisition of capital equipment. Excess demand created through any of these channels can impair labor productivity and managerial efficiency, thereby leading to increased instability caused by increased hiring during upswings to offset lowered efficiency and by reduced hiring during downswings as production pressures wane and productivity rises. Moreover, pressures from excess demand can lead to an expansion of overhead personnel, moving the economy "into a mode where more and more people are used to cope with the symptoms of shortages so that resources are diverted from actions that would alleviate the shortages."[53]

Investigations of business-cycle behavior, inflation, and economic stabilization policies need to focus on the multiple possible responses to excess demand. Actions designed to curtail inflation or temper business-cycle expansion can have inadvertent inflationary and destabilizing consequences if they tend simultaneously to impair productivity or the expansion of supply. More detailed dynamic models dealing with inflation and stabilization policies can be developed to expand upon these hypotheses.

## 3.6 Magnification of Inventory Demand Induced by Price Changes

Section 3.6 describes a general class of factors that cause temporary, nonsustainable increases in demand during periods of rising demand or inadequate supply. Such factors contribute to instability by first increasing the demand for goods and then reducing orders at a time when supply has adjusted to a higher indicated level of demand. To provide a concrete illustration of such destabilizing influences, section 3.6 discusses the magnification of production, employment, and inventory fluctuations caused by advanced ordering of inventories in expectation of price increases. The section next develops the equations that are added to the basic production sector to make desired inventory depend on price expectations. Finally, it illustrates the behavior of the basic production sector when desired inventory is assumed to depend on the expected growth rate of prices.

*Factors Causing Nonsustainable Increases in Demand.* As the economy moves to a higher level of output and employment during business-cycle upswings, several factors cause a temporary increase in aggregate demand that cannot be maintained once the higher level of output is achieved. The first such factor is the acceleration principle discussed in Chapter 2. John M. Clark has described the operation of the principle:

> Every producer of things to be sold to producers has two demands to meet. He must maintain the industrial equipment already in use and the stocks of materials and goods on their way to the final consumer, and he must also furnish any new equipment that is wanted for new construction, enlargements, or betterments, and any increase in the stocks of materials and unsold goods. Both these demands come ultimately from the consumer, but they follow different laws. The demand for maintenance and replacement of existing capital varies with the amount of the demand for finished products, while the demand for new construction or enlargement of stocks depends upon whether or not the sales of the finished product are growing. . . .

[53]Forrester (1973), pp. 12–13. If overhead personnel are not discharged during the subsequent business-cycle downswing, average unit costs of production may increase, placing upward pressure on prices.

> The demand for a certain product, let us say, begins to increase steadily, each year seeing an increment equal to 10 percent of the original demand. At the end of five years the increase stops and the demand remains stationary. If the productive equipment has kept pace with the need, it is now enlarged by 50 per cent and calls for 50 per cent more expenditure for maintenance and replacements. Meanwhile there has been an added demand for new construction equal in five years to half the entire original equipment. If renewals are at the rate of 5 per cent a year, the first effect of an increase in demand at the rate of 10 per cent in a year is to treble the demand for the means of production, since a demand for new construction has arisen twice as large as the previous demand for maintenance. At the end of a year the demand for maintenance has been increased because of the fact that there is now 10 per cent more capital to be maintained. . . . Under practical conditions the increase in maintenance would probably be considerably less than 10 per cent, as it takes some time for the new machines to be installed, and after that it is some time before it reaches an average condition of wear and tear. Until then the repair bills are comparatively light. However, this consideration does not affect the main feature of our problem, which is the suddenness of the increased demand for the means of production and the fact that it is far greater as a percentage change than the disturbance of demand that causes it.
>
> What happens at the end of the five years when the demand stops growing? By this time the requirements for maintenance are 50 per cent greater than they were, while new construction has been going on at a rate equal to twice the original maintenance account. The total output of capital equipment has grown to three and one-half times its former volume. But the demand for new construction now ceases abruptly. This means that if the producers engaged in construction work had enough capacity to meet the demand of the fifth year, the sixth year would see them running with four-sevenths of their capacity idle.
>
> This is a serious condition for any industry in the real world. It might well be serious enough to produce a panic if any considerable number of industries were in the same condition at the same time. And yet something like it is a normal effect, an inevitable effect, of changes in consumers' demands in a highly capitalistic industrial system.[54]

Figure 3–32 shows the pattern of investment demand described by Clark. Investment (derived) demand is high and increasing gradually as long as final demand is rising. However, once final demand levels off, investment demand declines because no new investment is needed to expand production capacity; the only investment needed is to offset depreciation of the fixed capital stock. In Figure 3–32, since capital stock and total depreciation have increased, investment will be higher at time $t_1$ than at $t_0$; however, the rate of investment will be below the values attained while final demand was still growing. The resulting decline in investment lowers incomes and, in accordance with the multiplier, leads to a net contraction of output. Therefore, the accelerator provides a first illustration of an increase in aggregate demand that is stimu-

[54]Clark (1917), in *American Economics Association* (1944), pp. 238–240.

lated during the business-cycle upswing, but one that cannot be sustained as the expansion progresses.

A second example of a transient increase in demand arising during the upswing was presented in section 3.2 in the discussion of Thomas W. Mitchell's theory of advance ordering of inventory due to rising delivery delays for intermediate goods and materials. The positive feedback loop shown in Figure 3–33 summarizes Mitchell's verbal description. An initial increase in inventory ordering raises the backlog; as long as production stays relatively fixed, the increased backlog raises the delivery delay for inventories and encourages advance inventory ordering, thereby accentuating the initial increase in inventory ordering. Eventually, production is expanded in response to a high order backlog; the adjustment is shown in Figure 3–33 by the positive link between backlog, desired production, and production. As production and shipments expand, however, the delivery delay is reduced; faster delivery eliminates the need for advance ordering, and inventory ordering is reduced as a result. Through this mechanism the coupled positive and negative feedback loops in Figure 3–33 can produce overexpansion in response to an initial increase in inventory demand (or, equivalently, through a temporary reduction in production).

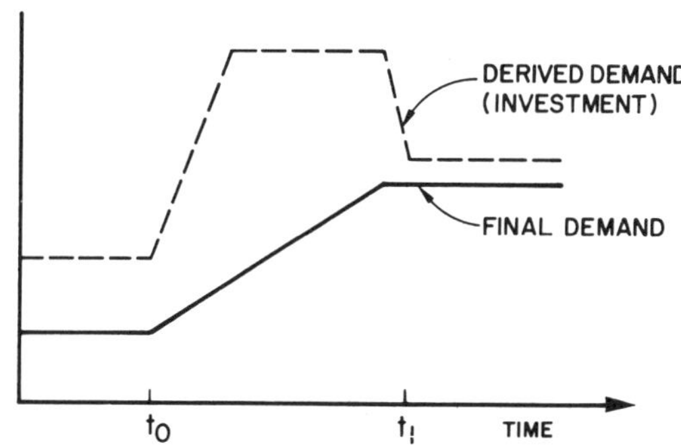


**Figure 3-32** Decline in investment caused by tapering off of final demand

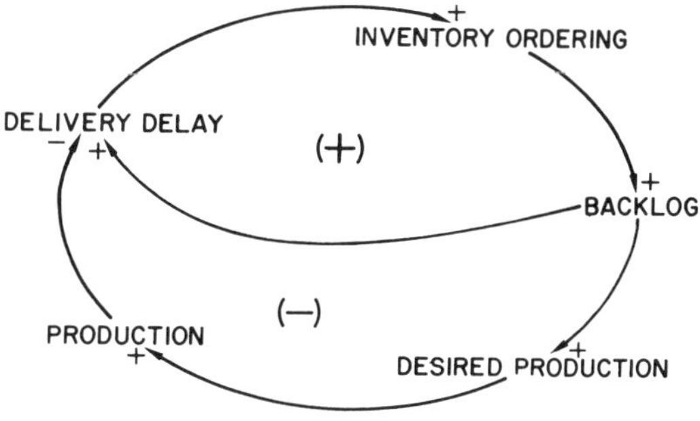


**Figure 3-33** Coupled negative and positive loops controlling delivery delay

A similar feedback structure can represent the effects of price expectations on desired inventory holdings. This structure is shown in Figure 3–34. In the inner loop of Figure 3–34, an increase in desired inventory raises desired production and places an upward pressure on price (shown in Figure 3–34 by a higher rate of price increase). The connection between the rate of price increase and desired inventory has been described by Ralph G. Hawtrey:

> When prices are rising, the holding of goods is itself profitable; when prices are falling, the holding of goods in stock is a source of loss. When prices are rising, a very high rate of interest may fail to deter merchants from borrowing; when they are falling, an apparently low rate of interest may fail to tempt them.[55]

According to Hawtrey, then, a positive rate of price increase raises desired inventory. In turn, a higher desired inventory generates upward pressures on price, thereby completing a positive feedback loop. The outer negative feedback loop in Figure 3–34 operates to counteract price changes: an increase in desired inventory raises desired production; after a delay, production increases, thereby tending to reduce price through expanded supply. Finally, the lower rate of increase in price encourages a reduction in desired inventory.

The structure shown in Figure 3–34 can independently cause oscillations in production. Consider the response of production to an increase in desired inventory. As long as production capacity is relatively fixed, increased demand is manifested in a higher price. Rising price, in turn, raises desired inventory, thus reinforcing the initial increase of demand. Gradually, production capacity expands, increasing output and lowering prices. However, the reduction in prices lowers desired inventory, leading to excess production. In this manner, price expectations can bring about cyclic changes in production and employment through their influence on desired inventory.

The importance of the influence of expected prices on desired inventories is suggested by the following quotation from Haberler:

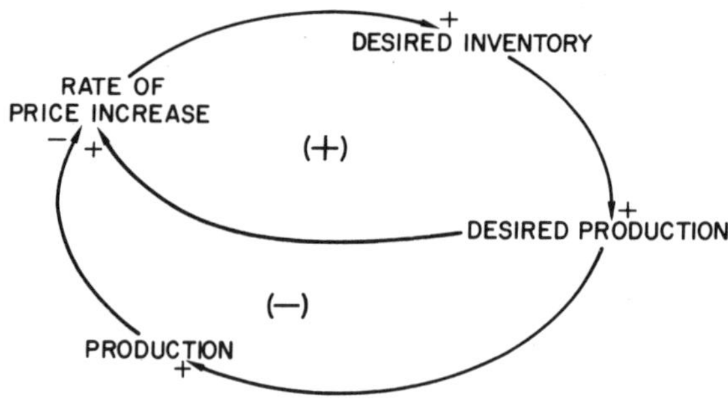


**Figure 3-34** Coupled negative and positive loops controlling price changes

[55] Hawtrey (1926), in ibid., p. 346.

> I suspect that the 'nonspeculative' inventory cycle based on a multiplier-acceleration mechanism (analyzed in masterly fashion in Metzler's celebrated articles) is only a small part of the real story and that inventory cycles without price speculation and monetary stimuli (elements which play no part in Metzler's theory) would be mild and uninteresting affairs.[56]

The practical importance of these issues is illustrated in an August 1974 article in the *Wall Street Journal,* which suggests that an excessive buildup of inventories due to advance ordering forebodes a severe reduction in inventory investment and production:

> A stream of revised statistics from the Commerce Department has led to increased worry among economists that the nation may, after all, be in for a classical case of what's known as an inventory recession. Coming on top of the current slump, this could mean that the economic downturn would be deeper and longer than has been expected. . . . Most of the accumulation so far this year has come in manufacturing, and most of that is in purchased materials and supplies. Some of the buildup undoubtedly stems from buying to beat price increases. Many firms are hoarding goods that already are scarce or that they fear may become so.[57]

*Determinants of Price.* Figure 3–35 contains a flow diagram describing the additions to the basic production sector needed to represent price expectations. The only equation change from section 3.3 is in the equation for desired inventory DINV. In the revised formulation, desired inventory, instead of reflecting a fixed number of months' coverage of production, depends on the perceived rate of increase in price PRIP. DINV now equals the average production rate APR multiplied by the normal inventory coverage NIC, which is in turn modified by the multiplier from price expectations on desired inventory MPEDI. In the equation for desired inventory (equation 11), MPEDI is activated by setting switch 2 SW2 equal to one in the simulations (see Appendix B for reference).

In equation 12, the multiplier from price expectations on desired inventory MPEDI (shown in Figure 3–36) is an increasing function of the perceived rate of increase in price PRIP. Thus desired inventory rises when prices are expected to rise, and falls when prices are expected to fall. MPEDI is assumed to have a fairly narrow range, varying desired inventory by ±10 percent. The assumption reflects Abramovitz's suggestion that

> It seems unlikely that during ordinary business cycles, manufacturers 'speculate' on price changes in the sense in which this word is appropriate to the operations of commodity traders. They are likely, however, to satisfy their routine desires for holding inventories somewhat more generously when the market for their raw material is firm and rising, somewhat less generously when it is weak and tending to drop . . . .[58]

[56]Haberler (1956), in Gordon and Klein (1965), p. 142.

[57]"Sharp Rise in Inventories Stirs Fears of Deep Slump—but May Slow Inflation," *Wall Street Journal,* August 16, 1974, p. 24.

[58]Abramovitz (1950), p. 315.

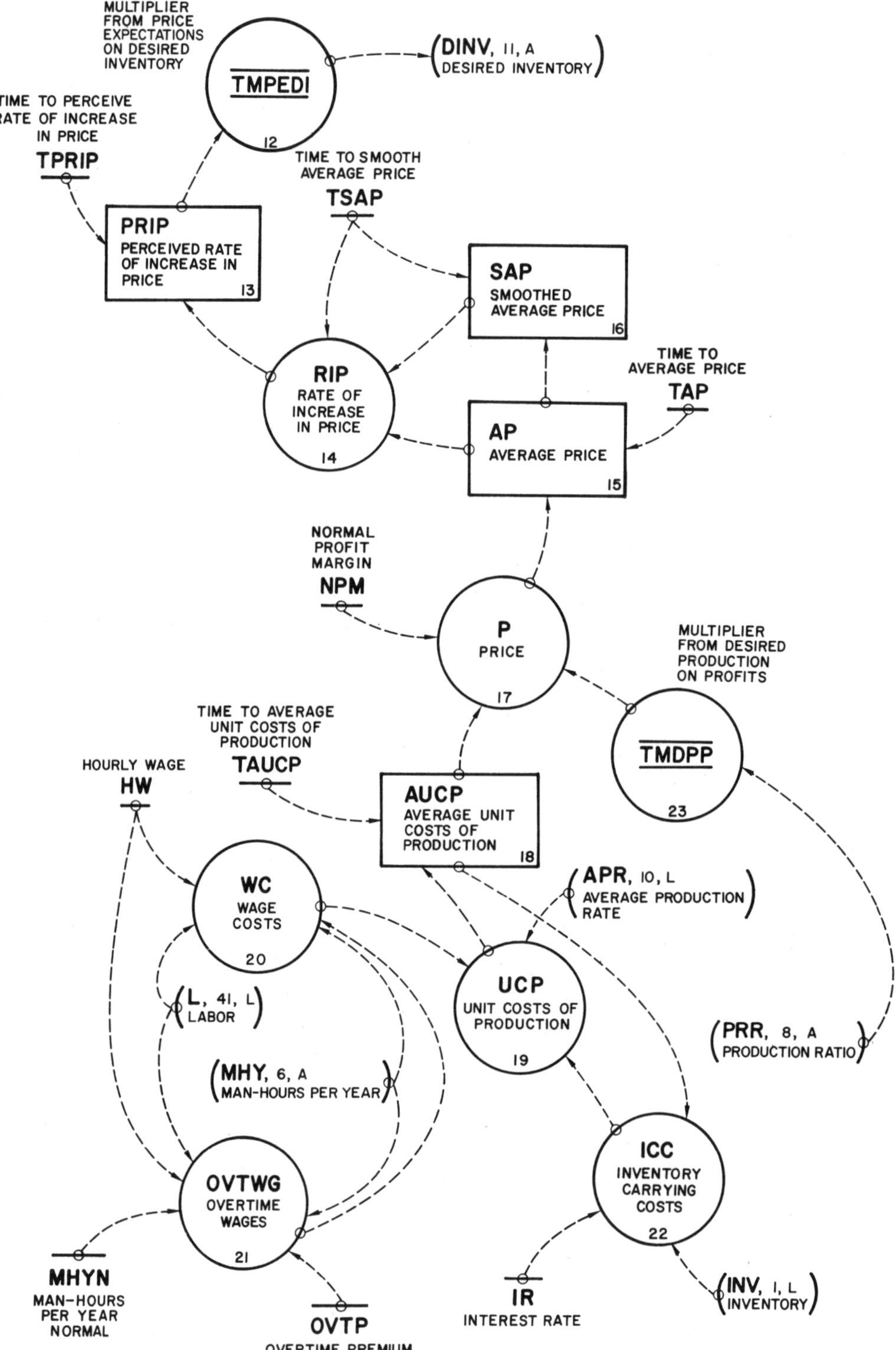


**Figure 3-35** Flow diagram of the influence of price expectations on inventory ordering

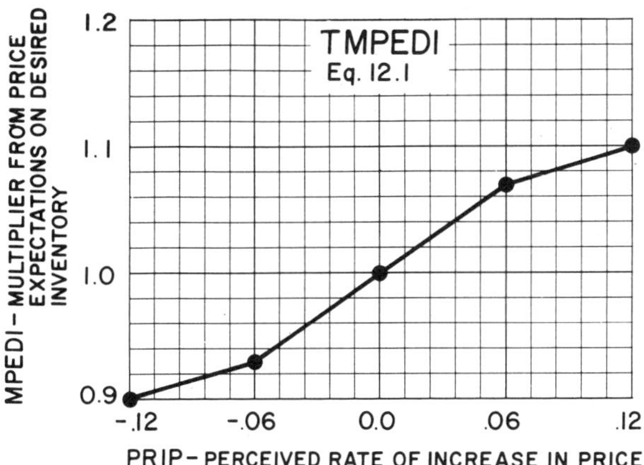


**Figure 3-36** Multiplier from price expectations on desired inventory

```
DINV.K=(APR.K)(NIC)(CLIP(MPEDI.K,1,SW2,1))            11, A
NIC=.5                                                11.1, C
SW2=0                                                 11.2, C
    DINV   - DESIRED INVENTORY  (UNITS)
    APR    - AVERAGE PRODUCTION RATE  (UNITS/YEAR)
    NIC    - NORMAL INVENTORY COVERAGE  (YEARS)
    MPEDI  - MULTIPLIER FROM PRICE EXPECTATIONS ON
               DESIRED INVENTORY (DIMENSIONLESS)
    SW2    - SWITCH 2  (DIMENSIONLESS)

MPEDI.K=TABLE(TMPEDI,PRIP.K,-.12,.12,.06)             12, A
TMPEDI=.9/.93/1/1.07/1.1                              12.1, T
MPEDI=1                                               12.2, N
    MPEDI  - MULTIPLIER FROM PRICE EXPECTATIONS ON
               DESIRED INVENTORY (DIMENSIONLESS)
    TMPEDI - TABLE FOR MULTIPLIER FROM PRICE
               EXPECTATIONS ON DESIRED INVENTORY
    PRIP   - PERCEIVED RATE OF INCREASE IN PRICE
               (FRACTION/YEAR)
```

The perceived rate of increase in price PRIP is computed in equation 13 as a one and one-half year exponential average of the actual rate of increase in price RIP.[59] The formulation implies that producers continuously adjust their expected rate of price increase toward the actual rate. Moreover, producers will extrapolate current price trends if a steady rate of price change is maintained. Thus, for example, if the rate of price increase rises from 1 percent to 3 percent per year, producers will gradually increase their expected rate of price increase from 1 percent toward 3 percent. If the actual 3 percent inflation is sustained, producers will eventually come to project 3 percent price rises each year.

```
PRIP.K=PRIP.J+(DT/TPRIP)(RIP.J-PRIP.J)                13, L
PRIP=RIP                                              13.1, N
TPRIP=1.5                                             13.2, C
    PRIP   - PERCEIVED RATE OF INCREASE IN PRICE
               (FRACTION/YEAR)
    TPRIP  - TIME TO PERCEIVE RATE OF INCREASE IN PRICE
               (YEARS)
    RIP    - RATE OF INCREASE IN PRICE  (FRACTION/YEAR)
```

[59]RIP is calculated in equations 14–16 as the average annual rate of change in price. See Forrester (1961), app. L, for a discussion of this form of computation.

```
RIP.K=(AP.K-SAP.K)/(SAP.K*TSAP)                          14, A
    RIP     - RATE OF INCREASE IN PRICE  (FRACTION/YEAR)
    AP      - AVERAGE PRICE  (DOLLARS/UNIT)
    SAP     - SMOOTHED AVERAGE PRICE  (DOLLARS/UNIT)
    TSAP    - TIME TO SMOOTH AVERAGE PRICE  (YEARS)

AP.K=AP.J+(DT/TAP)(P.J-AP.J)                             15, L
AP=P                                                     15.1, N
TAP=.33                                                  15.2, C
    AP      - AVERAGE PRICE  (DOLLARS/UNIT)
    TAP     - TIME TO AVERAGE PRICE  (YEARS)
    P       - PRICE  (DOLLARS/UNIT)

SAP.K=SAP.J+(DT/TSAP)(AP.J-SAP.J)                        16, L
SAP=AP                                                   16.1, N
TSAP=.33                                                 16.2, C
    SAP     - SMOOTHED AVERAGE PRICE  (DOLLARS/UNIT)
    TSAP    - TIME TO SMOOTH AVERAGE PRICE  (YEARS)
    AP      - AVERAGE PRICE  (DOLLARS/UNIT)
```

Price P is computed in equation 17 on the basis of a variable markup of average unit costs of production AUCP. The markup depends on the ratio of desired to actual production as an index of the relative balance of supply and demand.[60] In this respect, the formulation resembles the pricing equations developed by Franco Modigliani (1973) and Barbara R. Bergmann (1974). In equation 17, producers are assumed to maintain a normal markup of 10 percent when the multiplier from desired production on profits MDPP equals one, indicating that production equals desired production. Price P increases when excess demand arises within the sector, and it decreases in the face of excess production.

```
P.K=(AUCP.K)(1+NPM)(MDPP.K)                              17, A
NPM=.1                                                   17.1, C
    P       - PRICE  (DOLLARS/UNIT)
    AUCP    - AVERAGE UNIT COSTS OF PRODUCTION  (DOLLARS/
                UNIT)
    NPM     - NORMAL PROFIT MARGIN  (DIMENSIONLESS)
    MDPP    - MULTIPLIER FROM DESIRED PRODUCTION ON
                PROFITS  (DIMENSIONLESS)
```

Average unit costs of production AUCP (equation 18) is a one-year exponential average of actual unit costs of production UCP. The formulation bases prices on recent average costs instead of current costs alone.[61]

```
AUCP.K=AUCP.J+(DT/TAUCP)(UCP.J-AUCP.J)                   18, L
AUCP=WC/(APR-(INV)(IR))                                  18.1, N
TAUCP=1                                                  18.2, C
    AUCP    - AVERAGE UNIT COSTS OF PRODUCTION  (DOLLARS/
                UNIT)
    TAUCP   - TIME TO AVERAGE UNIT COSTS OF PRODUCTION
                (YEARS)
    UCP     - UNIT COSTS OF PRODUCTION  (DOLLARS/UNIT)
    WC      - WAGE COSTS  (DOLLARS/YEAR)
    APR     - AVERAGE PRODUCTION RATE  (UNITS/YEAR)
    INV     - INVENTORY  (UNITS)
    IR      - INTEREST RATE  (FRACTION/YEAR)
```

[60]Note that the desired production rate DPROD subsumes measures of inventory adequacy and order backlog level.

[61]AUCP is indirectly initialized equal to unit costs of production UCP. AUCP cannot be set directly equal to UCP because of simultaneity between inventory valuation, unit costs, and average unit costs (see equations 19 and 22). The initial (equilibrium) value for AUCP must therefore be derived algebraically as follows:

$$AUCP = ((INV)(AUCP)(IR) + WC)/APR$$
$$AUCP(1 - (INV)(IR)/APR)) = WC/APR$$
$$AUCP = WC/((APR)(1 - ((INV)(IR)/APR)))$$
$$AUCP = WC/(APR - (INV)(IR)).$$

Since labor is the only factor of production in the models discussed thus far, the cost of production has only two components: wage costs and inventory carrying costs. Equation 19 sets unit costs of production UCP equal to wage costs WC plus inventory carrying costs ICC, divided by the average production rate APR.

```
UCP.K=(WC.K+ICC.K)/APR.K                                   19, A
    UCP     - UNIT COSTS OF PRODUCTION   (DOLLARS/UNIT)
    WC      - WAGE COSTS   (DOLLARS/YEAR)
    ICC     - INVENTORY CARRYING COSTS   (DOLLARS/YEAR)
    APR     - AVERAGE PRODUCTION RATE   (UNITS/YEAR)
```

In equation 20, wage costs WC (measured in dollars per year) equals the product of labor L, man-hours per year MHY, and the hourly wage HW added to overtime wages OVTWG. The hourly wage has an assumed constant value of four dollars per hour. Overtime wages OVTWG is calculated in equation 21 as the excess of hours worked over normal hours worked, represented by the term (MHY — MHYN), multiplied by labor L and the additional hourly pay for overtime; this additional pay is calculated from the hourly wage and an assumed overtime premium OVTP of 30 percent. OVTWG is constrained to be greater than or equal to zero through use of the MAX function.[62] Therefore, overtime wages are paid if man-hours per year MHY exceed man-hours per year normal MHYN; no overtime pay is generated if MHY is less than MHYN.

```
WC.K=(L.K)(MHY.K)(HW)+OVTWG.K                              20, A
HW=4                                                       20.1, C
    WC      - WAGE COSTS   (DOLLARS/YEAR)
    L       - LABOR   (MEN)
    MHY     - MAN-HOURS PER YEAR   (HOURS/MAN-YEAR)
    HW      - HOURLY WAGE   (DOLLARS/HOUR)
    OVTWG   - OVERTIME WAGES   (DOLLARS/YEAR)

OVTWG.K=MAX(0,(L.K)(HW)(OVTP)(MHY.K-MHYN))                 21, A
OVTP=.3                                                    21.1, C
    OVTWG   - OVERTIME WAGES   (DOLLARS/YEAR)
    L       - LABOR   (MEN)
    HW      - HOURLY WAGE   (DOLLARS/HOUR)
    OVTP    - OVERTIME PREMIUM   (DIMENSIONLESS)
    MHY     - MAN-HOURS PER YEAR   (HOURS/MAN-YEAR)
    MHYN    - MAN-HOURS PER YEAR NORMAL   (HOURS/MAN-YEAR)
```

Inventory carrying costs ICC is computed in equation 22 from the dollar inventory valuation (equal to the number of physical units held in inventory), multiplied by the average unit costs of production and a constant interest rate IR of 6 percent per year.

```
ICC.K=(INV.K)(AUCP.K)(IR)                                  22, A
IR=.06                                                     22.1, C
    ICC     - INVENTORY CARRYING COSTS   (DOLLARS/YEAR)
    INV     - INVENTORY   (UNITS)
    AUCP    - AVERAGE UNIT COSTS OF PRODUCTION   (DOLLARS/
                UNIT)
    IR      - INTEREST RATE   (FRACTION/YEAR)
```

The multiplier from desired production on profits MDPP in equation 23 and Figure 3–37 reduces the profit margin when production exceeds desired production (indicated by a production ratio PRR below one) and raises profits when the sector comes under pressure to expand output.

[62]In DYNAMO language, the function MAX(a,b) assumes the value a if a≥b, and b if b>a.

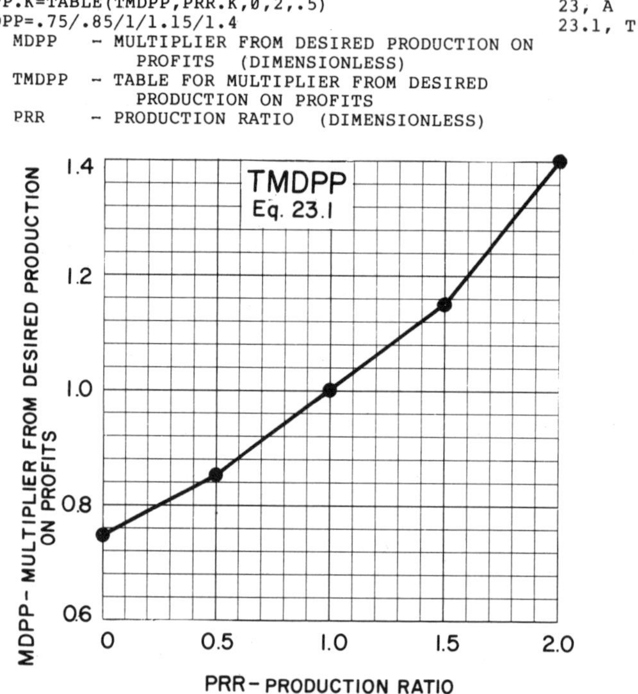

```
MDPP.K=TABLE(TMDPP,PRR.K,0,2,.5)                         23, A
TMDPP=.75/.85/1/1.15/1.4                                  23.1, T
    MDPP    - MULTIPLIER FROM DESIRED PRODUCTION ON
                PROFITS  (DIMENSIONLESS)
    TMDPP   - TABLE FOR MULTIPLIER FROM DESIRED
                PRODUCTION ON PROFITS
    PRR     - PRODUCTION RATIO  (DIMENSIONLESS)
```



**Figure 3-37** The influence of production demand on profit margins

*Behavior of the Production Sector with Price Expectations.* Figure 3–38 shows the response of the basic production sector, including price expectations, to a 15 percent step increase in consumption.[63] The strong destabilizing effects of price expectations on inventory and production behavior are apparent. The fluctuations exhibited in Figure 3–38 show about a four-year period, identical to that of the reference simulation (Figure 3–17), but they diverge slightly over the time horizon of the simulation. The relative decrease in stability in Figure 3–38 compared with Figure 3–17 is significant; however, the absolute divergence of the fluctuations is largely unrealistic, reflecting the omission of financial pressures, the limited availability of labor, and other factors that restrict wide excursions in production and inventory accumulation.[64] The addition of such factors would constitute useful extensions to the basic production sector.

In Figure 3–38A, as consumption is stepped upward, inventory begins to decline and backlog rises as in the previous simulations. Consequently, desired production exceeds the production rate. Price, plotted in Figure 3–38B, rises as a result of increased profit margins caused by excess demand; the increase in profit margins is reflected in Figure 3–38B in the multiplier from desired production on profits, which

[63]Figure 3–38 is plotted on a different set of vertical scales than the previous simulations due to the expanded range of variation in the production rate and other variables.

[64]The system becomes marginally stable, even given the present model structure, if the averaging time used in computing the perceived rate of increase in price PRIP is increased from one and one-half years to slightly over two years.

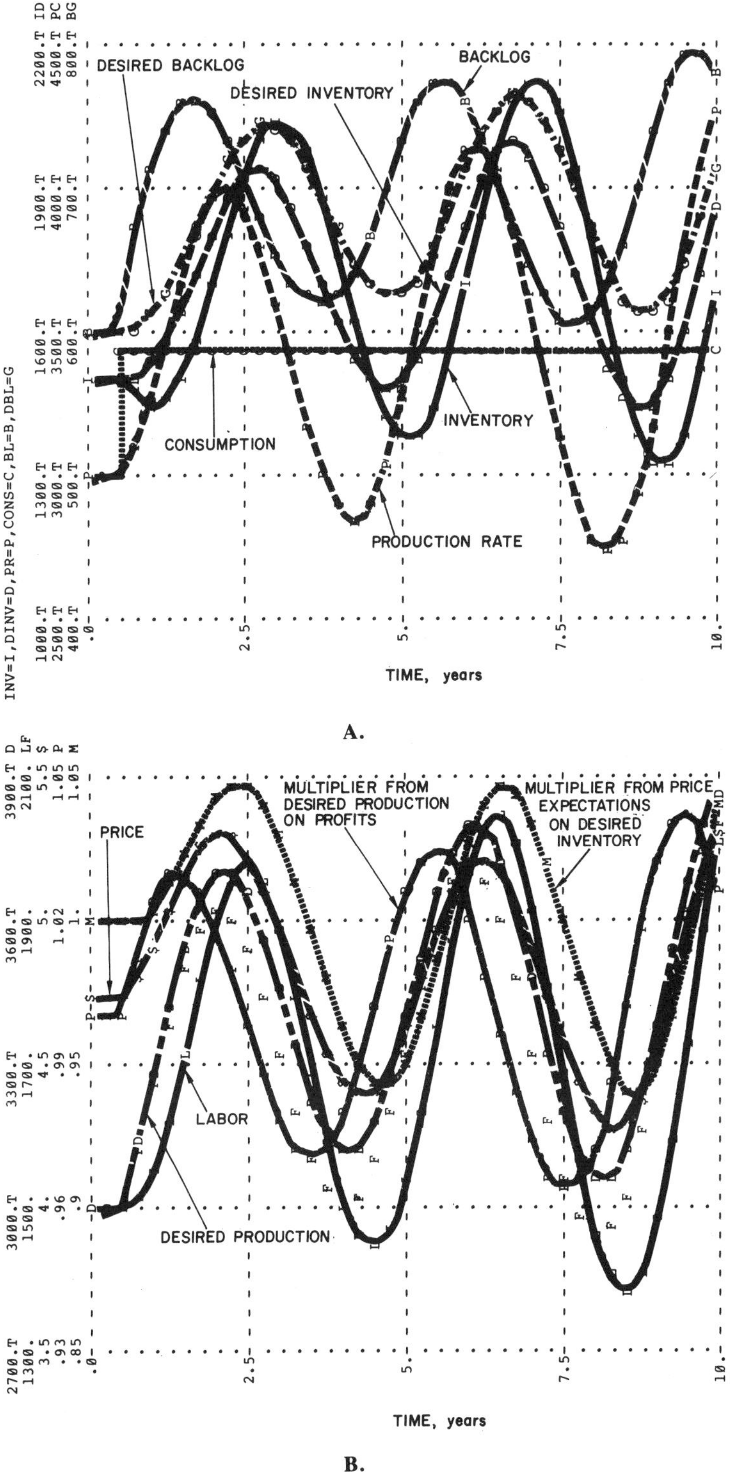


**Figure 3-38** Destabilizing effects of inventory ordering in response to price changes

rises from a normal value of 1 to about 1.03 at year 1.5. In addition to higher profit margins, an upward pressure on price also results from increased wage costs arising from overtime pay; overtime employment occurs because of the gap between actual production and desired production observable in the first two years of Figure 3–38. Price P increases from an initial value of approximately $4.70 per unit to $5.30 per unit at year 2, an increase of nearly 13 percent. The fluctuations in price roughly coincide with production-rate fluctuations, which is consistent with the evidence presented by Gordon.[65]

Figure 3–38B plots the multiplier from price expectations on desired inventory MPEDI, which varies between about 0.95 and 1.05 over the course of the ten-year simulation. MPEDI has a value greater than one, indicating expected price increases, from the time of the initial increase in consumption until approximately year 2.5. During this interval, MPEDI contributes to raising both desired inventory and desired production. As the production rate expands, increased needs for materials and goods in process further raise desired inventory, thereby placing some additional upward pressure on price. As a result, desired inventory in Figure 3–38A rises to over 1.9 million units at year 2.5, compared with a peak value of slightly over 1.8 million units in the reference simulation. Moreover, inventory attains an initial peak value of 2 million units, compared with a corresponding peak value of 1.9 million units in the reference simulation.

Price P peaks at year 2 in Figure 3–38B. After that year, a downward pressure on price results from an excess of production over desired production. In part, desired production declines because of a growing excess of inventory over desired inventory, which tends to promote a price reduction in order to liquidate inventory. As price declines, expectations of further reductions cause producers to lower their desired inventory stocks; in turn, the decline in desired inventory accentuates the fall in prices by discouraging inventory replenishment. The liquidation of inventory can continue, depressing output and prices, until inventory falls sufficiently to interfere with production through shortages of materials and to interfere with distribution through stock-outs, lengthened delivery delays, and poor customer service.

The destabilizing effects of increased variations in desired inventory on the production rate can be seen readily in Figure 3–38A. The production rate rises from an initial value of 3 million units per year to 4 million units per year around year 2, and subsequently declines to a value of 2.8 million units per year around year 4. Thus, in response to an increase of 0.45 million units per year in consumption, production rises by more than twice the increase in consumption and then declines below its initial equilibrium value. Employment (labor) similarly rises by about one-third before declining below its initial value of 1,500.[66]

The results of the simulation shown in Figure 3–38 suggest the major role of price expectations in generating short-term business cycles. Price expectations and their

[65] Gordon (1961), pp. 272–274.

[66] As noted previously, the hiring rate is unconstrained by labor availability in the basic production sector, as the delay in filling vacancies is assumed constant at one-quarter year. Preliminary efforts to add a simple labor-market structure to the production sector have not materially altered any of the conclusions or behavior modes described in the text.

impact on inventory investment decisions have been incorporated in rough form in several econometric models.[67] However, expectational factors have been largely neglected in developing the theory of the firm, since the theory is largely predicated on equilibrium relationships between current marginal prices and marginal costs. However, as pointed out by Thomas Sowell, expectations of future prices or sales are inherently subjective, and therefore volatile, because they depend on business optimism and similar factors.[68] As indicated in Figure 3–38, the volatility of expected prices and expected sales has an important influence on production behavior and must be dealt with in a disequilibrium theory of the business cycle.

### 3.7 A Model with Endogenous Consumption

All the models discussed until now have treated incoming order rate (consumption) as an exogenous test input to the production sector. Considering the order rate as a test input served the objectives of the analysis by showing how random fluctuations or minor variations in orders could initiate a cyclic production response. The assumption of an exogenous order rate may be appropriate for analyzing the behavior of a single firm or industry;[69] however, the assumption is less appropriate for analyzing a major segment of the economy in which factor payments by the sector exert a significant impact on the sector's sales. Therefore, section 3.7 expands the basic production sector to incorporate the simplest possible model of consumption, one in which wage earners spend a constant fraction of their average income.

An investigation of the effects of endogenous consumption in the basic production sector appears to be particularly important in light of the critical role played by consumption in the classical multiplier-accelerator theory of business cycles. In Samuelson's multiplier-accelerator model, for example, the multiplier is the principal source of amplification of production. According to the multiplier theory, an initial increase in production raises national income and generates increased consumption expenditures, thereby providing a further stimulus to production. The basic production sector analyzed thus far has not considered the multiplier process but has incorporated a second source of amplification: inventory- and backlog-management policies, as analyzed in sections 3.4 through 3.6.

To assess the relative amplification produced by endogenous consumption and by inventory and backlog policies, section 3.7 combines the multiplier and accelerator mechanisms, along with inventory and backlog adjustments, in a single model.[70] The multiplier concept is introduced through endogenous consumption that depends on consumer incomes. The analysis therefore adopts the framework of the standard

[67]For example, see Klein (1964) for a description of an inventory-investment equation that includes price changes as an explanatory variable. Klein, however, bases investment only on very recent price changes; a more reasonable procedure, as outlined in equations 12–16, would be to relate expected price changes to a longer time history of price movements and then to relate desired inventory stocks to expected price changes.

[68]Sowell (1972), p. 208. Sowell provides an interesting discussion contrasting Keynes's concept of the marginal efficiency of capital with the static concept of marginal productivity.

[69]Strictly speaking, even the order rate to a single firm is not in reality exogenous but depends on relative product newness, delivery delay, speed in responding to customer complaints, price, and other factors.

[70]An accelerator mechanism is already incorporated in the production sector, for example, through the influence of growth expectations on desired labor. As shown in equations 50 and 62, desired labor DL depends on the expected growth rate in production EGRP. According to the formulation, a decline in the expected growth rate, even though EGRP may still be positive, will lower desired labor, thereby placing a downward pressure on the production rate.

Keynesian consumption function, basing consumption only on income. Cash balances, wealth, availability of credit, and similar factors are omitted here as determinants of consumption because the purpose of the analysis is not to develop a detailed model of consumption behavior but, rather, to assess, as a first effort, the relative importance of the basic income-consumption link widely studied in the economic literature on business cycles. Section 3.7 develops the equations for the consumption sector and analyzes the resulting model behavior. Overall, section 3.7 illustrates a general procedure for evaluating alternative economic theories by incorporating them in a single model and testing model sensitivity to the component assumptions of each theory. Such a procedure could be used, for example, in analogous fashion to the analysis of income-consumption relationships presented here, to test the cyclic impacts of determinants of consumption such as wealth and liquidity.

*Equations for the Consumption Sector.* The consumption equations in the basic production sector are activated by setting switch 4 SW4 to one, thereby setting consumption CONS equal to consumption from income CONSI (equation 88). The consumption sector developed here is a minor variation of the consumption equation developed in Metzler's and Samuelson's articles on the multiplier and accelerator principles.[71] Both Samuelson and Metzler adopt D. H. Robertson's assumption that consumption depends upon income received during the past period.[72] However, such a discrete representation of consumption decisions fails to describe adequately the influence of previous income levels on consumption; moreover, the discrete formulation cannot capture the continuous process by which consumption habits and standards are gradually adapted to the levels dictated by current income. As an alternative to basing consumption on the income of some former period, consumption from income CONSI is represented in equation 91 as average real consumer income ARCI multiplied by a constant average propensity to consume APC.[73] ARCI, in turn, is formulated in equation 92 as an exponentially averaged value of current income. Current consumption is therefore related in a geometrically declining fashion to the incomes of all past periods.[74] The time to average real consumer income TARCI is 2.5 years, which is

[71]See Samuelson (1939) and Metzler (1941).

[72]Robertson (1926), pp. 168–191.

[73]CONSI is also multiplied by noise in consumption from income NCIN (equation 95). The latter is a noise input to the consumption rate that is activated later in section 3.7 to analyze model response to random variations in consumption.

```
NCIN.K=NCIN.J+(DT/TSNCI)(NORMRN(1,SDNCI)-NCIN.J)       95, L
NCIN=1                                                 95.1, N
TSNCI=1                                                95.2, C
SDNCI=0                                                95.3, C
     NCIN   - NOISE IN CONSUMPTION FROM INCOME
                (DIMENSIONLESS)
     TSNCI  - TIME TO SMOOTH NOISE IN CONSUMPTION FROM
                INCOME (YEARS)
     SDNCI  - STANDARD DEVIATION OF NOISE IN CONSUMPTION
                FROM INCOME (DIMENSIONLESS)
```

[74]Consumption CONS corresponds to the permanent component of consumption in Milton Friedman's formulation

$$\text{permanent consumption} = C_p(t) = (1 - b)\lambda \sum_{\tau=1}^{\infty} b^{\tau-1}Y(t-\tau), \tag{1}$$

where $0<b<1$ and $\lambda$ is the average propensity to consume. See Friedman (1957) for further discussion. Equation (1) yields the following value for $C_p(t-1)$:

$$C_p(t-1) = (1 - b)\lambda \sum_{\tau=1}^{\infty} b^{\tau-1}Y(t-\tau-1). \tag{2}$$

Multiplying equation (2) by b and subtracting from (1) yields

$$C_p(t) = C_p(t-1) + (1 - b)\,(\lambda Y(t-1) - C_p(t-1)). \tag{3}$$

close to the estimate of about 2.65 years obtained by Milton Friedman through econometric estimation.[75]

```
CONS.K=CLIP(CONSI.K,TCONS.K,SW4,1)                          88, A
SW4=0                                                       88.1, C
    CONS   - CONSUMPTION  (UNITS/YEAR)
    CONSI  - CONSUMPTION FROM INCOME  (UNITS/YEAR)
    TCONS  - TEST CONSUMPTION  (UNITS/YEAR)
    SW4    - SWITCH 4  (DIMENSIONLESS)

CONSI.K=(ARCI.K)(APC)(NCIN.K)                               91, A
APC=.9                                                      91.1, C
    CONSI  - CONSUMPTION FROM INCOME  (UNITS/YEAR)
    ARCI   - AVERAGE REAL CONSUMER INCOME  (UNITS/YEAR)
    APC    - AVERAGE PROPENSITY TO CONSUME
               (DIMENSIONLESS)
    NCIN   - NOISE IN CONSUMPTION FROM INCOME
               (DIMENSIONLESS)

ARCI.K=ARCI.J+(DT/TARCI)(RCI.J-ARCI.J)                      92, L
ARCI=RCI                                                    92.1, N
TARCI=2.5                                                   92.2, C
    ARCI   - AVERAGE REAL CONSUMER INCOME  (UNITS/YEAR)
    TARCI  - TIME TO AVERAGE REAL CONSUMER INCOME
               (YEARS)
    RCI    - REAL CONSUMER INCOME  (UNITS/YEAR)
```

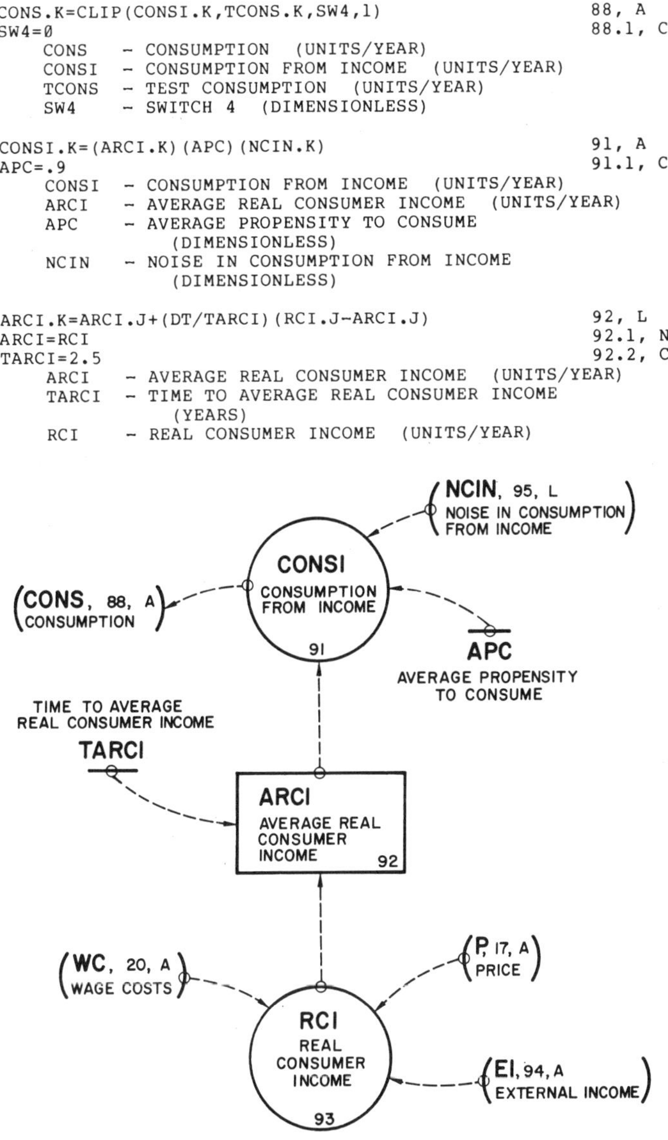


**Figure 3-39** Flow diagram of the determinants of the consumption rate

Real consumer income RCI (equation 93) is defined as the sum of wage costs WC (wage incomes received by labor) plus external income EI, divided by price P. Exter-

[75]Friedman (1957) and Evans (1969), pp. 22–23. Friedman found that the marginal propensity to consume out of current income is about 0.33, while the average propensity to consume is approximately 0.88. As shown in the previous footnote, the propensity to consume out of current income is $((1 - b)\lambda)$ where $\lambda$ is the average propensity to consume and $(1 - b)$ equals $(1/TC)$, where TC is the averaging time of the consumption distribution. These figures yield an estimate for TC of approximately 2.65 years.

nal income EI (equation 94) represents all income earned outside the sector, including transfer payments, interest income, and wages for government employment.[76] The price formulation used in the present analysis is identical to the formulation developed in section 3.6, except that the influence of price expectations on inventory investment is ignored for simplicity. Figure 3–39 contains a flow diagram of the consumption equations.

```
RCI.K=(WC.K+EI.K)/P.K                                      93, A
    RCI     - REAL CONSUMER INCOME   (UNITS/YEAR)
    WC      - WAGE COSTS   (DOLLARS/YEAR)
    EI      - EXTERNAL INCOME   (DOLLARS/YEAR)
    P       - PRICE   (DOLLARS/UNIT)
```

```
EI.K=(CEI+STEP(ISH,IST))                                   94, A
CEI=((PR*P)-(WC*APC))/APC                                  94.1, N
ISH=FISH*CEI                                               94.2, N
FISH=0                                                     94.3, C
IST=.2                                                     94.4, C
    EI      - EXTERNAL INCOME   (DOLLARS/YEAR)
    CEI     - CONSTANT EXTERNAL INCOME   (DOLLARS/YEAR)
    ISH     - INCOME STEP HEIGHT   (DOLLARS/YEAR)
    IST     - INCOME STEP TIME   (YEARS)
    PR      - PRODUCTION RATE   (UNITS/YEAR)
    P       - PRICE   (DOLLARS/UNIT)
    WC      - WAGE COSTS   (DOLLARS/YEAR)
    APC     - AVERAGE PROPENSITY TO CONSUME
                (DIMENSIONLESS)
    FISH    - FRACTION INCOME STEP HEIGHT
                (DIMENSIONLESS)
```

*Model Simulations with Endogenous Consumption.* Figure 3–40 shows the response of the production sector, including endogenous consumption, to small random variations in consumption.[77] The figure shows a four-year fluctuation in most system variables, identical to the periodicity of the reference simulation (Figure 3–17). Figure 3–40 clearly exhibits the amplification of production described in section 3.2. For example, over the twenty-five-year time horizon of the simulation, consumption varies over a fairly narrow range—roughly between 2.98 million and 3.04 million units per year—while production varies between approximately 2.97 million and 3.09 million units per year. Therefore, the production rate varies by about twice as much as consumption.

The amplification of production evidenced in Figure 3–40 principally reflects the effects of inventory and backlog policies on desired production. At year 8, for exam-

[76]External income EI equals constant external income CEI modified by a step-function input, normally set to zero. CEI is computed to equalize the production and consumption rates. Algebraically, the result can be derived as follows:

$$PR = CONS = (APC)(WC + CEI)/P$$
$$(PR*P)/APC = WC + CEI$$
$$CEI = (PR*P)/APC - WC,$$

where

PR = production rate
CONS = consumption
P = price
WC = wage costs
APC = average propensity to consume
CEI = constant external income

Note that consumption is proportional to (average) income in the present model. Therefore, testing model response to a step in external income corresponds to the procedure used previously in Chapter 3 of testing model response to a step change in consumption.

[77]The equation changes used to generate the simulation are listed in Appendix B to this volume.

ple, consumption is below production, so inventory rises (Figure 3–40A) and backlog declines (Figure 3–40B). As a result, in Figure 3–40C, desired production decreases from nearly 3.05 million to just below 3 million units per year in about year 10; as shown in Figure 3–40C, desired labor correspondingly declines from 1,525 to 1,490. The production rate falls between years 8 and 10 from 3.08 million to 2.97 million units per year (Figure 3–40A). The decline in production is caused by both reduced hiring, which lowers employment, and a reduced application of overtime.

In Figure 3–40A, the production rate eventually falls below consumption at year 10. As discussed previously, production must fall below consumption, for example, to work off the large inventory accumulated while production exceeded consumption. Such an inventory surplus can be seen in Figure 3–40B at year 9.5; at this point inventory equals about 1.54 million units, and desired inventory equals about 1.52 million units. The resulting inventory surplus of 0.02 million units lowers desired production by nearly 25,000 (= 0.025 million) units per year (see equation 9 for desired production).

In Figure 3–40, after about year 9.5, inventory declines (Figure 3–40A) and backlog begins to increase (Figure 3–40B) as a consequence of the production rate falling below consumption. Around year 10.5, backlog rises above desired backlog and inventory falls below desired inventory. As a result of the increased backlog and low inventory, the production rate once again starts to increase after year 10.5 and intersects consumption around year 11.5. In general, over the time span of the simulation, production fluctuates relative to consumption, alternately moving above and below the consumption rate.

Figure 3–40C shows that real consumer income varies between 3.32 million and 3.38 million units per year, exhibiting relatively minor oscillations. Wage payments to labor (not shown), which are based on labor and overtime pay, tend to vary procyclically. However, such payments are partially offset by price increases during the upswing and by price reductions in the downswing of the production cycle. During the upswing, for example, low inventory and a high order backlog lead to increased profit margins so that wage costs can largely be passed on in the form of higher prices; higher prices, in turn, lower real income. Figure 3–40B shows that price increases from approximately $4.68 to $4.77 per unit between about years 10 and 12, while Figure 3–40C shows employment rising from 1,490 to 1,540 men over the same period. Therefore, rising prices mitigate the changes in real purchasing power that result from higher employment.

In addition to the attenuation of spending rates caused by cyclic price changes, consumption is assumed to depend on real income averaged over two and one-half years; that is, households are assumed to base their spending not only on current incomes but on average incomes received over a period of two and one-half years. For example, households are reluctant to reduce their living standards significantly in the face of a temporary reduction in real income. The smoothing of income in consumption decisions further mitigates the impact of changes in income on consumption, damping

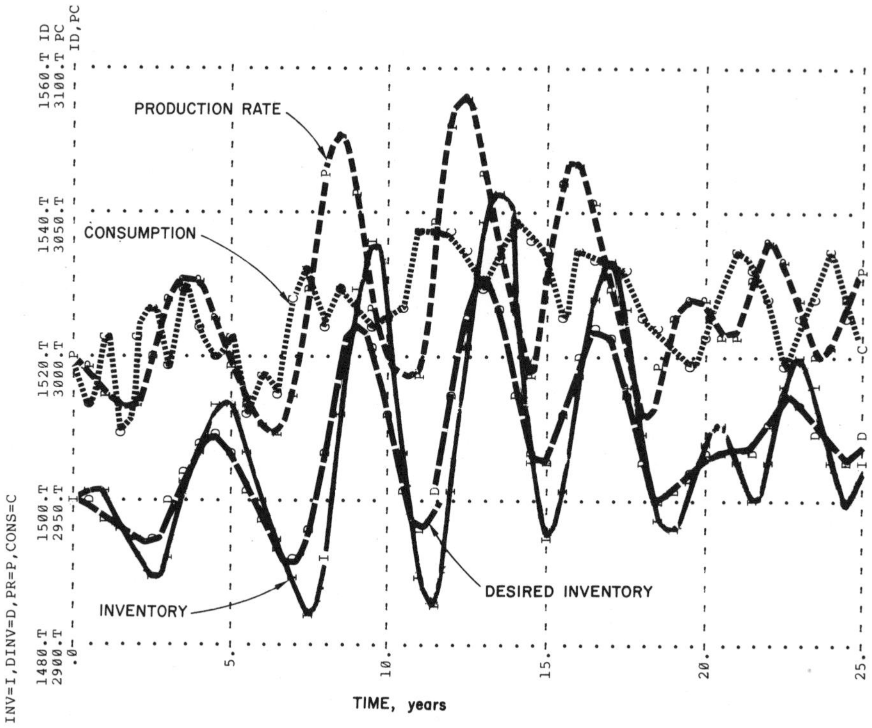
PRODUCTION RATE
CONSUMPTION
INVENTORY
DESIRED INVENTORY
TIME, years
INV=I,DINV=D,PR=P,CONS=C

A.

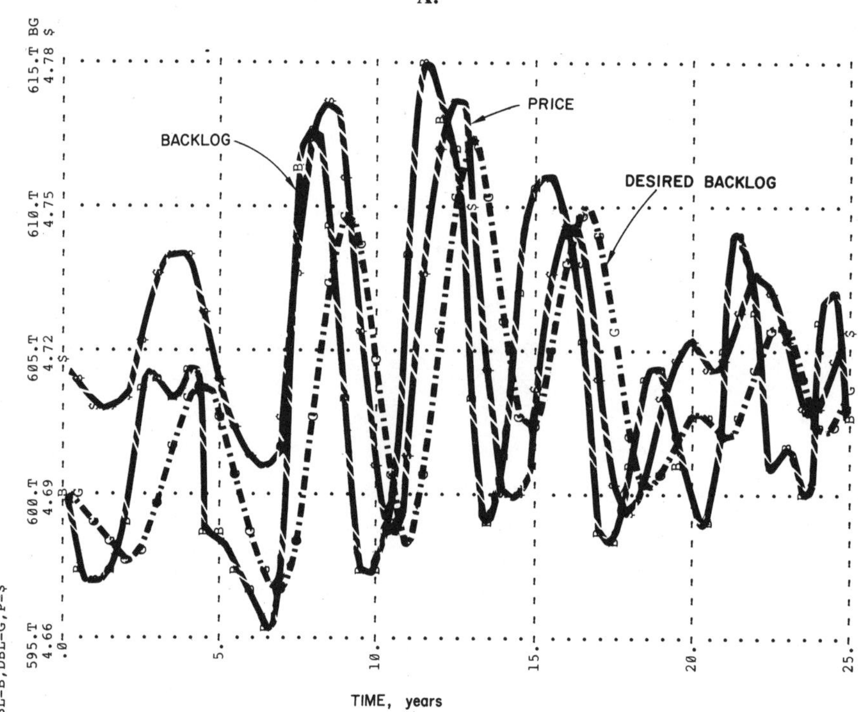
BACKLOG
PRICE
DESIRED BACKLOG
TIME, years
BL=B,DBL=G,P=$

B.

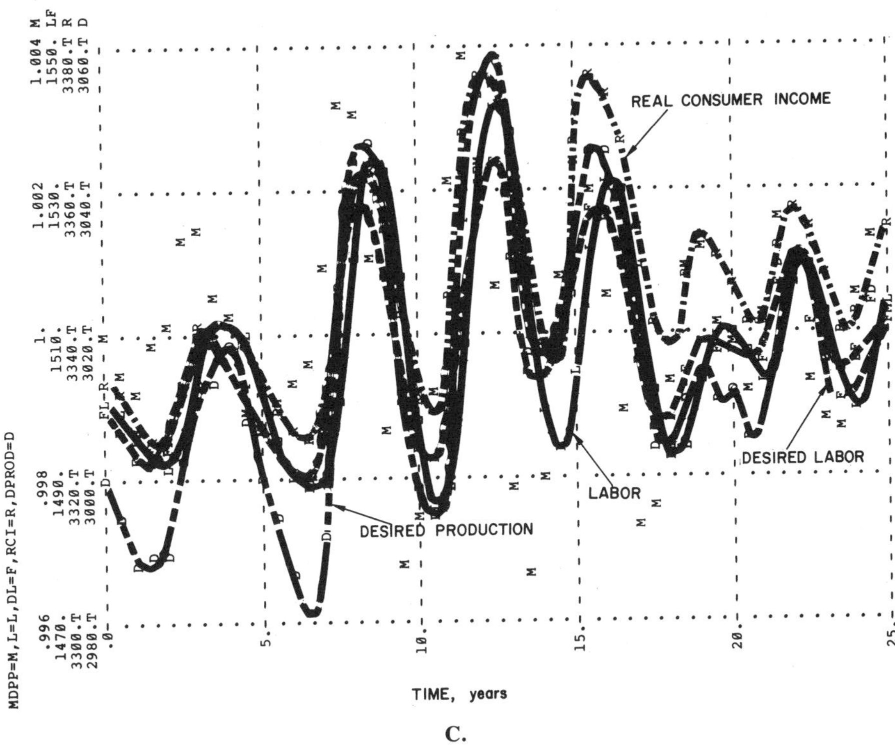


C.

**Figure 3-40** Noise response of the basic production sector including endogenous consumption

out roughly 80 percent of the fluctuations.[78] As a result, then, of cyclic price changes and the smoothing of income in consumption decisions, consumption tends to fluctuate much less than production, employment, and nominal income. In fact, Figure 3–40A exhibits no apparent fluctuations in consumption,[79] so the production-rate fluctuations in Figure 3–40 must be caused principally by inventory and backlog policies of the sector. In particular, these policies principally underlie the regular fluctuation in production relative to consumption observed in Figure 3–40.

It is interesting, in light of the minor role that endogenous consumption appears to have in generating inventory cycles in Figure 3–40, to note the disproportionate emphasis within the economic literature upon multiplier-accelerator theories of the business cycle. In accordance with the multiplier theory, the dependence of consumption upon income represents a potentially destabilizing influence on production. However, because of the relatively long smoothing delays involved in changing consumption

[78]A sinusoidal input of four-year periodicity passing through a two and one-half year first-order exponential delay will produce an output having the same period as the input sinusoid but roughly 20 percent of the amplitude. See Forrester (1961), p. 417.

[79]If the time to average real consumer income TARCI is reduced to around one to one and one-half years, more perceptible fluctuations in consumption appear. Such fluctuations, however, still appear to underlie only a small part of the variations in the production rate; inventory and backlog policies still constitute the major source of amplification.

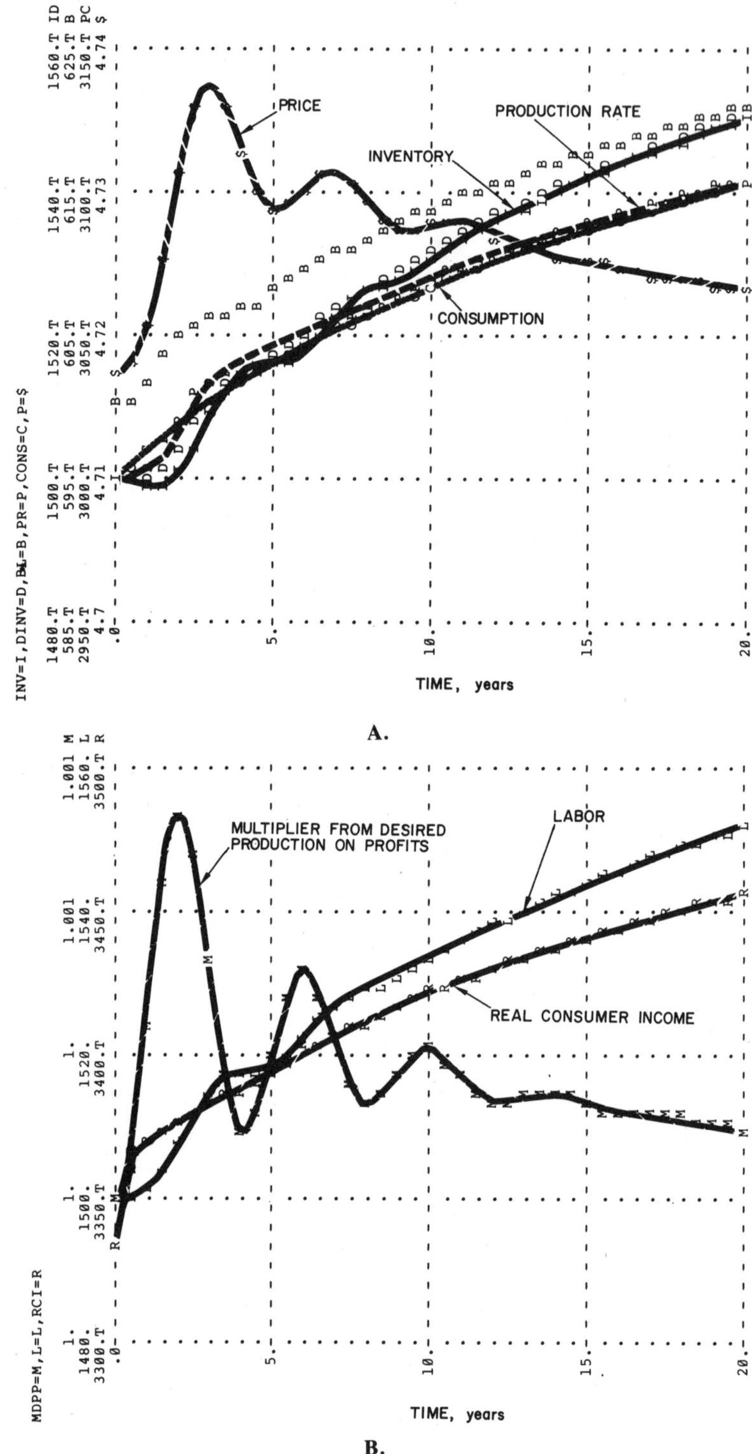


**Figure 3-41** Step response of the basic production sector including endogenous consumption

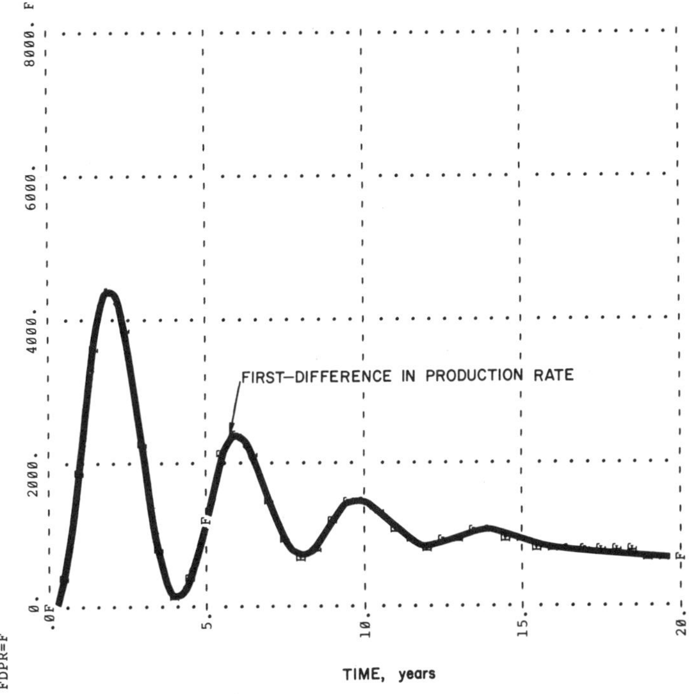


**Figure 3-42** Fluctuations in the growth rate of production induced by a step increase in income

patterns and because of the countervailing effects of price changes, the dependence of consumption on average income appears to be a less important source of amplification than changes in desired inventory brought about through price changes or similar processes endogenous to the firm. The effects of consumption on business-cycle behavior should be examined further in more detailed and realistic consumption models that incorporate determinants of consumption other than income.[80] For example, it may be found that consumption expenditures made in anticipation of price increases may exert a destabilizing impact on the production rate. However, from the analysis presented here, it appears that emphasis in the business-cycle literature on simple income-consumption relationships has not been directed at a major source of amplification in production. A simulation analysis, similar to that described in Figure 3–40, should be utilized in future business-cycle research to evaluate the importance of other factors and relationships hypothesized to underlie production cycles in the economy.

Finally, Figure 3–41 shows a system response to a 5 percent increase in external income. It exhibits a transient period of growth as production and consumption rise toward a new equilibrium level. The equilibrium increase in production equals the increase in external income times the production multiplier.[81] In Figure 3–41A, a

[80]In this context, the importance of income variations on consumption may be overstated in the multiplier-accelerator model because of both the assumed one-period lag in consumption and the neglect of price effects on real income changes.

[81]The multiplier is defined as the equilibrium change in nominal production resulting from a one-dollar increase in income. The multiplier for the system analyzed in Figure 3-41is calculated in the appendix to this chapter.

regular four-year cycle is clearly seen in the price. In contrast, the production rate, for example, is characterized by alternate periods of growth and stable output over the ten-year span.

A four-year cycle in production relative to a growth trend can be seen, however, by plotting first-differences in the production rate as in Figure 3–42. There the increase of production (measured as the production rate minus the average production rate over the previous quarter year)[82] exhibits regular fluctuations. Growth in production is always positive, however, since consumption is growing in accordance with the multiplier.

## Appendix: Derivation of the Production Multiplier

This appendix computes the production multiplier associated with Figure 3–41: In equilibrium, real production = real consumption. Using the equations for the production rate,

$$\begin{aligned}\text{(NPROD)}\ \text{(L/IL)} &= \text{(WC + EI)}\ \text{(APC)}\ /\text{P} \\ &= \text{((L*MHYN*HW)}\ \text{(APC)} + \text{(EI)}\ \text{(APC))}\ /\text{P},\end{aligned} \tag{1}$$

where

| | |
|---|---|
| NPROD | = normal production |
| IL | = initial labor |
| P | = price |
| L | = labor |
| MHYN | = man-hours per year normal |
| HW | = hourly wage |
| APC | = average propensity to consume |
| WC | = wage costs |
| EI | = external income. |

In equilibrium, price P is determined by a normal markup of costs:

$$\begin{aligned}\text{P} &= \text{AUCP(1 + NPM)} \\ &= \text{(WC/(APR} - \text{(INV)(IR)))(1 + NPM)} \\ &= \text{((L*MHYN*HW) (1 + NPM))/(PR} - \text{(PR*NIC) (IR))} \\ &= \text{((L*MHYN*HW) (1 + NPM))/(PR(1} - \text{(NIC) (IR)))} \\ &= \text{((L*MHYN*HW) (1 + NPM))/((NPROD) (L/IL) (1} - \text{(NIC)(IR)))} \\ &= \text{(HW*MHYN(1 + NPM))/((NPROD/IL) (1} - \text{(NIC) (IR))),}\end{aligned} \tag{2}$$

where

| | |
|---|---|
| AUCP | = average unit costs of production |
| NPM | = normal profit margin |

[82]The following model equations compute first-difference in production rate FDPR:

```
SPR.K=SMOOTH(PR.JK,.25)                              98, A
    SPR     - SMOOTHED PRODUCTION RATE  (UNITS/YEAR)
    PR      - PRODUCTION RATE  (UNITS/YEAR)

FDPR.K=PR.JK-SPR.K                                   99, S
    FDPR    - FIRST-DIFFERENCE IN PRODUCTION RATE
                 (UNITS/YEAR)
    PR      - PRODUCTION RATE  (UNITS/YEAR)
    SPR     - SMOOTHED PRODUCTION RATE  (UNITS/YEAR)
```

INV = inventory
NIC = normal inventory coverage
IR = interest rate.

Using equation (1) to solve for labor L, we obtain

L((NPROD/IL)P − MHYN*HW*APC) = EI*APC
L = (EI*APC)/((NPROD/IL)P − MHYN*HW*APC).

Therefore, nominal production = L*(NPROD/IL)*P
= (P*EI*APC*(NPROD/IL))/((NPROD/IL)P − MHYN*HW*APC)
= EI[((APC) (NPROD/IL)(P))/(NPROD/IL)P − MHYN*HW*APC)]. (3)

The expression in brackets in equation (3) is the multiplier, where P is given by equation (2). For the parameter values used in the text, the multiplier has an approximate value of 5.6.

# 4
# Inventory-Capital Interactions

## 4.1 Overview

Chapter 3 developed equations for the basic production sector with labor as the single factor of production. Simulations of the models described in Chapter 3 indicated that inventory-management and labor-hiring policies interact to produce fluctuations in production, inventory, and employment of approximately four years' duration.

As a prelude to the analysis of Chapter 5, which combines labor and fixed capital as joint factors of production, Chapter 4 treats fixed capital as the sole productive factor. Section 4.2 justifies altering the coefficients of the basic production sector, with the essential model structure left unchanged, to describe fixed capital plant and equipment rather than labor; this presentation also develops a set of parameter values appropriate for fixed capital. Section 4.3 analyzes the resulting model behavior and illustrates that capital-acquisition policies generate a cycle of fifteen to twenty years' duration or longer. Such a cycle resembles the Kuznets cycle or the long-term Kondratieff cycle observed in output and capital stock. Chapter 4 complements Chapter 3 by showing how the longer planning and depreciation delays for fixed capital equipment, as distinguished from labor, produce longer-term cycles in output and in factor input levels. Chapter 5 subsequently demonstrates that a model combining both labor and capital equipment exhibits short-term cycles in production, inventory, and employment and longer-term cycles in fixed capital and potential output.

## 4.2 Equations for Fixed Capital as a Factor of Production

*Differing Characteristics of Labor and Fixed Capital.* How can the basic production sector be adapted to describe a production process in which fixed plant and equipment is the only factor of production? This section outlines several differing characteristics of labor and fixed capital. It further suggests that these differences can be portrayed in terms of parameter changes in the basic production sector, leaving the model structure intact. The following analysis emphasizes the parallels among determinants of acquisition of diverse factors of production from the standpoint of the firm, and it affirms the utility of the basic production sector for studying the behavior modes associated with different factor inputs.

From a managerial viewpoint, labor and fixed capital have several mutually different attributes. For example, in the United States, as noted, labor can be readily acquired over a period of several weeks or months, while construction and the delivery of capital equipment require a longer period, perhaps one to three years. The acquisition of new capital equipment must also be preceded by an often long planning period. During that time, technical specifications are drawn up, plans are debated and modified, appropriations are approved, and credit is negotiated if the project is to be financed through debt or equity issues as distinguished from internal finance. Michael K. Evans describes the delays in planning for and obtaining new fixed capital in terms of an administrative lag and an appropriations lag.[1] The administrative (decision) lag subsumes the time required to formulate actual investment plans; the appropriations lag intervenes between appropriation and actual investment expenditures. Evans estimates the sum of the two lags at about one and a half to two years. In contrast to the delays for fixed capital, production labor can be added over a short period of time.

Labor and fixed capital also differ in the degree of commitment inherent in their acquisition. Labor can frequently be discharged on very short notice or reduced fairly quickly through attrition, since the average duration of employment is approximately two years.[2] Unlike labor, capital equipment, particularly buildings and heavy machinery, represents a relatively long-term commitment. Fixed capital can be reduced only through depreciation and discard, excepting the possibilities of sale, which are small because of (1) the high costs of transforming capital from one use to another and (2) the frequent simultaneous occurrence of capital excess in many firms within a particular industry. The long effective lifetime of fixed capital tends to increase still further the planning delay for capital. Since excess capital plant can be costly to maintain, fixed capital must be added more gradually than labor for a given discrepancy between the actual and desired production rates, that is, for a given probability of overbuilding total productive capacity.[3]

The preceding discussion has identified three principal differing attributes of labor and fixed capital. Compared with labor, fixed capital has (1) a longer average lifetime; (2) a longer planning and appropriations delay; and (3) a longer construction and delivery delay. All these differences can be represented in terms of parameter changes in the basic production sector, as distinguished from structural revisions. That is, the differences between labor and fixed capital do not involve fundamental differences in the criteria governing desired acquisitions of the two factor inputs; instead, they represent differences typified by the relative rapidity with which discrepancies between actual and desired factor levels can be eliminated. Therefore, the same model structure can be applied to study both the acquisition and the reduction of different factor inputs by

[1]Evans (1969), pp. 100–101.

[2]See Chapter 3, fn. 24.

[3]Bower (1972) provides several interesting case studies of capital investment decisions in actual firms. He emphasizes that the investment process involved in new product extensions is quite similar to the process for expanding productive capacity in existing product lines (p. 52). Moreover, Bower stresses that separate groups of individuals and separate pressures are typically involved in project definition ("context") and eventual acceptance or rejection of the project. The resulting delays in formulating an investment project and in developing an impetus for its ratification are important elements in the total planning and implementation period discussed here.

altering coefficient values to describe basic physical and technological attributes, such as construction delays and average lifetimes. The revised coefficients chosen to describe fixed capital are discussed in the following pages.

*Parameter Changes to Describe Fixed Capital.* This section briefly describes the structure and parameter values for the modified production sector with fixed capital as the single factor of production. The only equations described explicitly are those involving capital, for the others, such as inventory accounting equations, are the same as in Chapter 3. Emphasis is given to justifying the model parameters, since the structure of the basic production sector has already been presented in detail in Chapter 3. A complete documentor listing of the sector model appears in Appendix A.

Equation 2 for the production rate PR appears below. In Chapter 3 the production rate PR was assumed to be proportional to the available labor supply; analogously, in the current formulation, the production rate is proportional to capital stock. Setting the labor exponent LEX to zero in the production rate equation makes production independent of labor, as desired. With LEX equal to zero, the production equation is simplified as follows:[4]

production rate PR = (normal production NPROD) (normalized effective capital NECAP)

Figure 4–1 shows the impact of capital equipment on the production rate.

```
PR.KL=(NPROD)(EXP(LEX*LOGN(NEL.K)))(EXP(CEX*          2, R
  LOGN(NECAP.K)))(NPR.K)(CLIP(MLP.K,1,SW1,1))
NPROD=3E6                                             2.2, C
LEX=1                                                 2.3, C
CEX=1-LEX                                             2.4, N
SW1=0                                                 2.5, C
    PR      - PRODUCTION RATE  (UNITS/YEAR)
    NPROD   - NORMAL PRODUCTION (UNITS/YEAR)
    LEX     - LABOR EXPONENT  (DIMENSIONLESS)
    NEL     - NORMALIZED EFFECTIVE LABOR (DIMENSIONLESS)
    CEX     - CAPITAL EXPONENT  (DIMENSIONLESS)
    NECAP   - NORMALIZED EFFECTIVE CAPITAL
                (DIMENSIONLESS)
    NPR     - NOISE IN PRODUCTION RATE  (DIMENSIONLESS)
    MLP     - MULTIPLIER ON LABOR PRODUCTIVITY
                (DIMENSIONLESS)
    SW1     - SWITCH 1  (DIMENSIONLESS)
```

Normalized effective capital NECAP equals effective capital ECAP divided by initial capital ICAP. In equation 26, ICAP equals 7.5 million units, while normal production NPROD equals 3 million units per year (equation 2). These figures yield a normal capital-output ratio of 2.5, which is consistent with empirical evidence for the United States.[5]

Effective capital ECAP is defined in equation 27 as the level of capital CAP multiplied by the capital utilization factor CUF. The capital utilization factor CUF is

[4]In equation 2, the noise in production rate NPR is normally one and therefore exerts no influence on production. Analogously, switch 1 SW1 equals zero throughout Chapter 4, so that the multiplier on labor productivity MLP does not affect production. The labor exponent LEX is shown to equal one in equation 2 but is set to zero for the simulations in Chapter 4 (see Appendix B for the equations used to generate the simulations).

[5]Samuelson (1973), p. 745, shows that the capital-output ratio for the United States has tended to vary around a mean value of 2.5–3.0.

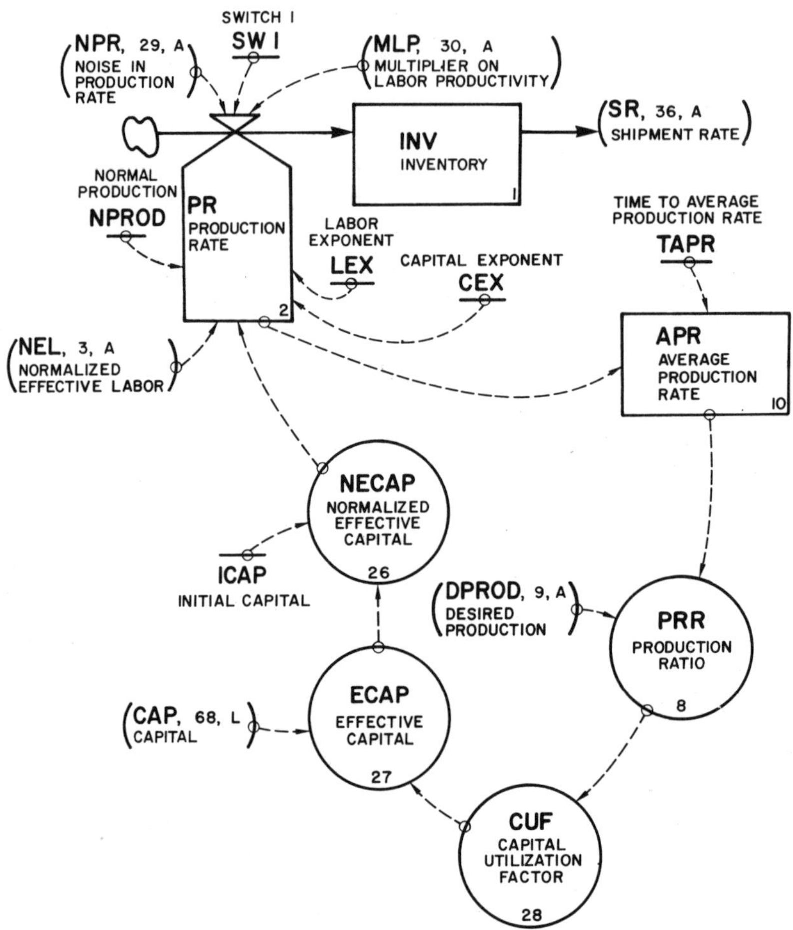


**Figure 4-1** Flow diagram of the influence of capital on production

```
NECAP.K=ECAP.K/ICAP                                         26, A
ICAP=7.5E6                                                  26.1, C
    NECAP  - NORMALIZED EFFECTIVE CAPITAL
               (DIMENSIONLESS)
    ECAP   - EFFECTIVE CAPITAL   (CAPITAL UNITS)
    ICAP   - INITIAL CAPITAL  (CAPITAL UNITS)
```

defined in equation 28 and shown in Figure 4–2. CUF is an increasing function of the production ratio PRR, the latter defined as the ratio of desired production to the average production rate.[6] CUF represents the use of additional work shifts, implying a longer work week for capital, when pressures arise to expand output. In addition, CUF subsumes variations in the fraction of capital stock utilized, since only 80–90 percent of the aggregate U.S. capital stock is utilized under normal conditions.[7] When desired

[6]See section 3.3, equation 8.

[7]Klein and Preston (1967), Creamer (1964), and Phillips (1963) describe measurements of capacity utilization.

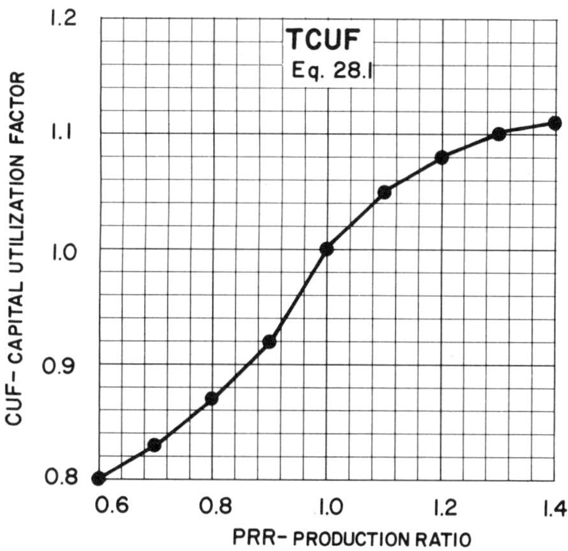


**Figure 4-2** The capital utilization factor

production exceeds the average production rate (indicated by a production ratio PRR of greater than unity), increased capacity utilization can expand the output derivable from a given capital stock, thereby raising total effective capital. Of course, as capital utilization rises, increased output is subject to diminishing returns as older and less efficient capital comes into operation. Analogously, excess production (indicated by a production ratio PRR of less than one) can lead to a reduction in net capital utilization, thereby lowering effective capital. In this respect, the formulation of effective capital is identical, both conceptually and algebraically, to the formulation of effective labor EL used in Chapter 3 (equation 4); in Chapter 3, effective labor equaled labor L multiplied by the relative length of work week RLWW, where RLWW was an increasing function of desired production relative to the average production rate.

```
ECAP.K=(CAP.K)(CUF.K)                                     27, A
    ECAP    - EFFECTIVE CAPITAL  (CAPITAL UNITS)
    CAP     - CAPITAL  (CAPITAL UNITS)
    CUF     - CAPITAL UTILIZATION FACTOR  (DIMENSIONLESS)

CUF.K=TABHL(TCUF,PRR.K,.6,1.4,.1)                         28, A
TCUF=.8/.83/.87/.92/1/1.05/1.08/1.1/1.11                  28.1, T
CUF=1                                                     28.2, N
    CUF     - CAPITAL UTILIZATION FACTOR  (DIMENSIONLESS)
    TCUF    - TABLE FOR CAPITAL UTILIZATION FACTOR
    PRR     - PRODUCTION RATIO  (DIMENSIONLESS)

PRR.K=DPROD.K/APR.K                                       8, A
    PRR     - PRODUCTION RATIO  (DIMENSIONLESS)
    DPROD   - DESIRED PRODUCTION  (UNITS/YEAR)
    APR     - AVERAGE PRODUCTION RATE  (UNITS/YEAR)
```

The variable capital utilization factor allows the production rate to expand somewhat in the short run, in response to an increase in demand, so that new orders for capital do not carry the entire burden of capacity adjustment. Haberler has described the importance of incorporating variable utilization rates in an investment function; he notes that variable utilization negates the assumption of a constant capital-output ratio inherent in the accelerator principle.[8] However, it is interesting to note that very few existing econometric investment functions embody variable usage of fixed capital plant, largely because of difficulties in measuring capacity utilization.[9]

The level of capital CAP (equation 68) is increased by capital arrivals CA and is decreased by capital depreciation CD. Since the level of capital is initially set to equal initial capital ICAP, normalized effective capital NECAP initially equals one;[10] consequently, the production rate equals normal production NPROD (see equations 2 and 26). Figure 4–3 shows the determinants of capital arrivals and depreciation.

```
CAP.K=CAP.J+(DT)(CA.JK-CD.JK)                               68, L
CAP=ICAP                                                    68.1, N
    CAP     - CAPITAL   (CAPITAL UNITS)
    CA      - CAPITAL ARRIVALS   (CAPITAL UNITS/YEAR)
    CD      - CAPITAL DEPRECIATION   (CAPITAL UNITS/YEAR)
    ICAP    - INITIAL CAPITAL   (CAPITAL UNITS)
```

Capital arrivals CA (equation 69) equals the level of capital on order CAPO divided by the delivery delay for capital DDC, which is assumed to be two years. The value of DDC is a compromise between the six- to twelve-month period required to receive machinery from suppliers and the several years required to construct new buildings or facilities, such as power plants and steel mills.[11] The structure of equation 69 for capital arrivals is identical to equation 42 in Chapter 3, where the hiring rate HR equals the level of vacancies (equivalent to unfilled orders for labor) divided by a delay in filling vacancies (a delivery delay for labor).

```
CA.KL=CAPO.K/DDC                                            69, R
DDC=2                                                       69.1, C
    CA      - CAPITAL ARRIVALS   (CAPITAL UNITS/YEAR)
    CAPO    - CAPITAL ON ORDER   (CAPITAL UNITS)
    DDC     - DELIVERY DELAY FOR CAPITAL   (YEARS)
```

Capital depreciation CD (equation 70) is modeled as the level of capital CAP divided by the average lifetime of capital ALC. In turn, the average lifetime of capital ALC (equation 71) equals a normal lifetime of fifteen years, modified by the multiplier from capital demand on lifetime of capital MCDLC.[12] Depending on the relative adequacy of capital, MCDLC represents the incentives for early discard of capital or, alternatively, for longer retention and maintenance.[13]

[8]Haberler (1964), pp. 96–97.

[9]For example, see the survey of investment functions in Bischoff (1971) and Jorgensen, Hunter, and Nadiri (1970); see also Evans (1969), pp. 255–256.

[10]Equation 26 defines NECAP as effective capital ECAP divided by initial capital ICAP.

[11]Mayer and Soneblum (1955) and Mayer (1958, 1960) present survey evidence on lags in fixed-capital investment.

[12]Modigliani (1973), p. 12, estimates the average lifetime of capital as being on the order of 15 years.

[13]Bain (1939) provides a good summary of monetary and technological factors that influence the optimal lifetime of fixed capital.

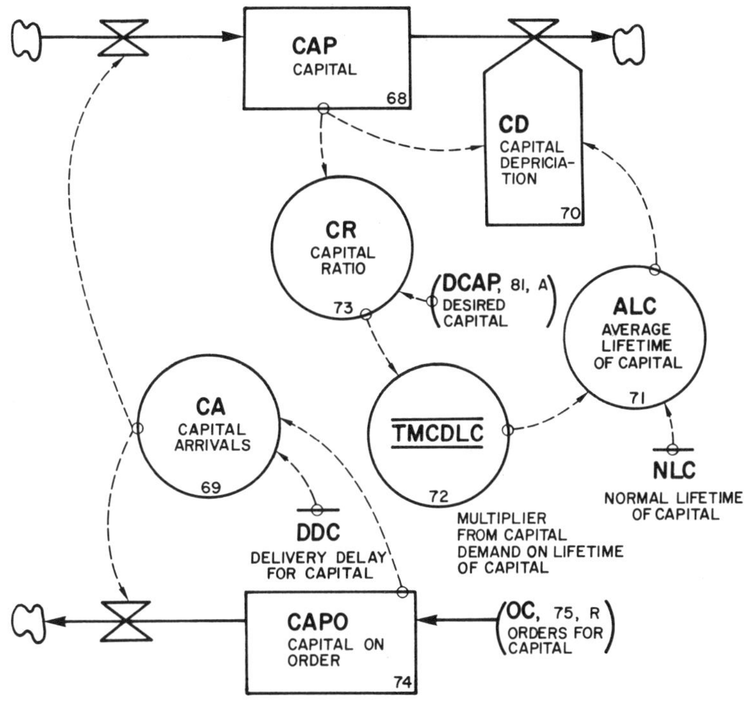


**Figure 4-3** Flow diagram of capital arrivals and depreciation

```
CD.KL=CAP.K/ALC.K                                        70, R
    CD      - CAPITAL DEPRECIATION  (CAPITAL UNITS/YEAR)
    CAP     - CAPITAL  (CAPITAL UNITS)
    ALC     - AVERAGE LIFETIME OF CAPITAL  (YEARS)

ALC.K=(NLC)(MCDLC.K)                                     71, A
NLC=15                                                   71.1, C
    ALC     - AVERAGE LIFETIME OF CAPITAL  (YEARS)
    NLC     - NORMAL LIFETIME OF CAPITAL  (YEARS)
    MCDLC   - MULTIPLIER FROM CAPITAL DEMAND ON LIFETIME
                OF CAPITAL (DIMENSIONLESS)
```

The multiplier from capital demand on lifetime of capital MCDLC (equation 72) is a decreasing function of the capital ratio CR (equation 73), defined as the ratio of capital CAP to desired capital DCAP. To the right of Figure 4-4, excess capital accelerates scrapping of capital plant and equipment, manifested by a reduction in the average lifetime of capital. Analogously, to the left of Figure 4-4, a strong demand for capital is assumed to prolong the use of existing capital equipment through increased maintenance. At the extreme left of the table, the average lifetime of capital is increased 40 percent above normal, to a maximum value of twenty-one years (= 15 × 1.4). The formulation is identical to equation 65 in Chapter 3 for the average duration

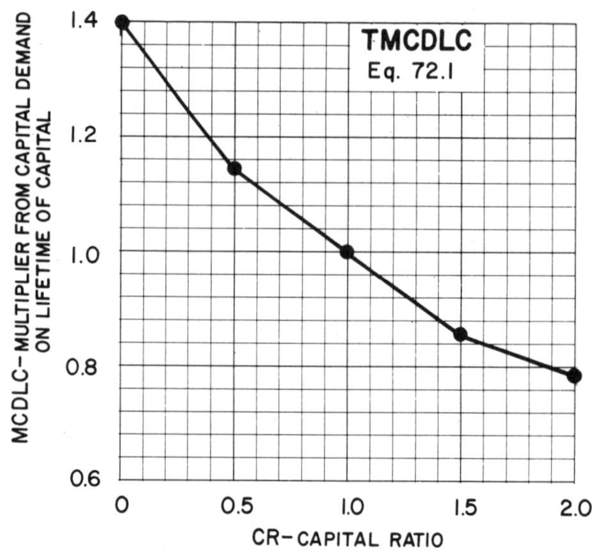


**Figure 4-4** The influence of capital demand on the average lifetime of capital

```
MCDLC.K=TABLE(TMCDLC,CR.K,0,2,.5)                           72, A
TMCDLC=1.4/1.15/1/.85/.75                                   72.1, T
    MCDLC  - MULTIPLIER FROM CAPITAL DEMAND ON LIFETIME
               OF CAPITAL (DIMENSIONLESS)
    TMCDLC - TABLE FOR MULTIPLIER FROM CAPITAL DEMAND ON
               LIFETIME OF CAPITAL
    CR     - CAPITAL RATIO  (DIMENSIONLESS)

CR.K=CAP.K/DCAP.K                                           73, A
    CR     - CAPITAL RATIO  (DIMENSIONLESS)
    CAP    - CAPITAL  (CAPITAL UNITS)
    DCAP   - DESIRED CAPITAL  (CAPITAL UNITS)
```

of employment ADE, where ADE (equivalent to the lifetime of labor within the sector) depends on the relative demand for labor.

Capital on order CAPO (equation 74) is a level variable that is increased by orders for capital OC and decreased through capital arrivals CA. The level of capital on order CAPO corresponds to an unfilled order backlog for capital goods; CAPO is therefore functionally equivalent to the level of vacancies in Chapter 3, which represents an order backlog for labor. Initially, capital on order is set to equal capital depreciation CD multiplied by the delivery delay for capital DDC. The initial value equation guarantees that the level of capital on order is just sufficient to equate capital arrivals CA and capital depreciation CD. In equilibrium, according to equation 69,

$$CA = CAPO/DDC = (CD*DDC)/DDC = CD.$$

```
CAPO.K=CAPO.J+(DT)(OC.JK-CA.JK)                             74, L
CAPO=(CD)(DDC)                                              74.1, N
    CAPO   - CAPITAL ON ORDER  (CAPITAL UNITS)
    OC     - ORDERS FOR CAPITAL  (CAPITAL UNITS/YEAR)
    CA     - CAPITAL ARRIVALS  (CAPITAL UNITS/YEAR)
    CD     - CAPITAL DEPRECIATION  (CAPITAL UNITS/YEAR)
    DDC    - DELIVERY DELAY FOR CAPITAL  (YEARS)
```

The formulation of orders for capital OC (equation 75), shown in Figure 4–5, is identical to the formulation in Chapter 3 for new vacancy creation NVC (see equation 44 and Figure 3–13). In equation 75, orders for capital OC equals average orders for capital AOC times the multiplier from capital demand on orders for capital MCDOC. AOC (equation 76) is a four-year exponential average of actual orders for capital OC. As will be explained, MCDOC increases the order rate above the average rate, thereby indicating a net expansion of capital, when production capacity is insufficient; analogously, MCDOC lowers orders of capital when production capacity becomes excessive.

```
OC.KL=(AOC.K)(MCDOC.K)                                    75, R
    OC      - ORDERS FOR CAPITAL   (CAPITAL UNITS/YEAR)
    AOC     - AVERAGE ORDERS FOR CAPITAL   (CAPITAL UNITS/
                YEAR)
    MCDOC   - MULTIPLIER FROM CAPITAL DEMAND ON ORDERS
                FOR CAPITAL (DIMENSIONLESS)
```

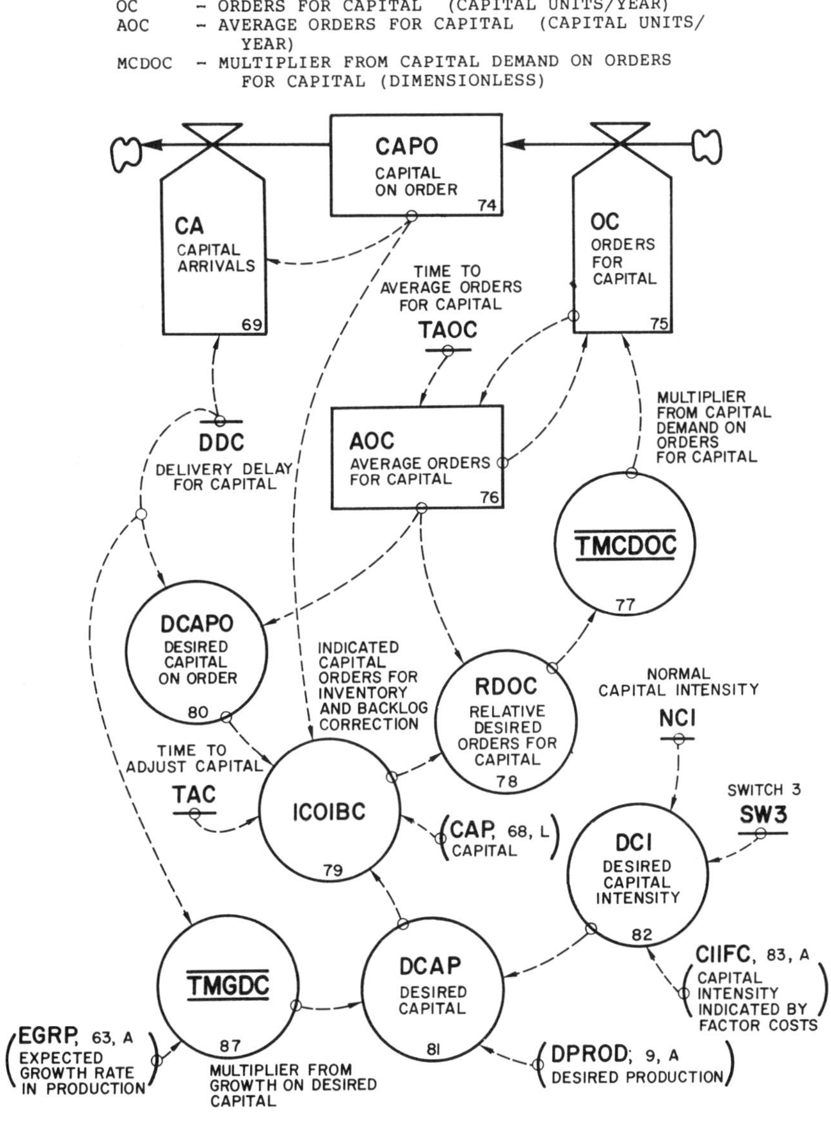


**Figure 4-5** Flow diagram of the determinants of orders for fixed capital

```
AOC.K=AOC.J+(DT/TAOC)(OC.JK-AOC.J)                      76, L
AOC=CD                                                  76.1, N
TAOC=4                                                  76.2, C
    AOC     - AVERAGE ORDERS FOR CAPITAL  (CAPITAL UNITS/
                YEAR)
    TAOC    - TIME TO AVERAGE ORDERS FOR CAPITAL  (YEARS)
    OC      - ORDERS FOR CAPITAL  (CAPITAL UNITS/YEAR)
    CD      - CAPITAL DEPRECIATION  (CAPITAL UNITS/YEAR)
```

The multiplier from capital demand on orders for capital MCDOC is an increasing function of relative desired orders for capital RDOC. As defined in equation 78,

RDOC = (average orders for capital AOC + indicated capital orders for inventory and backlog correction ICOIBC)/average orders for capital AOC

$$= 1 + \frac{\text{ICOIBC}}{\text{AOC}}$$

Indicated capital orders for inventory and backlog correction ICOIBC is a measure of the demand for fixed capital relative to the available supply. In equation 79, when capital equals desired capital, and capital on order equals desired capital on order, ICOIBC will equal zero; in turn, when ICOIBC equals zero, RDOC and MCDOC will have normal values of one. Under such circumstances, when current productive capacity is adequate to cover demand, orders for capital OC will equal average orders for capital AOC. On the other hand, suppose, for example, that desired capital exceeds capital; relative desired orders for capital RDOC will then exceed one, and MCDOC will increase, thereby signaling the expansion of orders for new capital equipment.

```
MCDOC.K=TABLE(TMCDOC,RDOC.K,0,2,.25)                    77, A
TMCDOC=.2/.35/.55/.75/1/1.25/1.45/1.6/1.7               77.1, T
    MCDOC   - MULTIPLIER FROM CAPITAL DEMAND ON ORDERS
                FOR CAPITAL (DIMENSIONLESS)
    TMCDOC  - TABLE FOR MULTIPLIER FROM CAPITAL DEMAND ON
                ORDERS FOR CAPITAL
    RDOC    - RELATIVE DESIRED ORDERS FOR CAPITAL
                (DIMENSIONLESS)

RDOC.K=(AOC.K+ICOIBC.K)/AOC.K                           78, A
    RDOC    - RELATIVE DESIRED ORDERS FOR CAPITAL
                (DIMENSIONLESS)
    AOC     - AVERAGE ORDERS FOR CAPITAL  (CAPITAL UNITS/
                YEAR)
    ICOIBC  - INDICATED CAPITAL ORDERS FOR INVENTORY AND
                BACKLOG CORRECTION (CAPITAL UNITS/YEAR)

ICOIBC.K=(DCAPO.K-CAPO.K+DCAP.K-CAP.K)/TAC              79, A
TAC=4                                                   79.1, C
    ICOIBC  - INDICATED CAPITAL ORDERS FOR INVENTORY AND
                BACKLOG CORRECTION (CAPITAL UNITS/YEAR)
    DCAPO   - DESIRED CAPITAL ON ORDER  (CAPITAL UNITS)
    CAPO    - CAPITAL ON ORDER  (CAPITAL UNITS)
    DCAP    - DESIRED CAPITAL  (CAPITAL UNITS)
    CAP     - CAPITAL  (CAPITAL UNITS)
    TAC     - TIME TO ADJUST CAPITAL  (YEARS)
```

Figure 4-6 exhibits saturation toward the extreme right of the table function; saturation reflects increasing organizational difficulties in absorbing progressively larger new infusions of capital and a corresponding reluctance to continue the rapid expansion of orders for capital in the presence of severe capital shortages.

To the left of Figure 4-6, orders for capital decrease as aggregate capital stock or capital on order becomes excessive. The multiplier from capital demand on orders for capital MCDOC approaches zero, but it remains positive even when the stock of fixed

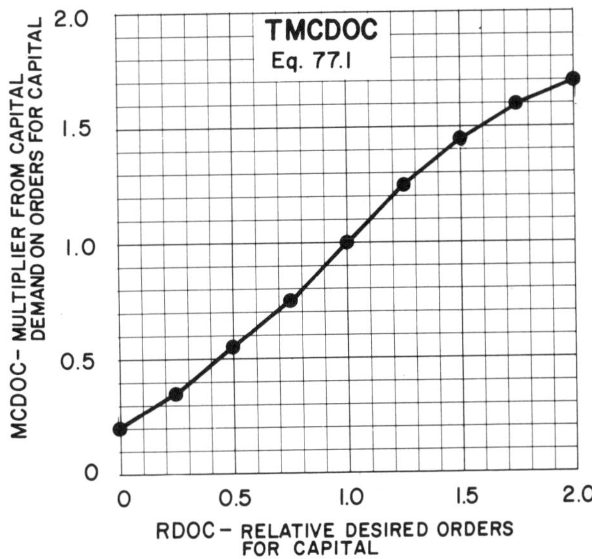


**Figure 4-6** Multiplier from capital demand on orders for capital

capital substantially exceeds desired capital. The continuous nature of the curve largely reflects the process of model aggregation. At any point in time the economy is characterized by a wide spectrum among individual product lines, firms, and industries with respect to their perceived levels of sales and desired capital stock. Some firms would continue to invest while others would maintain a zero (gross) investment rate. Therefore, a curve representing aggregate behavior should exhibit a gradual and continuous decline in the investment multiplier as the aggregate fixed capital stock exceeds the average desired capital.[14]

In equation 80, desired capital on order DCAPO equals average orders for capital AOC multiplied by the delivery delay for capital DDC. The formulation is identical to equation 49 in Chapter 3 for desired vacancies.

```
DCAPO.K=(AOC.K)(DDC)                                    80, A
     DCAPO   - DESIRED CAPITAL ON ORDER   (CAPITAL UNITS)
     AOC     - AVERAGE ORDERS FOR CAPITAL   (CAPITAL UNITS/
                 YEAR)
     DDC     - DELIVERY DELAY FOR CAPITAL   (YEARS)
```

In equation 81, desired capital DCAP equals desired production DPROD multiplied by the desired capital intensity DCI (equation 82) and the multiplier from growth on desired capital MGDC (equation 87).[15] This formulation is identical to equation 50 in Chapter 3 computing desired labor DL from desired production and growth expectations. The formulation of desired capital also broadly resembles the generalized ac-

[14]Analogously, Haberler (1964) notes that the labor force is a broad aggregate of individuals differing in skills, motivations, and other attributes. Thus "the existence of a large total does not in the least preclude the possibility of a shortage of labor in many special fields" (p. 359).

[15]Desired capital intensity DCI is represented, as in Chapter 3, using a CLIP function. DCI, which is equivalent to the desired capital-output ratio of the sector, here equals a constant normal capital intensity NCI, defined as the ratio of initial capital ICAP to normal production NPROD, as switch 3 SW3 is set to zero. In Chapter 5, the investment function is extended to include variations in the input mix of capital and labor.

celerator model described by Bischoff (1971), except that inventories and backlogs, rather than just sales, influence desired production.[16] Growth expectations are accounted for explicitly in equation 81; moreover, as discussed previously, variable capital utilization is included in the sector model so that orders for capital do not carry the full burden of adjusting production to desired production.

```
DCAP.K=(DPROD.K)(DCI.K)(MGDC.K)                          81, A
    DCAP    - DESIRED CAPITAL  (CAPITAL UNITS)
    DPROD   - DESIRED PRODUCTION  (UNITS/YEAR)
    DCI     - DESIRED CAPITAL INTENSITY (CAPITAL UNITS/
                OUTPUT UNIT/YEAR)
    MGDC    - MULTIPLIER FROM GROWTH ON DESIRED CAPITAL
                (DIMENSIONLESS)

DCI.K=CLIP(CIIFC.K,NCI,SW3,1)                            82, A
NCI=ICAP/NPROD                                           82.1, N
    DCI     - DESIRED CAPITAL INTENSITY (CAPITAL UNITS/
                OUTPUT UNIT/YEAR)
    CIIFC   - CAPITAL INTENSITY INDICATED BY FACTOR COSTS
                (CAPITAL UNITS/OUTPUT UNIT/YEAR)
    NCI     - NORMAL CAPITAL INTENSITY  (CAPITAL UNITS/
                OUTPUT UNIT/YEAR)
    SW3     - SWITCH 3  (DIMENSIONLESS)
    ICAP    - INITIAL CAPITAL  (CAPITAL UNITS)
    NPROD   - NORMAL PRODUCTION (UNITS/YEAR)

MGDC.K=1+(EGRP.K)(DDC)                                   87, A
    MGDC    - MULTIPLIER FROM GROWTH ON DESIRED CAPITAL
                (DIMENSIONLESS)
    EGRP    - EXPECTED GROWTH RATE IN PRODUCTION
                (FRACTION/YEAR)
    DDC     - DELIVERY DELAY FOR CAPITAL  (YEARS)
```

## 4.3 Simulation of the Inventory-Capital Model

Section 4.2 listed the parameter changes used to adapt the basic production sector to describe fixed capital rather than labor. Figure 4–7 summarizes the parameter changes.

Figure 4–8 exhibits the response of the basic production sector, including fixed capital, to a 15 percent step increase in consumption beginning at year 2.[17] All system variables exhibit a cycle of approximately fifteen-year periodicity,[18] which is well beyond the range of short-term business-cycle fluctuations but closely resembles the periodicities characteristic of long-term Kuznets cycles. The Kuznets cycle, according to Hickman, is a fifteen- to twenty-year fluctuation in the rate of growth of capital stock, output, productivity, and other variables.[19] The Kuznets cycle is also characterized by long swings in growth rate of the labor force and in the unemployment rate. Figure 4–8 illustrates the average annual changes in output for the United States from 1860 to 1960. Figure 4–9 shows Kuznets-cycle peaks occurring roughly in 1865, 1885, 1900, 1920, and 1940.

[16]Bischoff (1971), pp. 15–16. For further discussion of the generalized accelerator model see Chenery (1952), Koyck (1954), and Jorgensen and Siebert (1968).

[17]Appendix A lists the complete set of parameter changes required to generate the simulation.

[18]Note that Figure 4–8 spans forty years on the horizontal axis.

[19]Hickman (1963), pp. 490-492. The original empirical work supporting the existence of 18–20 year swings in capital growth appears in Wardwell (1927) and Kuznets (1930). Lewis and O'Leary (1955) have conducted a more recent study indicating the existence of Kuznets-type cycles in a variety of countries.

| Parameter | Value in Production Sector Including Labor | Value in Production Sector Including Capital |
|---|---|---|
| 1. Delay in acquiring factor | Delay in filling vacancies DFV = 0.25 year | Delivery delay for capital DDC = 2 years |
| 2. Normal factor intensity | Normal labor intensity NLI = 2,000 men/output unit/year | Normal capital intensity NCI = 2.5 capital units/output unit/year |
| 3. Time to average orders for factor | Time to average new vacancy creation TANVC = 0.5 year | Time to average orders for capital TAOC = 4 years |
| 4. Time to adjust factor | Time to adjust labor TAL = 0.5 year | Time to adjust capital TAC = 4 years |
| 5. Average lifetime of factor | Normal duration of employment NDE = 2 years | Normal lifetime of capital NLC = 15 years |

**Figure 4-7** Parameter changes adapting the basic production sector to describe fixed capital as a factor of production

As mentioned, Kuznets-cycle fluctuations appear in the rate of growth of output and capital stock. Superficially, they differ from the capital-production cycle exhibited in Figure 4–8, which exhibits a cycle in absolute levels of output and fixed capital. However, available data on the Kuznets cycle are drawn from a growing economy; such data therefore measure fluctuations in output and capital around a long-term growth trend. To produce comparable data, the basic production sector can be subjected to a steady ramp increase in incoming orders. Figure 4–10 shows the response of capital, the production rate, inventory, and other variables to a ramp increase in consumption (orders); the ramp input generates an annual growth of approximately 2 percent in consumption. A long-term cycle in the capital growth rate can be seen clearly in Figure 4–11, which plots first-differences of data on capital stock drawn from Figure 4–10. Figure 4–11 exhibits a fifteen-year cycle in capital growth, which is identical to the period of the cycle induced by a step increase in consumption (see Figure 4–8).[20]

A detailed analysis of the results shown in Figures 4–8, 4–10, and 4–11 completely parallels the analysis given in Chapter 3; the only significant difference between model behavior in Chapters 3 and 4 is that the response of the production sector containing fixed capital, rather than labor, as a factor of production, is drawn out over a much longer period, and the magnitude of the lead and lag relationships differs accordingly. Nonetheless, a brief analysis is provided here to emphasize the parallels between the causes of the oscillations in the models presented in Chapters 3 and 4.

In Figure 4–8, as incoming orders are increased, inventory begins to decline and backlog increases. Desired production (plotted in Figure 4–8B) rises as a result,

[20]The basic production sector including fixed capital also responds to random noise in consumption with a fifteen-year cycle. The result probably has greater practical significance than the step or ramp responses illustrated here, because random variation is necessarily superimposed on all consumption streams.

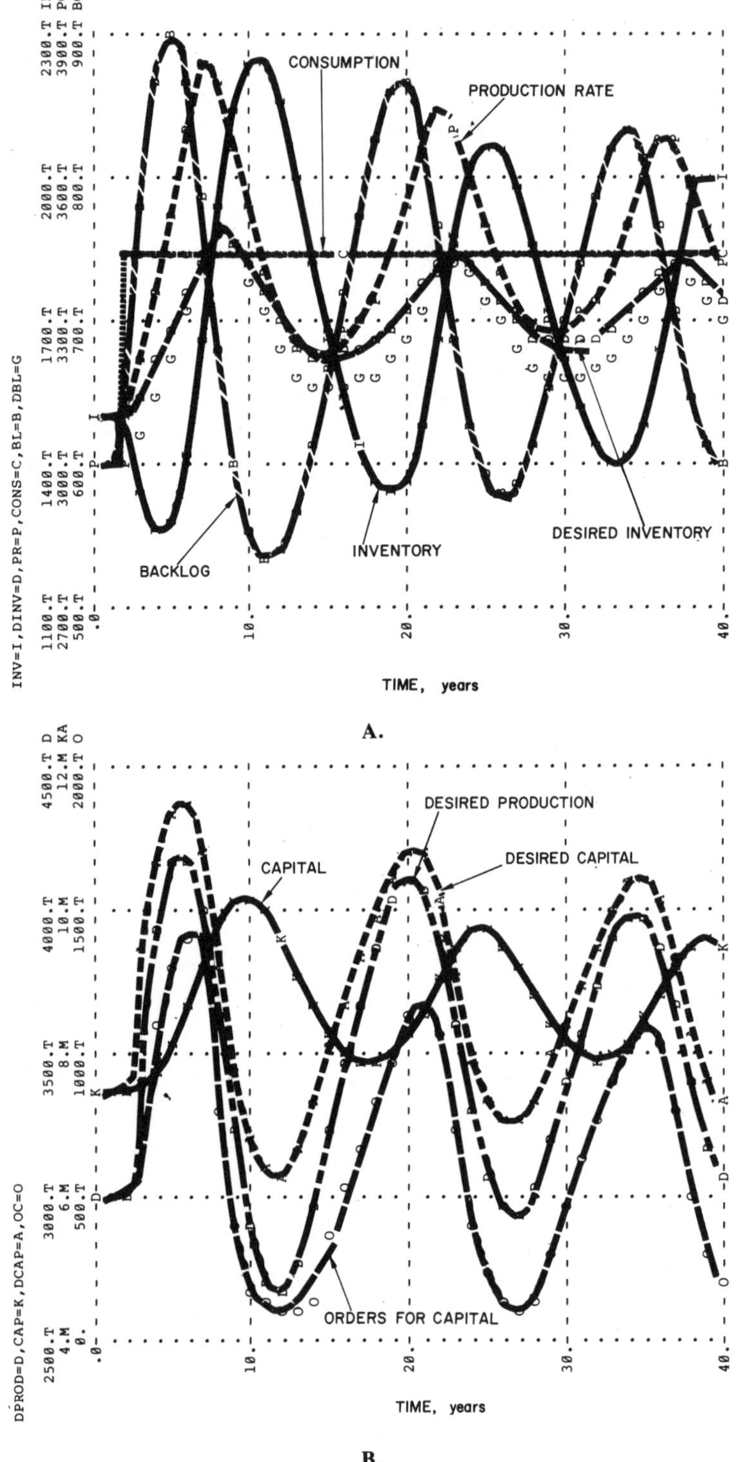


**Figure 4-8** Step response of the basic production sector including fixed capital

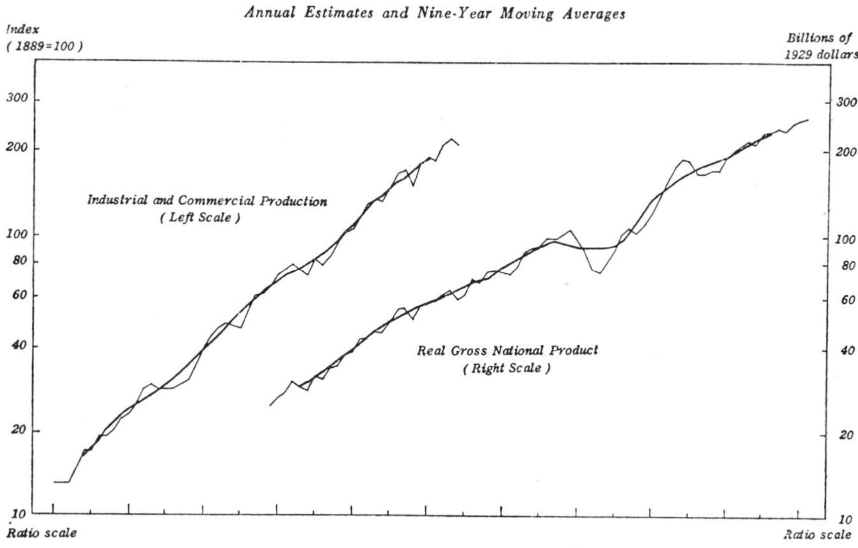


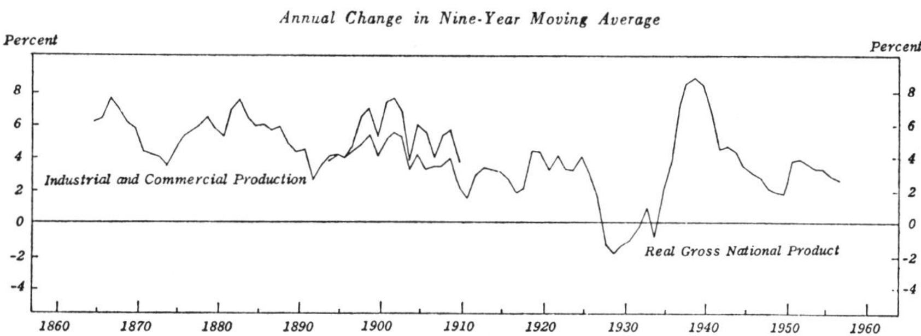


**Figure 4-9** Long swings in aggregate production in the United States
Source: Hickman (1963), p. 491

thereby increasing desired capital and leading to increased orders for capital. However, the long time delays involved in the planning and construction of fixed capital delay the actual increase in capital stock. By around year 5, the production rate has increased sufficiently to equal consumption, thereby terminating the fall in inventory. But inventory has been steadily depleted between years 1 and 5, while desired inventory has risen in response to increased production. At year 5, for example, inventory equals 1.25 million units while desired inventory equals nearly 1.7 million units (see Figure 4–8A). Analogously, Figure 4–8A exhibits a large backlog discrepancy at year 5 with backlog equaling 0.9 million units and desired backlog equaling 0.68 million units.

To eliminate the inventory and backlog discrepancies caused by increased consumption, production must rise above consumption. Thus, in Figure 4–8B, capital rises from an initial value of 7.5 million units to about 10 million units at year 10 and continues to expand as long as desired production exceeds the average production rate.

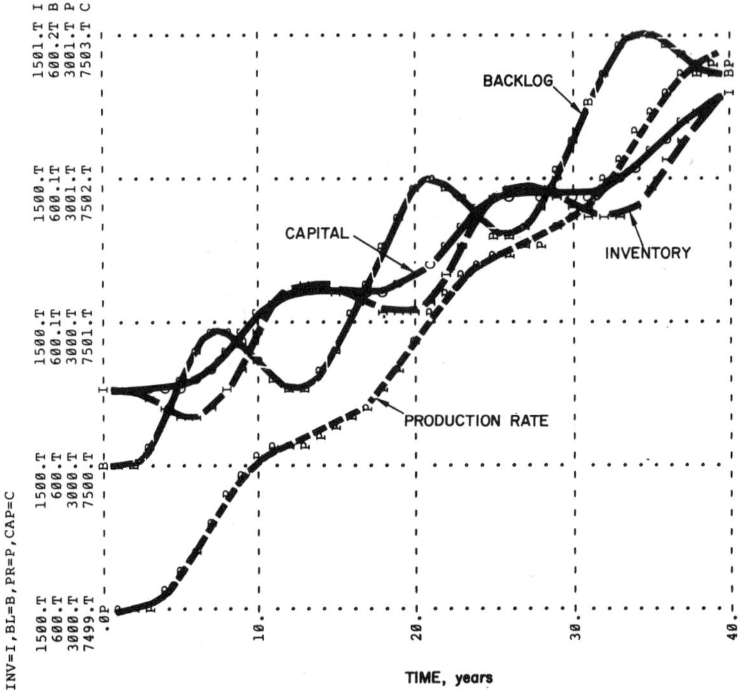


**Figure 4-10** Response of the basic production sector including fixed capital to a ramp increase in orders

However, as inventory builds up once more and backlog declines, desired production drops off, thereby gradually leading to excess capacity. Capacity remains in excess for several years as a consequence of the long delay in capital depreciation. Consequently, Figure 4–8 displays a cyclic adjustment similar to that of the reference simulation in Chapter 3 (Figure 3–17). However, the response in Figure 4–8 is protracted, compared with the four-year cycles exhibited in Chapter 3.[21] Compared with the models in Chapter 3, the addition of capacity is delayed in the production upturn because of the increased acquisition delays; moreover, the reduction of capacity occurs slowly on the downturn because of the gradual runoff of capital through depreciation.[22]

The capital and production cycle exhibited in Figure 4–8, although considerably longer than the four-year business cycle, probably still lies on the short range of cycles induced by fixed capital investment. For example, the production sector underlying Figure 4–8 resembles a consumer-goods sector characterized by a relatively short

[21]Chapter 2 noted that Pigou (1927) and Robertson (1915) attributed the period of the business cycle to the "gestation delay," or construction period, of capital equipment. The results in Figures 4–8, 4–10, 4–11, and 4–12 indicate the role of such construction delays, in addition to the planning and depreciation delays, in generating capital cycles. However, contrary to Pigou and Robertson, cycles induced by fixed capital investment appear to have a much longer period than the four-year trade cycle.

[22]Tinbergen (1938), noting that the reduction of capital stock is limited by the rate of depreciation, originally criticized the accelerator formulation for assuming symmetry in capital acquisition and disposal. The investment function described in section 4.2 embodies such asymmetry by treating the determinants of gross investment and depreciation separately.

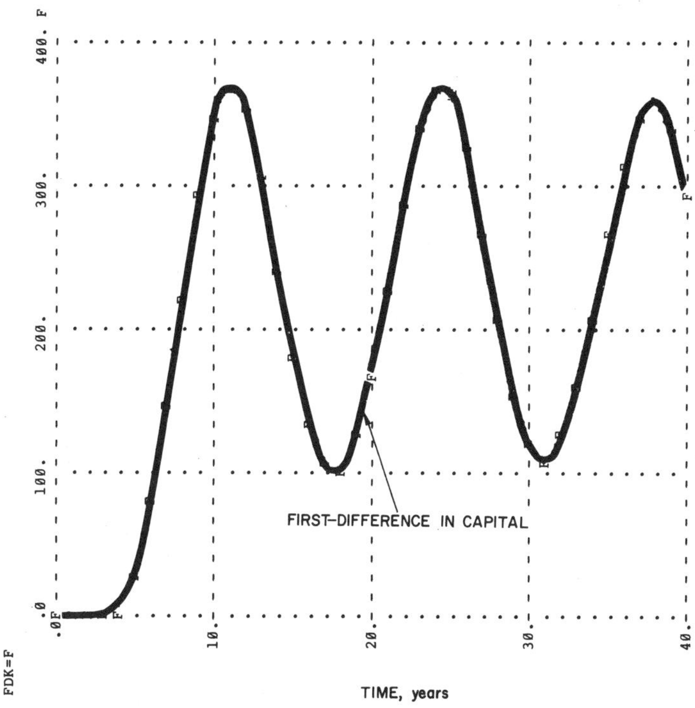


**Figure 4-11** Growth cycle in capital stock induced by ramp increase in incoming orders

delivery delay and a short delay for in-process inventory between initiation and completion of production. Because of these short production and delivery delays, a consumer-goods sector can normally adjust production to consumption fairly rapidly. To study the behavior modes characteristic of a capital-producing sector, rather than a goods sector, the parameter values of the sector model can be adapted to describe a capital sector. Compared with the goods-producing sector, the capital sector is assumed to have a longer production and delivery delay for its output. Because of the increased adjustment delays, the capital sector also requires a longer time to correct inventory and backlog discrepancies. Moreover, the capital sector is assumed to adjust production gradually because of fears of overbuilding capacity if adjustment proceeds too rapidly; such risks of overexpansion tend to rise steeply as the delivery delay of the sector increases.[23]

Figure 4–12 shows the response of the capital-sector model to a 15 percent step increase in consumption. Figure 4–12 exhibits a twenty-year cycle in capital and the production rate, which is longer than the fifteen-year capital cycle observed in Figure 4–8. In a model of an economy combining both goods-producing sectors and capital-producing sectors, the long-term capital cycles characteristic of the two individual

[23]The corresponding model changes are as follows: first, normal backlog coverage NBC is increased from 0.2 to 2 years, yielding a delivery delay of two years for sector output. In addition, the time to correct inventories and backlogs TCIB is increased from 0.8 to 2.5 years, and the time to average production rate TAPR is increased from 1 to 5 years. Appendix B lists all the model changes used for the simulations.

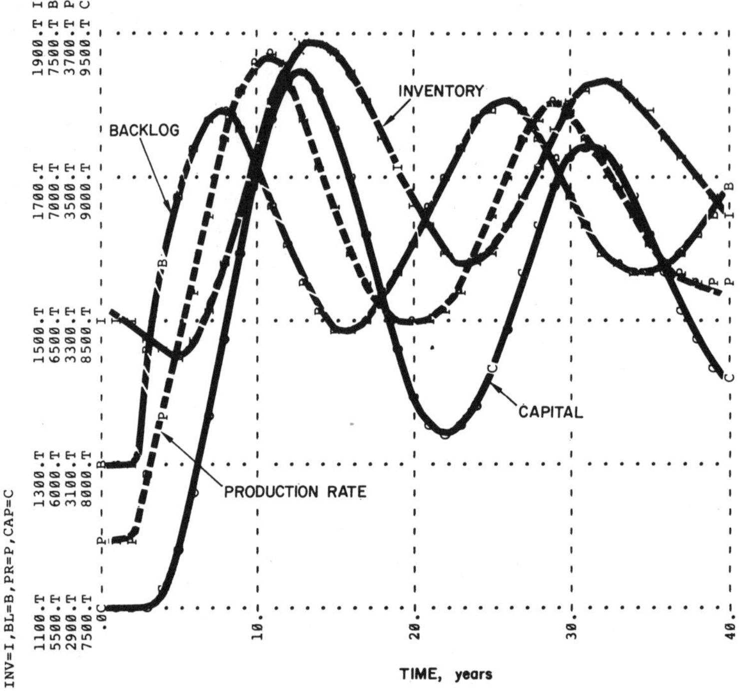


**Figure 4-12** Step response of the capital-sector model

sectors would probably be mutually entrained to form a single capital cycle with a periodicity of about eighteen years.

The capital cycle exhibited by the aggregate economy might even be much longer than eighteen to twenty years in a model including structural elements that were omitted from the basic production sector analyzed in Chapters 3 and 4. For example, a model containing a limited supply of labor should tend to exhibit a longer-term capital cycle, as more of the burden of adjusting production to desired production would be accomplished through capital ordering rather than through short-term changes in employment. In addition, a more detailed model would represent the process of self-ordering, whereby production sectors generate orders for their own output, which they use as a factor of production; for example, an increased demand for capital equipment in the economy would induce capital producers to expand their production, thus further stimulating the demand for capital, because capital is a factor of production. Self-ordering therefore represents an additional source of amplification not included in the basic sector model. Adding such factors as limited labor supply and self-ordering to the model could well extend the period of the long-term capital cycle close to the fifty-year span of the so-called Kondratieff cycle.[24] A future examination along these lines can be conducted within the framework of the basic production sector.

[24]See Kondratieff (1935) and Garvy (1943) for descriptions.

In terms of the classification scheme proposed in Chapter 2, the results described in section 4.3 cast doubts upon the validity of any theory centered around fixed capital investment as an essential cause of the short-term business cycle. Instead, Chapters 3 and 4 suggest that labor adjustments chiefly underlie short-term cycles in output and employment, while fixed capital investment generates longer-term cycles in the growth of capital stock.

The practical and theoretical significance of these issues is well described by Gordon:

> Economists have not yet developed a generally accepted explanation of these intermediate swings, nor is there full agreement that these swings constitute a separate order of cycles distinct from business cycles. One uncertainty arises from the fact that these "cycles" are obviously related to the severe depressions of the past century. It is not surprising that expansion should be particularly rapid as the economy comes out of a deep depression, and the "downswings" of these long cycles may reflect in part the fact that we have experienced severe depressions. It is significant, however, that in the past, deep depressions have been associated with substantial retardation in the rate of growth of output.[25]

From a theoretical standpoint, Chapters 3 and 4 suggest a common structure underlying both business cycles and longer-term capital cycles. Moreover, according to this analysis, differences in the characteristics of the factors of production—differences that can be represented simply in terms of changed parameter values—suffice to explain the different periodicities of fluctuation.

From a policy standpoint, Gordon suggests that the relative amplitude of business-cycle peaks and troughs is critically dependent on the phase of the Kuznets cycle in which short-term cycles appear.[26] For example, a business-cycle trough occurring during a Kuznets-cycle downturn may be far more severe than a trough appearing in the midst of a Kuznets-cycle upswing. Moreover, for a given rate of growth of labor, the rate of capital accumulation determines the growth of potential output. Thus long-term changes in capital stock can exert a significant impact on productivity growth, unemployment, and inflationary pressures within the aggregate economy. For these reasons, it is critical that policy makers consider the effects of alternative stabilization policies on both short-term and long-term cyclic trends. Such an analysis, in turn, must reflect an adequate theory of the factors underlying fluctuations of different periodicities. Chapters 5 and 6 further discuss these issues, thereby synthesizing the analyses in Chapters 3 and 4.

[25]Gordon (1961), p. 243.

[26]A similar point is made in Daly (1969).

# 5
# A Production Sector Including Labor and Capital as Factors of Production

## 5.1 Background and Summary

Chapter 3 demonstrated that labor adjustments in response to inventory and backlog discrepancies produce an inventory, production, and employment cycle of approximately four years' duration. Chapter 4 altered the coefficients of the basic production sector developed in Chapter 3 to describe a production process in which fixed capital is the only factor of production. Chapter 4 showed that a highly capital-intensive production sector is likely to exhibit longer-term swings, of approximately twenty years' duration, in potential output rate and in fixed capital stock. As noted previously, the long periodicities associated with fixed capital investment render it highly unlikely that such investment is an essential force in generating typical four-year business cycles.

Chapter 5 integrates the analyses in Chapters 3 and 4, which dealt with capital and labor individually in order to study the cyclic modes arising from each factor input. Chapter 5 combines labor and capital in a joint production process. It primarily investigates the question: When capital and labor are combined, do the periodicities associated with each input factor remain distinct or are they mutually entrained to yield a single cycle of intermediate length? Section 5.2 overviews the parametric and structural changes necessary to adapt the basic production sector to encompass both fixed capital and labor. Section 5.3 explores model behavior, showing that labor adjustments still produce a four-year cycle in the production rate, inventory, and employment when both capital and labor contribute to production. However, these short-run fluctuations are superimposed on a longer-term cycle in fixed capital induced by capital-investment policies. The results tend, once again, to confirm the importance of employment and inventory-management policies, and the relatively minor role of fixed capital investment, in generating business cycles. Moreover, the results demonstrate the importance of evaluating alternative economic stabilization policies for the national economy or for individual firms from the point of view of their likely impacts on labor and capital adjustments. Chapter 6 expands upon the implications of the research results presented in this volume.

## 5.2 Formulation of the Two-Factor Input Model

*Overview of the Two-Factor Model.* The equations described in section 5.2 essentially merge the formulations for labor ordering and capital ordering developed in Chapters 3 and 4, respectively, into a single production unit. In the revised production sector containing two factor inputs, both labor and fixed capital contribute to production. Labor and capital are assumed to be substitutable factors of production. For example, a constant output rate can be maintained by increasing labor somewhat as the stock of capital declines. The optimal long-run proportions of capital and labor are determined by the marginal costs and productivities associated with each factor input.[1]

Figure 5–1 provides an overview of the revised production sector. Within the production sector, a desired production rate is calculated on the basis of an average production rate and inventory and backlog conditions. This formulation is identical to that used in Chapters 3 and 4. However, according to the assumptions outlined here,

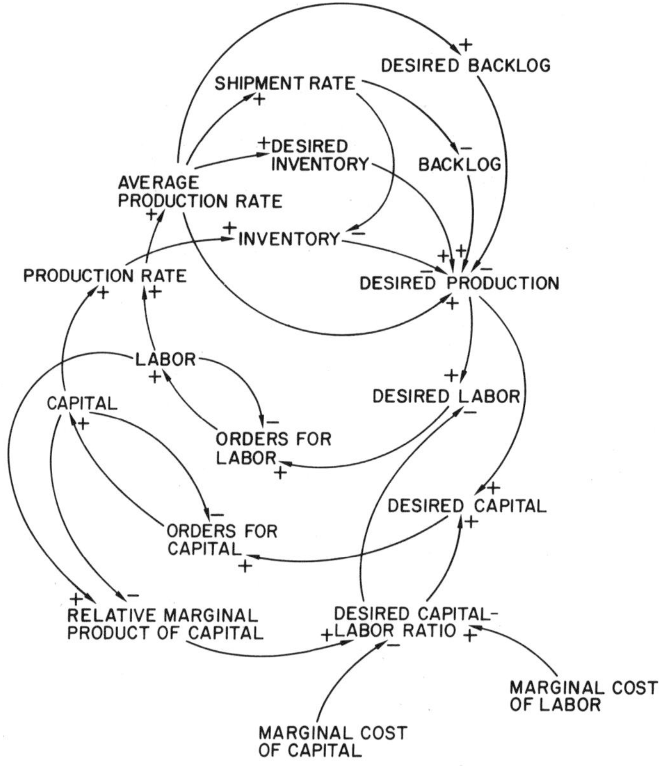


**Figure 5-1** A simplified causal-loop diagram of the two-factor input model

[1]Production processes cannot be reorganized immediately in response to a change in the optimal factor mix. A change in desired factor proportions therefore has the principal effect of altering the capital-labor composition of new projects, thereby only gradually changing the aggregate capital-labor ratio. These ideas are discussed in more detail later in this chapter.

the sector can now maintain a given production rate using many different combinations of capital and labor. As a result, desired production cannot be translated easily into desired holdings of capital and labor. The situation contrasts with the single-factor models developed in Chapters 3 and 4, where desired labor or desired capital could be computed readily on the basis of desired production and a constant long-run factor productivity.

The production sector's desired stocks of labor and capital now depend on the profitability of producing with different combinations of factor inputs. In other words, a desired balance of capital and labor must be determined to relate desired labor and desired capital to desired production. In turn, once desired labor and desired capital are calculated, orders for the two factor inputs can be determined as in Chapters 3 and 4.

From the preceding discussion, five distinct processes illustrated in Figure 5–1 can be identified. First, desired production is determined, as in Chapters 3 and 4, by the average production rate, inventory adequacy, and the discrepancy between backlog and desired backlog. Second, desired stocks of labor and capital are determined by desired production and by desired factor proportions. Third, the desired levels of labor and capital determine orders for labor and capital. Fourth, the available supplies of labor and capital determine the production rate for the sector. Fifth, the production rate alters inventory and backlog. Figure 5–2 summarizes the preceding processes and illustrates their broad interconnection in a feedback structure.

Of the five processes shown in Figure 5–2, only (b) and (d) have not been described in the context of the models in Chapters 3 and 4. The two processes account for the joint determination of desired labor and desired capital on the basis of desired production and the determination of production rate from available labor and capital. Process (a), which computes desired production, has been described in both Chapters 3 and 4; its formulation is independent of the number of factor inputs under considera-

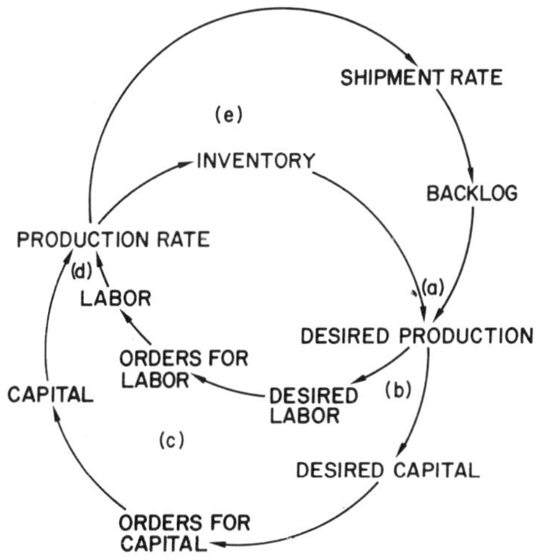


**Figure 5-2** Feedback structure governing levels of labor and fixed capital

tion. Analogously, process (e), which defines the accounting relationships among production rate, shipment rate, inventory, and backlog, is independent of the number of factors of production. Finally, process (c) describes the acquisition of capital and labor. The equations for vacancy creation and the hiring rate have already been developed in Chapter 3, while equations for capital ordering and investment have been developed in Chapter 4. Because most of the equations for the two-factor input model have already been described, section 5.2 provides a detailed explanation of only the previously undefined equations. Appendix A provides a complete documentor listing of the complete production sector.

*New Equations in the Revised Production Sector.* This section describes the new equations used to convert from one to two factors of production in the basic production sector.[2] The new equations, as noted, determine the production rate for the sector, as well as the desired stocks of labor and fixed capital.

As described in Chapter 3, the production sector utilizes a modified Cobb-Douglas production function. In equation 2 for the production rate PR, setting the labor exponent LEX at a value between zero and one makes the production rate dependent on both effective labor and effective capital. In the two-factor model, a value of 0.5 is assumed for LEX.[3] Therefore, excluding the multiplier for labor productivity MLP that is inactive in the simulations, the production rate equation simplifies to:

$$\text{production rate PR} = (\text{normal production NPROD})(\text{normalized effective labor NEL})^{\frac{1}{2}}\,(\text{normalized effective capital NECAP})^{\frac{1}{2}}\,(\text{noise in production rate NPR}).$$

In this equation, normalized effective labor NEL and normalized effective capital NECAP are defined as described in Chapters 3 and 4, respectively.

```
PR.KL=(NPROD)(EXP(LEX*LOGN(NEL.K)))(EXP(CEX*          2, R
  LOGN(NECAP.K)))(NPR.K)(CLIP(MLP.K,1,SW1,1))
NPROD=3E6                                             2.2, C
LEX=1                                                 2.3, C
CEX=1-LEX                                             2.4, N
SW1=0                                                 2.5, C
    PR      - PRODUCTION RATE  (UNITS/YEAR)
    NPROD   - NORMAL PRODUCTION (UNITS/YEAR)
    LEX     - LABOR EXPONENT  (DIMENSIONLESS)
    NEL     - NORMALIZED EFFECTIVE LABOR (DIMENSIONLESS)
    CEX     - CAPITAL EXPONENT  (DIMENSIONLESS)
    NECAP   - NORMALIZED EFFECTIVE CAPITAL
                (DIMENSIONLESS)
    NPR     - NOISE IN PRODUCTION RATE  (DIMENSIONLESS)
    MLP     - MULTIPLIER ON LABOR PRODUCTIVITY
                (DIMENSIONLESS)
    SW1     - SWITCH 1  (DIMENSIONLESS)
```

Figure 5–3 illustrates the determinants of desired capital DCAP; the structure underlying desired labor DL is analogous to the structure for desired capital and therefore does not appear. In equation 81, desired capital DCAP equals desired pro-

[2]The production sector could readily be expanded to encompass more than two factors of production in accordance with the procedures outlined.

[3]Solow (1962) estimates the exponent of the labor term at about one-half. LEX is shown to equal one in equation 2, but it is set to one-half for the simulations in Chapter 5 (see Appendix B).

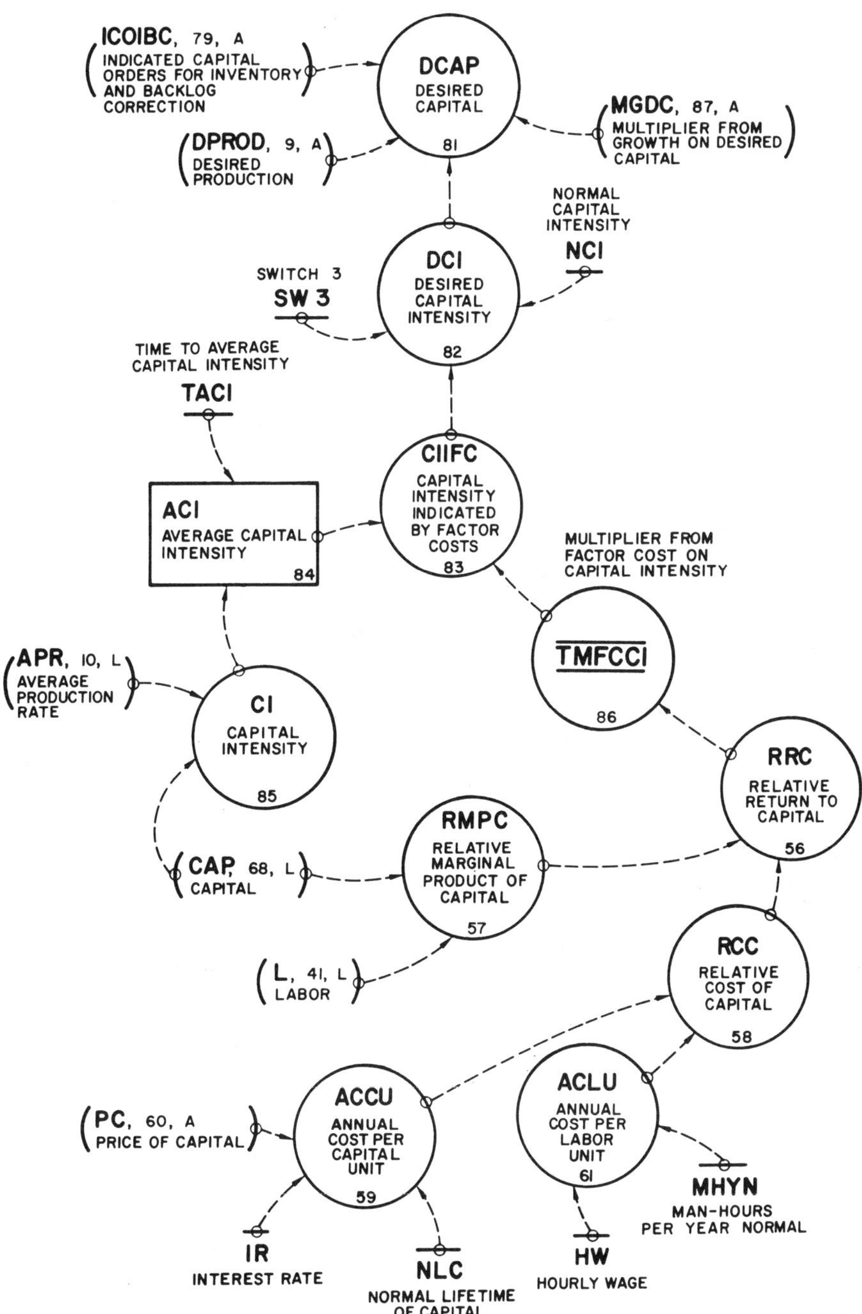


**Figure 5-3** Flow diagram of the determinants of desired capital stock

duction DPROD multiplied by desired capital intensity DCI and the multiplier from growth on desired capital MGDC. As explained in Chapter 4, desired capital intensity DCI is equivalent to a desired capital-output ratio. Thus the product of DPROD and

DCI represents the amount of fixed capital desired to produce current output. The multiplier from growth on desired capital MGDC modulates desired capital, as described in Chapter 4, in light of expectations of future growth or decline in the demand for sector output.

```
DCAP.K=(DPROD.K)(DCI.K)(MGDC.K)                            81, A
    DCAP    - DESIRED CAPITAL   (CAPITAL UNITS)
    DPROD   - DESIRED PRODUCTION   (UNITS/YEAR)
    DCI     - DESIRED CAPITAL INTENSITY (CAPITAL UNITS/
                OUTPUT UNIT/YEAR)
    MGDC    - MULTIPLIER FROM GROWTH ON DESIRED CAPITAL
                (DIMENSIONLESS)
```

A variable capital-output ratio is implemented in the sector model by setting switch 3 SW3 to one in the simulations (see Appendix B) so that desired capital intensity DCI (equation 82) equals capital intensity indicated by factor costs CIIFC (equation 83). The latter equals average capital intensity ACI times the multiplier from factor cost on capital intensity MFCCI. The formulation for desired capital intensity assumes that the sector will maintain its current proportions of capital and labor (and therefore its current capital-output ratio) if production is no more profitable with capital than with labor. On the other hand, desired capital intensity increases, raising desired capital DCAP, when capital becomes relatively more profitable—more productive per dollar of expenditure—than labor.

```
DCI.K=CLIP(CIIFC.K,NCI,SW3,1)                              82, A
NCI=ICAP/NPROD                                             82.1, N
    DCI     - DESIRED CAPITAL INTENSITY (CAPITAL UNITS/
                OUTPUT UNIT/YEAR)
    CIIFC   - CAPITAL INTENSITY INDICATED BY FACTOR COSTS
                (CAPITAL UNITS/OUTPUT UNIT/YEAR)
    NCI     - NORMAL CAPITAL INTENSITY  (CAPITAL UNITS/
                OUTPUT UNIT/YEAR)
    SW3     - SWITCH 3  (DIMENSIONLESS)
    ICAP    - INITIAL CAPITAL   (CAPITAL UNITS)
    NPROD   - NORMAL PRODUCTION (UNITS/YEAR)

CIIFC.K=(ACI.K)(MFCCI.K)                                   83, A
    CIIFC   - CAPITAL INTENSITY INDICATED BY FACTOR COSTS
                (CAPITAL UNITS/OUTPUT UNIT/YEAR)
    ACI     - AVERAGE CAPITAL INTENSITY (CAPITAL UNITS/
                OUTPUT UNIT/YEAR)
    MFCCI   - MULTIPLIER FROM FACTOR COST ON CAPITAL
                INTENSITY (DIMENSIONLESS)
```

Average capital intensity ACI is defined in equation 84 as a fifteen-year exponential average of actual capital intensity CI, which in turn is defined as the ratio of capital stock to the average production rate APR (equation 85). The smoothing time for average capital intensity ACI is identical to the fifteen-year normal lifetime of capital NLC. The formulation prevents a rapid adjustment of the aggregate capital-output ratio in the face of changing factor costs. It presumes that existing capital equipment is characterized technologically by a relatively fixed capital-labor ratio and that an adjustment in aggregate capital intensity takes place predominately through new investment (including replacement investment) that embodies changed factor proportions.[4] The long averaging time for ACI subsumes the time required to shift from one production technique to another.

```
ACI.K=ACI.J+(DT/TACI)(CI.J-ACI.J)                      84, L
ACI=CI                                                 84.1, N
TACI=15                                                84.2, C
    ACI     - AVERAGE CAPITAL INTENSITY (CAPITAL UNITS/
                OUTPUT UNIT/YEAR)
    TACI    - TIME TO AVERAGE CAPITAL INTENSITY  (YEARS)
    CI      - CAPITAL INTENSITY  (CAPITAL UNITS/OUTPUT
                UNIT/YEAR)

CI.K=CAP.K/APR.K                                       85, A
    CI      - CAPITAL INTENSITY  (CAPITAL UNITS/OUTPUT
                UNIT/YEAR)
    CAP     - CAPITAL   (CAPITAL UNITS)
    APR     - AVERAGE PRODUCTION RATE   (UNITS/YEAR)
```

The multiplier from factor cost on capital intensity MFCCI (equation 86 and Figure 5–4) increases desired capital intensity when the relative return to capital RRC exceeds one. A value of RRC greater than one indicates that capital is relatively more productive than labor per dollar of factor expenditure, thereby raising desired capital intensity DCI. Analogously, MFCCI lowers DCI when the relative return to capital falls below one.

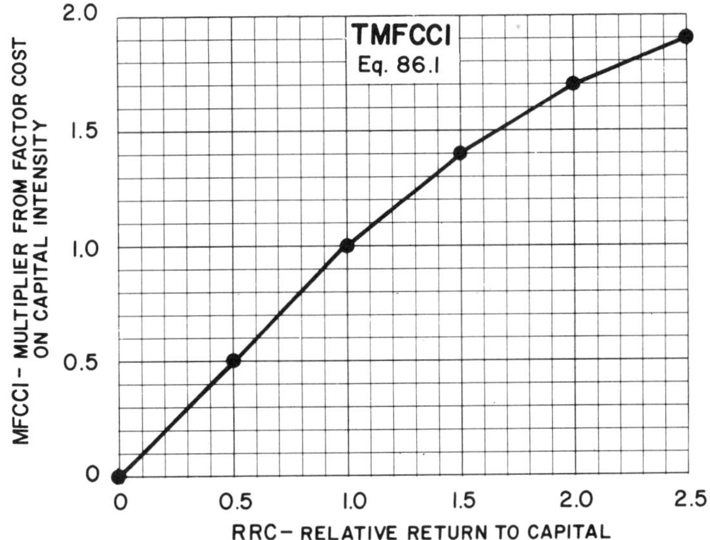


**Figure 5-4** Multiplier from factor cost on capital intensity

```
MFCCI.K=TABLE(TMFCCI,RRC.K,0,2.5,.5)                   86, A
TMFCCI=0/.5/1/1.4/1.7/1.9                              86.1, T
    MFCCI   - MULTIPLIER FROM FACTOR COST ON CAPITAL
                INTENSITY (DIMENSIONLESS)
    TMFCCI  - TABLE FOR MULTIPLIER FROM FACTOR COST ON
                CAPITAL INTENSITY
    RRC     - RELATIVE RETURN TO CAPITAL   (DIMENSIONLESS)
```

[4]The economic literature defines a putty-clay production function as follows: "In this model the equipment in which the investment at any given point of time is embodied is characterized by fixed proportions, and in particular by a fixed output-labor ratio, although the proportions embodied in the equipment can be chosen from a set of alternatives described by an ex-ante production function allowing for continuous factor substitution." See Ando et al. (1973), p. 1.

The relative return to capital RRC is defined in equation 56 as the relative marginal product of capital RMPC divided by the relative cost of capital RCC. Thus, for example, if an incremental unit of capital yields twice as much output as an additional unit of labor but capital is twice as costly, RRC equals one, and producers would have no incentive to substitute capital for labor or labor for capital. On the other hand, if capital is twice as productive as labor but only one and one-half times as costly, producers would profit from substituting capital for labor in new investment projects.

```
RRC.K=RMPC.K/RCC.K                                      56, A
    RRC     - RELATIVE RETURN TO CAPITAL   (DIMENSIONLESS)
    RMPC    - RELATIVE MARGINAL PRODUCT OF CAPITAL (MEN/
                CAPITAL UNIT)
    RCC     - RELATIVE COST OF CAPITAL   (MEN/CAPITAL
                UNIT)
```

The relative marginal product of capital RMPC equals the marginal product of capital divided by the marginal product of labor. The following expression for RMPC can be derived from the production-rate equation (equation 2):

$$\text{production rate PR} = (\text{NPROD})\,(\text{NEL})^{\frac{1}{2}}\,(\text{NECAP})^{\frac{1}{2}},$$

where NPROD = normal production
NEL = normalized effective labor
NECAP = normalized effective capital.

In the preceding equation, normalized effective capital NECAP equals effective capital ECAP divided by initial capital ICAP. Effective capital ECAP, in turn, equals capital CAP multiplied by the capital utilization factor CUF. Analogously, normalized effective labor NEL equals effective labor EL divided by initial labor IL, and EL equals labor L times the relative length of work week RLWW. Differentiating the production rate with respect to labor and capital yields:

$$\text{marginal product of labor } MP_L = \frac{1}{2}\cdot L^{-\frac{1}{2}}\cdot CAP^{\frac{1}{2}}\cdot RLWW^{\frac{1}{2}}\cdot CUF^{\frac{1}{2}} \cdot NPROD\cdot IL^{-\frac{1}{2}}\cdot ICAP^{-\frac{1}{2}}$$

$$\text{marginal product of capital } MP_C = \frac{1}{2}\cdot L^{\frac{1}{2}}\cdot CAP^{-\frac{1}{2}}\cdot RLWW^{\frac{1}{2}}\cdot CUF^{\frac{1}{2}} \cdot NPROD\cdot IL^{-\frac{1}{2}}\cdot ICAP^{-\frac{1}{2}}$$

The equation for the relative marginal product of capital RMPC now follows directly from computing the ratio $MP_C/MP_L$.

```
RMPC.K=L.K/CAP.K                                        57, A
    RMPC    - RELATIVE MARGINAL PRODUCT OF CAPITAL (MEN/
                CAPITAL UNIT)
    L       - LABOR   (MEN)
    CAP     - CAPITAL   (CAPITAL UNITS)
```

The relative cost of capital RCC equals the annual cost per capital unit ACCU divided by the annual cost per labor unit ACLU:

```
RCC.K=ACCU.K/ACLU.K                                    58, A
    RCC     - RELATIVE COST OF CAPITAL    (MEN/CAPITAL
                UNIT)
    ACCU    - ANNUAL COST PER CAPITAL UNIT (DOLLARS/
                CAPITAL UNIT/YEAR)
    ACLU    - ANNUAL COST PER LABOR UNIT    (DOLLARS/MAN/
                YEAR)
```

The annual cost per capital unit ACCU consists of two parts: an annual interest charge and a charge for fixed capital depreciation.[5] Therefore, in equation 59, ACCU equals the price of capital multiplied by the sum of the interest rate IR and the inverse of the normal lifetime of capital NLC. The first term, (PC)(IR), represents the interest cost of capital measured in dollars per year; the second term, (PC)(1/NLC), represents the annual loss of value of the capital stock through depreciation.[6]

```
ACCU.K=(PC.K)(IR+(1/NLC))                              59, A
    ACCU    - ANNUAL COST PER CAPITAL UNIT (DOLLARS/
                CAPITAL UNIT/YEAR)
    PC      - PRICE OF CAPITAL (DOLLARS/CAPITAL/UNIT)
    IR      - INTEREST RATE    (FRACTION/YEAR)
    NLC     - NORMAL LIFETIME OF CAPITAL    (YEARS)

PC.K=CPC                                               60, A
CPC=(HW*MHYN)/((ICAP/IL)(IR+(1/NLC)))                  60.1, N
    PC      - PRICE OF CAPITAL (DOLLARS/CAPITAL/UNIT)
    CPC     - CONSTANT PRICE OF CAPITAL    (DOLLARS/CAPITAL
                UNIT)
    HW      - HOURLY WAGE    (DOLLARS/HOUR)
    MHYN    - MAN-HOURS PER YEAR NORMAL    (HOURS/MAN-YEAR)
    ICAP    - INITIAL CAPITAL    (CAPITAL UNITS)
    IL      - INITIAL LABOR    (MEN)
    IR      - INTEREST RATE    (FRACTION/YEAR)
    NLC     - NORMAL LIFETIME OF CAPITAL    (YEARS)
```

Finally, the annual cost per labor unit ACLU (equation 61) equals the hourly wage multiplied by man-hours per year normal MHYN.

```
ACLU.K=(HW)(MHYN)                                      61, A
    ACLU    - ANNUAL COST PER LABOR UNIT    (DOLLARS/MAN/
                YEAR)
    HW      - HOURLY WAGE    (DOLLARS/HOUR)
    MHYN    - MAN-HOURS PER YEAR NORMAL    (HOURS/MAN-YEAR)
```

[5]The formulation of capital costs presented here parallels the neoclassical investment function described by Jorgensen (1967), and Jorgensen, Hunter, and Nadiri (1970). Overall, the investment function used in Chapter 5, including variable proportions of capital and labor, resembles the neoclassical investment function and also the investment function of the Federal Reserve—MIT—Penn (FMP) econometric model of the United States. See Modigliani (1973) and Bischoff (1971) for a description. Several important differences are recognizable, however. First, like the FMP model, and unlike the neoclassical model, the investment function of Chapter 5 directly generates orders for capital equipment rather than actual investment expenditures; the orders for capital enter into a backlog and are filled according to a delivery delay; the delivery delay for capital, although assumed constant here for simplicity, can vary widely over the business cycle in response to the adequacy of capacity in capital-producing sectors. Second, as discussed in Chapter 4, desired production explicitly depends on the relative size of inventories and backlogs, in addition to final sales. Third, growth expectations are assumed to influence the desired stock of capital. Finally, as also discussed in Chapter 4, the formulation takes into account the aggregation of diverse forms by having investment fall off gradually toward zero as capital stock exceeds aggregate desired capital.

[6]In equation 60, the price of capital PC equals a constant price of capital CPC. In turn, CPC is chosen so that the relative return to capital initially equals one. The relationship can be expressed algebraically as follows:

$$\text{RRC} = 1 \text{ implies RMPC} = \text{RCC}.$$

Therefore,

$$\text{IL/ICAP} = [(\text{CPC})(\text{IR} + (1/\text{NLC}))]/(\text{HW*MHYN}).$$

Solving for PC yields

$$\begin{aligned}\text{CPC} &= (\text{IL/ICAP})(\text{HW*MHYN})/(\text{IR} + (1/\text{NLC})).\\ &= (\text{HW*MHYN})/((\text{ICAP/IL})(\text{IR} + (1/\text{NLC}))).\end{aligned}$$

## 5.3 Simulation of the Two-Factor Input Model

Section 5.3 analyzes the behavior of the revised production sector developed in section 5.2. In contrast to the simpler models analyzed in Chapter 3 and 4, the revised production sector includes both labor and capital as joint factors of production. As described in section 5.2, labor and capital are combined in variable proportions dictated by the marginal cost and marginal productivity associated with each factor of production.

The simulations presented in this section are intended to demonstrate whether or not, when labor and capital are combined, the periodicities associated with adjustments in each factor either remain distinct or become mutually entrained to form a single cycle of intermediate duration. Figure 5–5 illustrates the revised production sector's response to random variations in the production rate.[7] Random noise, which contains components of all frequencies, can usually excite the different oscillatory modes inherent in a system structure.[8] Ragnar Frisch has provided a cogent description of this property of "random shocks." In discussing the "impulse problem," that is, the process through which oscillations in a system are sustained by outside disturbances, Frisch writes:

> The most important feature of the free oscillations is that the length of the cycles and the tendency towards dampening are determined by the intrinsic structure of the swinging system, while the intensity (the amplitude) of the fluctuations is determined primarily by the exterior impulse. An important consequence of this is that a more or less regular fluctuation may be produced by a cause which operates irregularly. There need not be any synchronism between the initiating force or forces and the movement of the swinging system. This fact has frequently been overlooked in economic cycle analysis . . . .
>
> There are several alternative ways in which one may approach the impulse problem and try to reconcile the results of the determinate dynamic analysis with the facts. One way which I believe is particularly fruitful and promising is to study what would become of the solution of a determinate dynamic system if it were exposed to a stream of erratic shocks that constantly upsets the continuous evolution, and by so doing introduces into the system the energy necessary to maintain the swings. If fully worked out, I believe that this idea will give an interesting synthesis between the stochastical point of view and the point of view of rigidly dynamic laws.
>
> Knut Wicksell seems to be first who has been definitely aware of the two types of problems in economic cycle analysis—the propagation problem and the impulse problem—and also the first who has formulated explicitly the theory that the source of energy which maintains the economic cycles are erratic shocks. He conceived more or less definitely of the economic system as being pushed along irregularly, jerkingly. New innovations and exploita-

[7]To activate the noise input, the standard deviation of noise in production rate SDNPR is set at 0.1 As shown later in section 5.3, fairly similar results are obtained if random noise is added to the consumption rate. See Appendix B for further details on parameter changes for the simulations.

[8]Forrester (1961), p. 412.

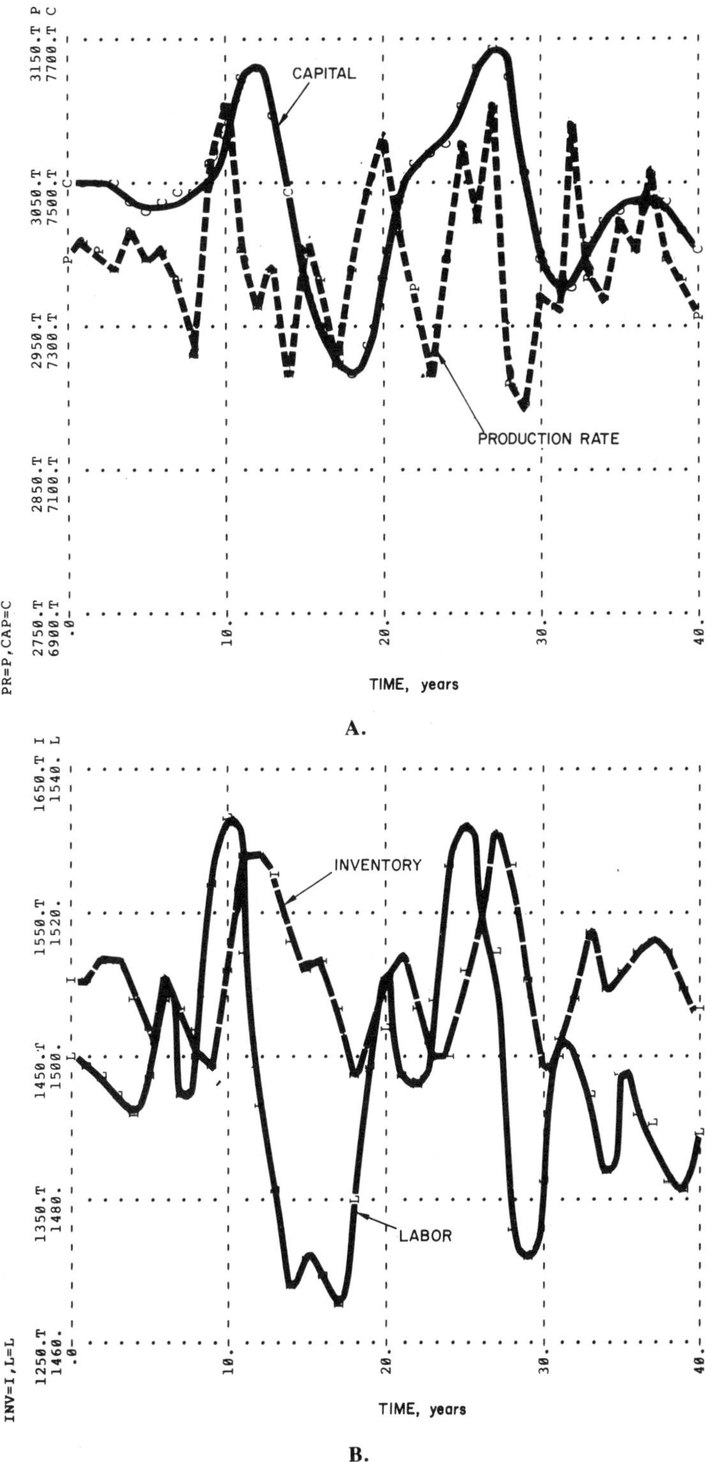


**Figure 5-5** Response of the two-factor model to noise in the production rate

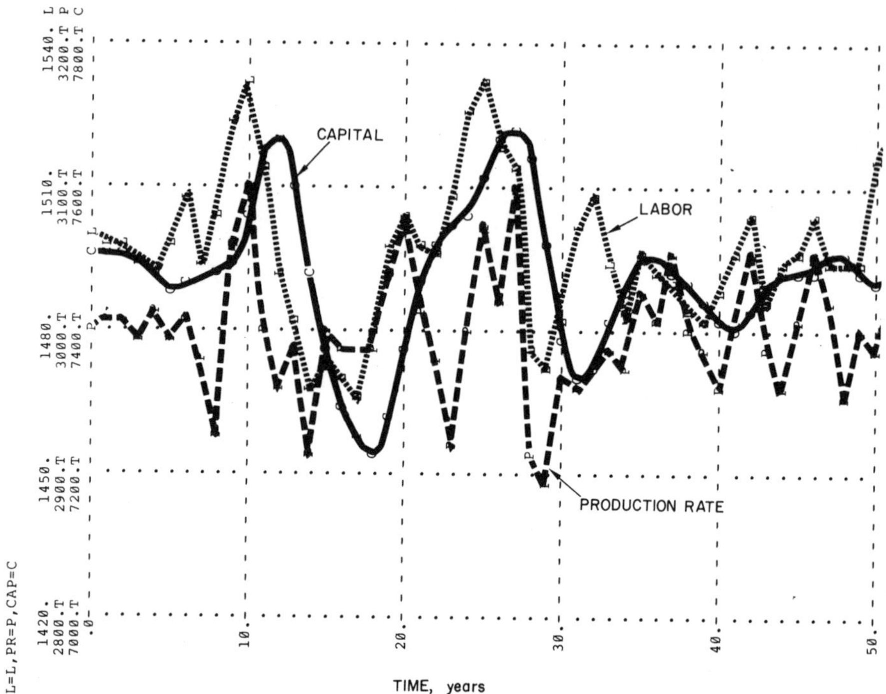


**Figure 5-6** Response of the two-factor model over a 100-year period to noise in the production rate

tions do not come regularly he says. But, on the other hand, these irregular jerks may cause more or less regular cyclical movements. He illustrates it by one of those perfectly simple and yet profound illustrations: "If you hit a wooden rocking horse with a club, the movement of the horse will be very different to that of the club."[9]

Figure 5–5 shows that random noise can simultaneously excite the short-term cycle induced by labor adjustment and the longer-term cycle resulting from fixed capital investment. In Figure 5–5, approximately a four-year cycle in the production rate, labor, and inventory is superimposed on an approximately fourteen-year fluctuation in the level of capital. Apparently, the periodicities induced by labor and capital are sufficiently separated from one another to remain distinct, instead of merging together, when labor and fixed capital both contribute to production.

Figure 5–6, plotting only fixed capital, labor, and the production rate, extends the simulation shown in Figure 5–5 over a 100-year period. It very clearly illustrates the different periodicities associated with labor and fixed capital;[10] these results are in accordance with the analysis conducted in Chapters 3 and 4 on models containing single factors of production.

[9]Frisch (1933), in Gordon and Klein (1965), pp. 155, 178.

[10]As suggested in Chapter 4, considerably longer capital cycles could appear in more detailed sector models or even in modifications of the sector model that describe a capital-producing sector rather than a goods sector.

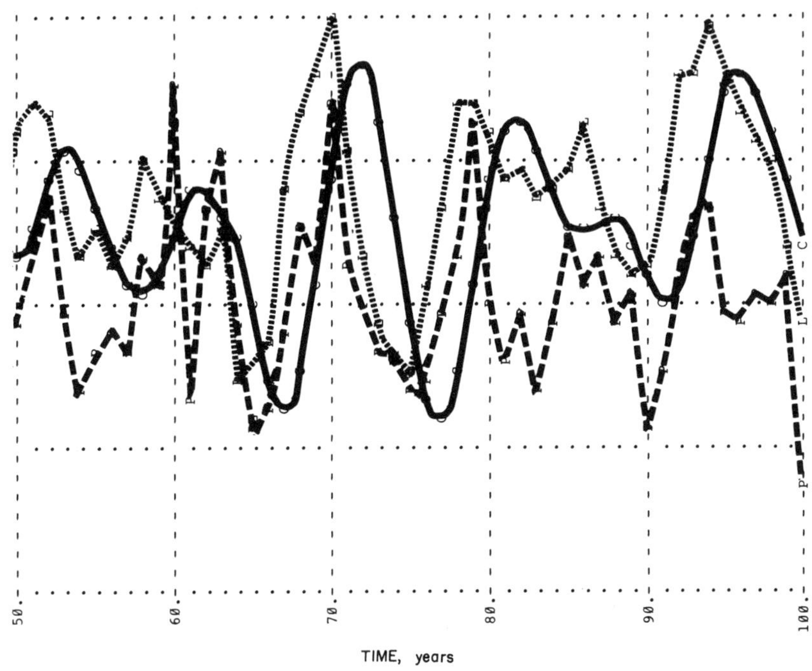


**Figure 5-6** cont'd.

Figure 5–7 is the final simulation of the revised sector model. The conditions underlying Figure 5–7 are identical to those in Figure 5–6 except that a noise disturbance in consumption, rather than in the production rate, is tested. Figure 5–7 displays both the short-term and the long-term periodicities associated with labor and capital, respectively. The results shown in Figures 5–6 and 5–7 lend further support to the hypotheses that labor adjustments principally underlie short-term business cycles and that fixed capital investment is not an intrinsic factor in generating business cycles.[11]

Because of the numerous simplifying assumptions, the revised production sector cannot be used for a detailed analysis of the interaction between long-term and short-term economic cycles. To deal with such issues effectively, a model would need, for example, to incorporate an endogenous labor market and a limited labor supply. In contrast, the present model has an essentially infinite supply of labor implicit in the

[11]The business cycle is, in fact, characterized by short-term fluctuations in capital spending. Such observed fluctuations are consistent with the behavior of the revised production sector model (orders for capital were not plotted in Figures 5–5 or 5–6). According to the model, short-term investment cycles are the result of fluctuations in the relative balance of capital and desired capital within the economy. Fluctuations in capital relative to desired capital stock in turn reflect short-term changes in the balance of production and desired production caused by corporate policies governing overtime and labor adjustment. In other words, short-term employment and overtime policies adjust the production rate toward desired production over the business cycle, thereby creating varying incentives for capital investment. However, the resulting short-term fluctuations in capital investment are directly caused by labor policies; capital investment policies still cannot independently generate short-term business cycles. Any future examination should aim at further clarifying these interactions of production, employment, and investment policies during the business cycle.

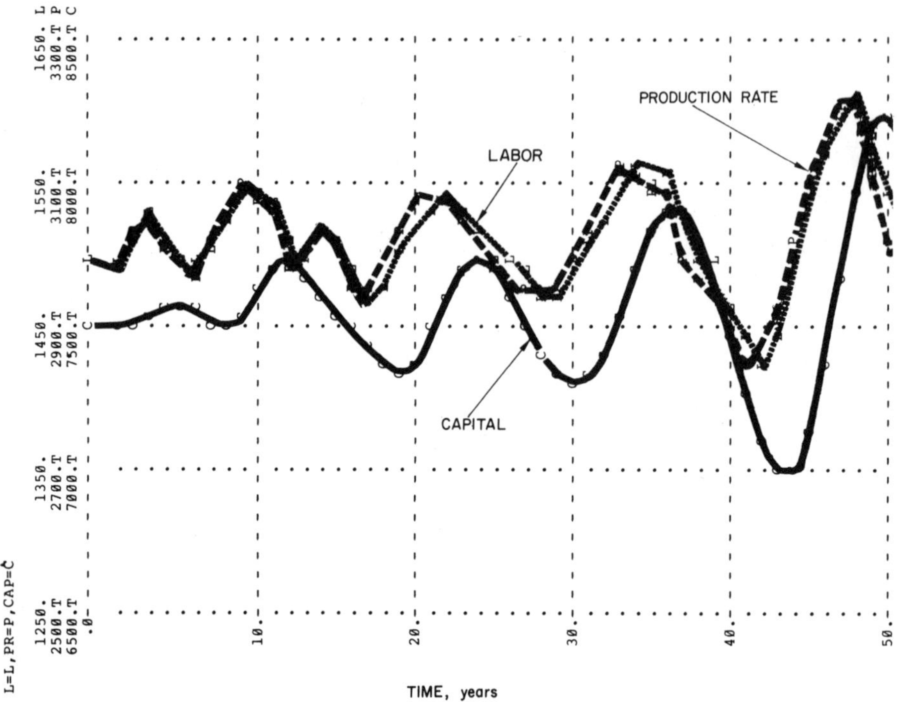


**Figure 5-7** Response of the two-factor model over a 100-year period to noise in the incoming order rate

assumption of a constant delay in filling vacancies. Moreover, an adequate model would need to include determinants of interest rates, credit availability, and factor costs. Such extensions are beyond the scope of the present work, and must be deferred to future investigations.

Nonetheless, the analysis in Chapters 4 and 5 indicates the importance of reassessing the fundamental assumptions underlying business-cycle theory and stabilization policies. Many prevalent economic stabilization policies, particularly monetary policies, are largely predicated on a capital-investment theory of business-cycle behavior. However, if business cycles are attributable for the most part to short-term employment and inventory decisions, policies that attempt to control fixed capital investment may have relatively little leverage or at least may be less effective than policies directly aimed at employment and inventories. Moreover, if fixed capital investment generates cycles of fifteen to twenty years or longer in capital plant, policies designed to regulate capital investment can have significant long-term impacts on output and productivity.

A brief example may help to clarify the hypotheses just presented. The Federal Reserve frequently applies tight monetary policies in efforts to reduce investment and consumption expenditures and thereby lower aggregate demand and dampen business-cycle upswings. However, as noted in section 3.5 of Chapter 3, such efforts to curtail fixed capital investment may result in lower labor efficiency. Declining production

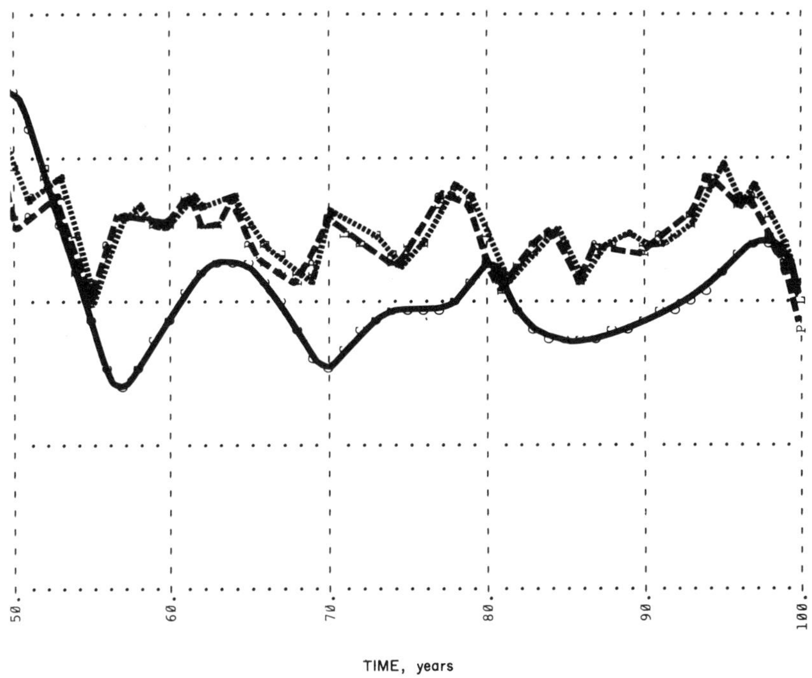


**Figure 5-7** cont'd.

rates or increased delivery delays may in turn raise labor demand in consumer-goods sectors, thus accentuating short-term swings in wages and employment. Moreover, by discouraging fixed capital investment, sustained tight money policies can interact with the long-term capital cycle to restrict capital growth, thereby lowering long-term output and labor productivity.

The preceding example, although speculative, suggests the need for a critical assessment of proposed economic stabilization policies according to (1) their short-term impacts on labor and inventory adjustments and (2) their longer-term effects on capital investment and potential output. Such an evaluation may contribute to a better understanding of the impacts and probable effectiveness of discretionary monetary and fiscal policies and the various "automatic stabilizers."[12]

[12]Evans (1969) defines automatic stabilizers as "relationships that reduce the amplitude of cyclical fluctuations in the economy without any direct action by government, businesses, or individuals" (p. 531). An example is the progressive income tax, which raises tax receipts more than proportionately to GNP, thereby dampening increases in spending by households.

# 6 Summary and Suggestions for Further Work

This book has developed a generic model of the production sector of the economy as a means of exploring the causes of business-cycle behavior. In particular, the study has focused on the periodicities of oscillation associated with the acquisition of different factors of production. The analysis is intended to establish a framework suitable for future examination of monetary and fiscal stabilization policies. Chapter 6 briefly summarizes the results of the research and then suggests additional areas for theoretical business-cycle research and policy-related studies.

## 6.1 Summary of the Research

Chapter 2 reviewed the principal theories of the business cycle and showed that most business-cycle theories emphasize the determinants of fixed capital investment. However, in accordance with the hypotheses advanced by Moses Abramovitz,[1] Chapter 2 argues that fixed capital investment cannot be an intrinsic cause of the four-year business cycle because of the long delays in fixed capital construction and depreciation. These arguments motivate an analysis of the effects of different factors of production on the cyclic behavior of the economy.

Chapter 3 developed a generic model of a production process. The model interrelates factor-input levels, production, product inventory, and unfilled order backlog. Simulations of the basic production sector with labor treated as the only factor of production show that, within reasonable parameter variations, labor adjustments tend to cause a three- to five-year fluctuation in employment, inventory, and production. Such periodicities are representative of real-world business-cycle fluctuations.

Chapter 4 analyzed the behavior of the basic production sector with the parameters altered to describe fixed capital plant and equipment, rather than labor, as the single factor of production. The characteristics of fixed capital contrast with the characteristics of labor. Capital is a durable (long-lived) asset from the standpoint of the firm, whereas, in countries such as the United States, labor represents a shorter-term commitment because of the opportunities for terminating employment. Moreover, the

[1]Abramovitz (1961).

delays in constructing fixed capital equipment are much longer than the corresponding delays in acquiring labor. The simulations of the basic production sector including fixed capital yield an eighteen- to twenty-year periodicity of oscillation resembling the so-called Kuznets cycle.

The results of Chapter 4 are significant for three principal reasons. First, the results suggest that the economic cycles associated with capital investment have a much longer duration than those induced by labor-hiring policies. This viewpoint contrasts with the failure of much theoretical business-cycle research and many discussions of stabilization policies to recognize the distinct behavior modes associated with different factors of production.

Second, Chapter 4 provides a possible explanation of the long-term Kuznets cycle. As noted by R. A. Gordon and Moses Abramovitz, explanations of the Kuznets cycle in the theoretical economic literature are far less advanced and enjoy even less consensus than extant theories of the short-term business cycle.[2] However, the longer-term fluctuations are important because of the observed changes in unemployment rates, labor productivity, output, and inflation that characterize the Kuznets-cycle expansions and contractions.[3] Moreover, the effectiveness of short-term stabilization policies is likely to vary according to the prevailing phase of the long-term cycle. As noted by Abramovitz, for example, "each [Kuznets cycle] period of retardation in the rate of growth of output has culminated in a protracted depression or in a period of stagnation in which business cycle recoveries were disappointing, failing to lift the economy to a condition of full employment or doing so only transiently."[4]

Finally, the results of Chapters 3 and 4 suggest that an explanation of long-term capital cycles may parallel a theory of the four-year business cycle, except for the focus on different factors of production. Moreover, as discussed in Chapter 4, the only model changes required to describe fixed capital rather than labor are parameter changes that reflect increased delivery delays and similar factors. This observation is significant from a theoretical and an educational viewpoint, for it provides a simple illustration of the transferability of structure, that is, the application of a single model structure to explain diverse phenomena.[5]

Chapter 5 builds upon Chapters 3 and 4, combining labor and fixed capital as joint factors of production. The resulting system exhibits roughly four-year fluctuations in inventory, employment, and production. The four-year cycle is, in turn, superimposed on a longer-term cycle in capital equipment. The analysis confirms that the periodicities associated with labor and fixed capital are sufficiently different so that the individual cycles remain distinct (rather than merge together to form an intermediate cycle of, for example, ten-year periodicity) when labor and fixed capital are combined. The broader question of analyzing interactions between long-term and short-term economic cycles must be deferred to future work.

[2]Gordon (1961) and Abramovitz (1961).

[3]See Hickman (1963).

[4]Abramovitz (1961), p. 529.

[5]Emphasizing the educational value of the concept, Forrester (1968) provides examples of the transferability of structure between disciplines.

## 6.2 Extensions of the Present Work

Useful successor studies to the present work might take a number of forms. Several model refinements might be undertaken, for example, to improve upon several simplifying assumptions contained in the models developed in Chapters 3 through 5. First, the basic production sector developed in Chapter 3 assumes an unlimited supply of labor, as reflected in the assumption of a constant delay in filling vacancies. The addition of an endogenous labor market, involving both wage-determination equations and a finite labor supply, would be a useful extension to the production sector, especially in light of the major role attributed in the present work to employment fluctuations in generating four-year business cycles.

The inclusion of an endogenous labor market in the basic production sector should permit an analysis of the effects of labor availability on the stability of economic cycles. For example, in the United States since World War II, tight labor markets have accompanied a reduced magnitude of business-cycle fluctuations. Similar tight labor-market conditions also characterize several West European nations. If business cycles are chiefly generated as a result of employment changes and short-term production policies, as suggested in Chapter 3, increased short-run stability could be the result of tight labor markets that limit employment increases and, therefore, business-cycle upswings. At the same time, however, a reduced ability on the part of producers to obtain labor would tend to increase the demand for capital equipment, thereby accentuating the long-term capital cycle. An increase in short-term stability may occur, therefore, at the cost of increased vulnerability to severe recession. An extension of the basic production sector to encompass such issues could shed considerable light on secular influences on relative economic stability.

A second possible extension of the basic production sector might involve endogenous interest-rate determination. Following the identification of instruments of monetary policy, the addition of a simple monetary sector could permit a preliminary investigation of the probable effects of monetary policies on short-term and long-term cycles.[6] Such an investigation might help to illuminate the current debates over the role of monetary variables in generating business cycles.[7]

A third area of research, related to problems of both cyclic instability and inflation, concerns the multiple responses to excess demand discussed in section 3.5. That discussion showed how production efficiency can decline during periods of excess demand as a result of (1) diverting management attention from direct production and investment planning, (2) weariness attributable to sustained overtime, and (3) expanded hiring that may lead to a higher proportion of less-skilled workers. Such responses, which tend to prolong conditions of excess demand, can be examined in more detail using the basic production sector as a framework of analysis.

[6]The monetary sector of the national socioeconomic model under construction by the M.I.T. System Dynamics Group is described in William W. Behrens III, Alan K. Graham, Gilbert W. Low, and Nathaniel J. Mass, "A Model of the Monetary and Financial Sector," System Dynamics Group Memorandum D-2028-1 (Cambridge, Mass., August 1974). Simpler models of the monetary and banking system could be developed from insights gained through experimentation with the national socioeconomic model.

[7]For a statement of the monetarist theory of monetary interaction in business cycles, see Friedman and Schwartz (1963).

Several substudies might also be performed by applying the basic production sector model to analyze issues at the level of the individual firm or corporation. The results of the parameter sensitivity tests described in section 3.4 suggest a fourth area for research: the effects of lags in inventory, backlog, production, and employment decisions on corporate and economic stability. Section 3.4 shows that a faster correction of inventory and backlog discrepancies somewhat enhances production stability. Similar results have been obtained in several industrial dynamics studies. For example, Forrester writes:

> If production rate appears to be running ahead of sales, compassion for the welfare of employees and reluctance to upset carefully laid procurement and production plans may result in delaying employment changes. It is easy to hope that the conditions calling for reduced production rate will disappear and that one can "ride through" the presently developing crisis. There can be situations where this reluctance to act is actually one of the key factors in creating system instability. The reluctance to make small present cutbacks in employment can be one of the causes for still greater employment reductions in the future.[8]

In contrast to the results discussed above, several industrial dynamics models have shown that increased stability derives from longer employment, inventory, and production adjustment times.[9] Such apparently conflicting results require an explanation in depth. In this light, a distinction seems to be necessary between delays in forming norms about desired inventory or the desired production rate and adjustment delays in correcting for a given discrepancy between desired and actual conditions. For example, testing increased aggressiveness in inventory correction involves reducing a delay of the latter type—the delay in adjusting inventory to desired inventory. As described in section 3.4, faster adjustment of inventory tends to have a stabilizing effect on the production rate. On the other hand, sensitivity experiments not reported in the present volume indicate that greatly *increasing* the time to average production rate TAPR has a stabilizing effect on production behavior; TAPR, representing the delay in forming decisions about an appropriate production rate based on the past production rate, belongs to the former category of delays. Efforts to categorize different situations in which increased reaction delays can stabilize or destabilize a system should contribute significantly to developing improved corporate policies.

A final, and more ambitious, area for research entails an examination of the effects of different stabilization policies on the acquisition of labor, capital, and other factor inputs. In accordance with the results of Chapters 3 through 5, short-term policy effects tend to be associated with labor adjustments, while longer-term effects reflect changes in capital investment and fixed capital stock. One approach to the proposed examination might involve the following steps:

1. Identification of major fiscal and monetary policy instruments.
2. Representation of such policy instruments in the national socioeconomic model.

[8] Forrester (1961), p. 269.

[9] See, for example, Forrester (1961), sec. 15.7.7, and Mass (1974), "A Dynamic Model of Managerial Recruitment and Attrition."

3. Simulation and detailed analysis of the resulting model behavior.
4. Construction of simpler models, perhaps extending the basic production sector, to illustrate the principal policy impacts.

In this procedure, the analysis phase (step 3) is particularly critical. Initial simulations should alternatively hold capital and labor constant in order to study the separate policy impacts on short-term and long-term cycles. Later, simulations should allow both capital and labor to vary in order to study the interaction between cyclic modes. The response of other factors of production besides capital and labor can be similarly analyzed. Such an analysis might provide a framework for examining the short-term stabilization effectiveness of different policies, as well as the possible impacts of policies on capital growth and on the level of potential output.

# Appendix A
# Documentor and Analyzer Listings of the Business-Cycle Model

## A.1 Documentor Listing

```
  GOODS SECTOR

  BASIC PRODUCTION SECTOR

INV.K=INV.J+(DT)(PR.JK-SR.J)                             1, L
INV=DINV                                                 1.1, N
    INV    - INVENTORY  (UNITS)
    PR     - PRODUCTION RATE  (UNITS/YEAR)
    SR     - SHIPMENT RATE  (UNITS/YEAR)
    DINV   - DESIRED INVENTORY  (UNITS)

PR.KL=(NPROD)(EXP(LEX*LOGN(NEL.K)))(EXP(CEX*             2, R
  LOGN(NECAP.K)))(NPR.K)(CLIP(MLP.K,1,SW1,1))
NPROD=3E6                                                2.2, C
LEX=1                                                    2.3, C
CEX=1-LEX                                                2.4, N
SW1=0                                                    2.5, C
    PR     - PRODUCTION RATE  (UNITS/YEAR)
    NPROD  - NORMAL PRODUCTION (UNITS/YEAR)
    LEX    - LABOR EXPONENT  (DIMENSIONLESS)
    NEL    - NORMALIZED EFFECTIVE LABOR (DIMENSIONLESS)
    CEX    - CAPITAL EXPONENT  (DIMENSIONLESS)
    NECAP  - NORMALIZED EFFECTIVE CAPITAL
               (DIMENSIONLESS)
    NPR    - NOISE IN PRODUCTION RATE  (DIMENSIONLESS)
    MLP    - MULTIPLIER ON LABOR PRODUCTIVITY
               (DIMENSIONLESS)
    SW1    - SWITCH 1  (DIMENSIONLESS)

NEL.K=EL.K/IL                                            3, A
IL=1500                                                  3.1, C
    NEL    - NORMALIZED EFFECTIVE LABOR (DIMENSIONLESS)
    EL     - EFFECTIVE LABOR  (MEN)
    IL     - INITIAL LABOR  (MEN)

EL.K=(L.K)(RLWW.K)                                       4, A
    EL     - EFFECTIVE LABOR  (MEN)
    L      - LABOR  (MEN)
    RLWW   - RELATIVE LENGTH OF WORK WEEK
               (DIMENSIONLESS)

RLWW.K=MHY.K/MHYN                                        5, A
MHYN=2080                                                5.1, C
    RLWW   - RELATIVE LENGTH OF WORK WEEK
               (DIMENSIONLESS)
    MHY    - MAN-HOURS PER YEAR  (HOURS/MAN-YEAR)
    MHYN   - MAN-HOURS PER YEAR NORMAL  (HOURS/MAN-YEAR)
```

```
MHY.K=(MHYN)(MLDO.K)                                     6, A
MHY=MHYN                                                 6.1, N
    MHY    - MAN-HOURS PER YEAR  (HOURS/MAN-YEAR)
    MHYN   - MAN-HOURS PER YEAR NORMAL  (HOURS/MAN-YEAR)
    MLDO   - MULTIPLIER FROM LABOR DEMAND ON OVERTIME
               (DIMENSIONLESS)

MLDO.K=TABHL(TMLDO,PRR.K,.6,1.4,.1)                      7, A
TMLDO=.85/.87/.9/.94/1/1.07/1.14/1.18/1.2                7.1, T
    MLDO   - MULTIPLIER FROM LABOR DEMAND ON OVERTIME
               (DIMENSIONLESS)
    TMLDO  - TABLE FOR MULTIPLIER FROM LABOR DEMAND ON
               OVERTIME
    PRR    - PRODUCTION RATIO  (DIMENSIONLESS)

PRR.K=DPROD.K/APR.K                                      8, A
    PRR    - PRODUCTION RATIO  (DIMENSIONLESS)
    DPROD  - DESIRED PRODUCTION  (UNITS/YEAR)
    APR    - AVERAGE PRODUCTION RATE  (UNITS/YEAR)

DPROD.K=APR.K+(DINV.K-INV.K+BL.K-DBL.K)/TCIB             9, A
TCIB=.8                                                  9.1, C
    DPROD  - DESIRED PRODUCTION  (UNITS/YEAR)
    APR    - AVERAGE PRODUCTION RATE  (UNITS/YEAR)
    DINV   - DESIRED INVENTORY  (UNITS)
    INV    - INVENTORY  (UNITS)
    BL     - BACKLOG  (UNITS)
    DBL    - DESIRED BACKLOG  (UNITS)
    TCIB   - TIME TO CORRECT INVENTORIES AND BACKLOGS
               (YEARS)

APR.K=APR.J+(DT/TAPR)(PR.JK-APR.K)                       10, L
APR=PR                                                   10.1, N
TAPR=1                                                   10.2, C
    APR    - AVERAGE PRODUCTION RATE  (UNITS/YEAR)
    TAPR   - TIME TO AVERAGE PRODUCTION RATE  (YEARS)
    PR     - PRODUCTION RATE  (UNITS/YEAR)

DINV.K=(APR.K)(NIC)(CLIP(MPEDI.K,1,SW2,1))               11, A
NIC=.5                                                   11.1, C
SW2=0                                                    11.2, C
    DINV   - DESIRED INVENTORY  (UNITS)
    APR    - AVERAGE PRODUCTION RATE  (UNITS/YEAR)
    NIC    - NORMAL INVENTORY COVERAGE  (YEARS)
    MPEDI  - MULTIPLIER FROM PRICE EXPECTATIONS ON
               DESIRED INVENTORY (DIMENSIONLESS)
    SW2    - SWITCH 2  (DIMENSIONLESS)

MPEDI.K=TABLE(TMPEDI,PRIP.K,-.12,.12,.06)                12, A
TMPEDI=.9/.93/1/1.07/1.1                                 12.1, T
MPEDI=1                                                  12.2, N
    MPEDI  - MULTIPLIER FROM PRICE EXPECTATIONS ON
               DESIRED INVENTORY (DIMENSIONLESS)
    TMPEDI - TABLE FOR MULTIPLIER FROM PRICE
               EXPECTATIONS ON DESIRED INVENTORY
    PRIP   - PERCEIVED RATE OF INCREASE IN PRICE
               (FRACTION/YEAR)

PRIP.K=PRIP.J+(DT/TPRIP)(RIP.J-PRIP.J)                   13, L
PRIP=RIP                                                 13.1, N
TPRIP=1.5                                                13.2, C
    PRIP   - PERCEIVED RATE OF INCREASE IN PRICE
               (FRACTION/YEAR)
    TPRIP  - TIME TO PERCEIVE RATE OF INCREASE IN PRICE
               (YEARS)
    RIP    - RATE OF INCREASE IN PRICE  (FRACTION/YEAR)

RIP.K=(AP.K-SAP.K)/(SAP.K*TSAP)                          14, A
    RIP    - RATE OF INCREASE IN PRICE  (FRACTION/YEAR)
    AP     - AVERAGE PRICE  (DOLLARS/UNIT)
    SAP    - SMOOTHED AVERAGE PRICE  (DOLLARS/UNIT)
    TSAP   - TIME TO SMOOTH AVERAGE PRICE  (YEARS)
```

```
AP.K=AP.J+(DT/TAP)(P.J-AP.J)                                15, L
AP=P                                                        15.1, N
TAP=.33                                                     15.2, C
    AP      - AVERAGE PRICE  (DOLLARS/UNIT)
    TAP     - TIME TO AVERAGE PRICE  (YEARS)
    P       - PRICE  (DOLLARS/UNIT)

SAP.K=SAP.J+(DT/TSAP)(AP.J-SAP.J)                           16, L
SAP=AP                                                      16.1, N
TSAP=.33                                                    16.2, C
    SAP     - SMOOTHED AVERAGE PRICE  (DOLLARS/UNIT)
    TSAP    - TIME TO SMOOTH AVERAGE PRICE  (YEARS)
    AP      - AVERAGE PRICE  (DOLLARS/UNIT)

P.K=(AUCP.K)(1+NPM)(MDPP.K)                                 17, A
NPM=.1                                                      17.1, C
    P       - PRICE  (DOLLARS/UNIT)
    AUCP    - AVERAGE UNIT COSTS OF PRODUCTION  (DOLLARS/
                UNIT)
    NPM     - NORMAL PROFIT MARGIN  (DIMENSIONLESS)
    MDPP    - MULTIPLIER FROM DESIRED PRODUCTION ON
                PROFITS  (DIMENSIONLESS)

AUCP.K=AUCP.J+(DT/TAUCP)(UCP.J-AUCP.J)                      18, L
AUCP=WC/(APR-(INV)(IR))                                     18.1, N
TAUCP=1                                                     18.2, C
    AUCP    - AVERAGE UNIT COSTS OF PRODUCTION  (DOLLARS/
                UNIT)
    TAUCP   - TIME TO AVERAGE UNIT COSTS OF PRODUCTION
                (YEARS)
    UCP     - UNIT COSTS OF PRODUCTION  (DOLLARS/UNIT)
    WC      - WAGE COSTS  (DOLLARS/YEAR)
    APR     - AVERAGE PRODUCTION RATE  (UNITS/YEAR)
    INV     - INVENTORY  (UNITS)
    IR      - INTEREST RATE  (FRACTION/YEAR)

UCP.K=(WC.K+ICC.K)/APR.K                                    19, A
    UCP     - UNIT COSTS OF PRODUCTION  (DOLLARS/UNIT)
    WC      - WAGE COSTS  (DOLLARS/YEAR)
    ICC     - INVENTORY CARRYING COSTS  (DOLLARS/YEAR)
    APR     - AVERAGE PRODUCTION RATE  (UNITS/YEAR)

WC.K=(L.K)(MHY.K)(HW)+OVTWG.K                               20, A
HW=4                                                        20.1, C
    WC      - WAGE COSTS  (DOLLARS/YEAR)
    L       - LABOR  (MEN)
    MHY     - MAN-HOURS PER YEAR  (HOURS/MAN-YEAR)
    HW      - HOURLY WAGE  (DOLLARS/HOUR)
    OVTWG   - OVERTIME WAGES  (DOLLARS/YEAR)

OVTWG.K=MAX(0,(L.K)(HW)(OVTP)(MHY.K-MHYN))                  21, A
OVTP=.3                                                     21.1, C
    OVTWG   - OVERTIME WAGES  (DOLLARS/YEAR)
    L       - LABOR  (MEN)
    HW      - HOURLY WAGE  (DOLLARS/HOUR)
    OVTP    - OVERTIME PREMIUM  (DIMENSIONLESS)
    MHY     - MAN-HOURS PER YEAR  (HOURS/MAN-YEAR)
    MHYN    - MAN-HOURS PER YEAR NORMAL  (HOURS/MAN-YEAR)

ICC.K=(INV.K)(AUCP.K)(IR)                                   22, A
IR=.06                                                      22.1, C
    ICC     - INVENTORY CARRYING COSTS  (DOLLARS/YEAR)
    INV     - INVENTORY  (UNITS)
    AUCP    - AVERAGE UNIT COSTS OF PRODUCTION  (DOLLARS/
                UNIT)
    IR      - INTEREST RATE  (FRACTION/YEAR)

MDPP.K=TABLE(TMDPP,PRR.K,0,2,.5)                            23, A
TMDPP=.75/.85/1/1.15/1.4                                    23.1, T
    MDPP    - MULTIPLIER FROM DESIRED PRODUCTION ON
                PROFITS  (DIMENSIONLESS)
    TMDPP   - TABLE FOR MULTIPLIER FROM DESIRED
                PRODUCTION ON PROFITS
    PRR     - PRODUCTION RATIO  (DIMENSIONLESS)
```

```
BL.K=BL.J+(DT)(CONS.J-SR.J)                                 24, L
BL=DBL                                                      24.1, N
    BL      - BACKLOG  (UNITS)
    CONS    - CONSUMPTION  (UNITS/YEAR)
    SR      - SHIPMENT RATE  (UNITS/YEAR)
    DBL     - DESIRED BACKLOG  (UNITS)

DBL.K=(APR.K)(NBC)                                          25, A
NBC=.2                                                      25.1, C
    DBL     - DESIRED BACKLOG  (UNITS)
    APR     - AVERAGE PRODUCTION RATE  (UNITS/YEAR)
    NBC     - NORMAL BACKLOG COVERAGE  (YEARS)

NECAP.K=ECAP.K/ICAP                                         26, A
ICAP=7.5E6                                                  26.1, C
    NECAP   - NORMALIZED EFFECTIVE CAPITAL
                (DIMENSIONLESS)
    ECAP    - EFFECTIVE CAPITAL  (CAPITAL UNITS)
    ICAP    - INITIAL CAPITAL  (CAPITAL UNITS)

ECAP.K=(CAP.K)(CUF.K)                                       27, A
    ECAP    - EFFECTIVE CAPITAL  (CAPITAL UNITS)
    CAP     - CAPITAL  (CAPITAL UNITS)
    CUF     - CAPITAL UTILIZATION FACTOR  (DIMENSIONLESS)

CUF.K=TABHL(TCUF,PRR.K,.6,1.4,.1)                           28, A
TCUF=.8/.83/.87/.92/1/1.05/1.08/1.1/1.11                    28.1, T
CUF=1                                                       28.2, N
    CUF     - CAPITAL UTILIZATION FACTOR  (DIMENSIONLESS)
    TCUF    - TABLE FOR CAPITAL UTILIZATION FACTOR
    PRR     - PRODUCTION RATIO  (DIMENSIONLESS)

NPR.K=NPR.J+(DT/TSNPR)(NORMRN(1,SDNPR)-NPR.J)               29, L
NPR=1                                                       29.1, N
TSNPR=1                                                     29.2, C
SDNPR=0                                                     29.3, C
    NPR     - NOISE IN PRODUCTION RATE  (DIMENSIONLESS)
    TSNPR   - TIME TO SMOOTH NOISE IN PRODUCTION RATE
                (YEARS)
    SDNPR   - STANDARD DEVIATION OF NOISE IN PRODUCTION
                RATE (DIMENSIONLESS)

MLP.K=(MOLP.K)(MPPLP.K)                                     30, A
    MLP     - MULTIPLIER ON LABOR PRODUCTIVITY
                (DIMENSIONLESS)
    MOLP    - MULTIPLIER FROM OVERTIME ON LABOR
                PRODUCTIVITY (DIMENSIONLESS)
    MPPLP   - MULTIPLIER FROM PRODUCTION PRESSURE ON
                LABOR PRODUCTIVITY (DIMENSIONLESS)

MOLP.K=TABLE(TMOLP,ARLWW.K,.8,1.2,.1)                       31, A
TMOLP=1.06/1.04/1/.95/.9                                    31.1, T
    MOLP    - MULTIPLIER FROM OVERTIME ON LABOR
                PRODUCTIVITY (DIMENSIONLESS)
    TMOLP   - TABLE FOR MULTIPLIER FROM OVERTIME ON LABOR
                PRODUCTIVITY
    ARLWW   - AVERAGE RELATIVE LENGTH OF WORK WEEK
                (DIMENSIONLESS)

ARLWW.K=ARLWW.K+(DT/TARLWW)(RLWW.J-ARLWW.J)                 32, L
ARLWW=1                                                     32.1, N
TARLWW=.33                                                  32.2, C
    ARLWW   - AVERAGE RELATIVE LENGTH OF WORK WEEK
                (DIMENSIONLESS)
    TARLWW  - TIME TO AVERAGE RELATIVE LENGTH OF WORK
                WEEK  (YEARS)
    RLWW    - RELATIVE LENGTH OF WORK WEEK
                (DIMENSIONLESS)

MPPLP.K=TABLE(TMPPLP,RDDG.K,0,2,.5)                         33, A
TMPPLP=1.1/1.07/1/.8/.7                                     33.1, T
    MPPLP   - MULTIPLIER FROM PRODUCTION PRESSURE ON
                LABOR PRODUCTIVITY (DIMENSIONLESS)
    TMPPLP  - TABLE FOR MULTIPLIER FROM PRODUCTION
                PRESSURE ON LABOR PRODUCTIVITY
    RDDG    - RELATIVE DELIVERY DELAY FOR GOODS
                (DIMENSIONLESS)
```

```
RDDG.K=DDG.K/NBC                                       34, A
RDDG=1                                                 34.1, N
    RDDG    - RELATIVE DELIVERY DELAY FOR GOODS
                (DIMENSIONLESS)
    DDG     - DELIVERY DELAY FOR GOODS  (YEARS)
    NBC     - NORMAL BACKLOG COVERAGE  (YEARS)

DDG.K=BL.K/SR.K                                        35, A
    DDG     - DELIVERY DELAY FOR GOODS  (YEARS)
    BL      - BACKLOG  (UNITS)
    SR      - SHIPMENT RATE  (UNITS/YEAR)

SR.K=(APR.K)(IMS.K)(BLMS.K)                            36, A
    SR      - SHIPMENT RATE  (UNITS/YEAR)
    APR     - AVERAGE PRODUCTION RATE  (UNITS/YEAR)
    IMS     - INVENTORY MULTIPLIER FOR SHIPMENTS
                (DIMENSIONLESS)
    BLMS    - BACKLOG MULTIPLIER FOR SHIPMENTS
                (DIMENSIONLESS)

IMS.K=TABHL(TIMS,INVR.K,0,2,.5)                        37, A
TIMS=0/.6/1/1.4/1.6                                    37.1, T
IMS=1                                                  37.2, N
    IMS     - INVENTORY MULTIPLIER FOR SHIPMENTS
                (DIMENSIONLESS)
    TIMS    - TABLE FOR INVENTORY MULTIPLIER FOR
                SHIPMENTS
    INVR    - INVENTORY RATIO  (DIMENSIONLESS)

INVR.K=INV.K/DINV.K                                    38, A
    INVR    - INVENTORY RATIO  (DIMENSIONLESS)
    INV     - INVENTORY  (UNITS)
    DINV    - DESIRED INVENTORY  (UNITS)

BLMS.K=TABHL(TBLMS,BLR.K,0,2,.5)                       39, A
TBLMS=0/.6/1/1.4/1.6                                   39.1, T
    BLMS    - BACKLOG MULTIPLIER FOR SHIPMENTS
                (DIMENSIONLESS)
    BLR     - BACKLOG RATIO  (DIMENSIONLESS)

BLR.K=BL.K/DBL.K                                       40, A
    BLR     - BACKLOG RATIO  (DIMENSIONLESS)
    BL      - BACKLOG  (UNITS)
    DBL     - DESIRED BACKLOG  (UNITS)

L.K=L.J+(DT)(HR.J-TR.JK)                               41, L
L=IL                                                   41.1, N
    L       - LABOR  (MEN)
    HR      - HIRING RATE  (MEN/YEAR)
    TR      - TERMINATION RATE  (MEN/YEAR)
    IL      - INITIAL LABOR  (MEN)

HR.K=VAC.K/DFV                                         42, A
DFV=.25                                                42.1, C
    HR      - HIRING RATE  (MEN/YEAR)
    VAC     - VACANCIES  (MEN)
    DFV     - DELAY IN FILLING VACANCIES  (YEARS)

VAC.K=VAC.J+(DT)(NVC.JK-HR.J)                          43, L
VAC=(L/NDE)(DFV)                                       43.1, N
    VAC     - VACANCIES  (MEN)
    NVC     - NEW VACANCY CREATION  (MEN/YEAR)
    HR      - HIRING RATE  (MEN/YEAR)
    L       - LABOR  (MEN)
    NDE     - NORMAL DURATION OF EMPLOYMENT  (YEARS)
    DFV     - DELAY IN FILLING VACANCIES  (YEARS)

NVC.KL=(ANVC.K)(MLDOL.K)                               44, R
    NVC     - NEW VACANCY CREATION  (MEN/YEAR)
    ANVC    - AVERAGE NEW VACANCY CREATION  (MEN/YEAR)
    MLDOL   - MULTIPLIER FROM LABOR DEMAND ON ORDERS FOR
                LABOR (DIMENSIONLESS)
```

```
ANVC.K=ANVC.J+(DT/TANVC)(NVC.JK-ANVC.J)                   45, L
ANVC=L/NDE                                                45.1, N
TANVC=.5                                                  45.2, C
    ANVC   - AVERAGE NEW VACANCY CREATION  (MEN/YEAR)
    TANVC  - TIME TO AVERAGE NEW VACANCY CREATION
               (YEARS)
    NVC    - NEW VACANCY CREATION  (MEN/YEAR)
    L      - LABOR  (MEN)
    NDE    - NORMAL DURATION OF EMPLOYMENT  (YEARS)

MLDOL.K=TABLE(TMLDOL,RDOL.K,0,2,.25)                      46, A
TMLDOL=.2/.35/.55/.75/1/1.25/1.45/1.6/1.7                 46.1, T
    MLDOL  - MULTIPLIER FROM LABOR DEMAND ON ORDERS FOR
               LABOR (DIMENSIONLESS)
    TMLDOL - TABLE FOR MULTIPLIER FROM LABOR DEMAND ON
               ORDERS FOR LABOR
    RDOL   - RELATIVE DESIRED ORDERS FOR LABOR
               (DIMENSIONLESS)

RDOL.K=(ANVC.K+IVCIBC.K)/ANVC.K                           47, A
    RDOL   - RELATIVE DESIRED ORDERS FOR LABOR
               (DIMENSIONLESS)
    ANVC   - AVERAGE NEW VACANCY CREATION  (MEN/YEAR)
    IVCIBC - INDICATED VACANCY CREATION FOR INVENTORY
               AND BACKLOG CORRECTION (MEN/YEAR)

IVCIBC.K=(DVAC.K-VAC.K+DL.K-L.K)/TAL                      48, A
TAL=.5                                                    48.1, C
    IVCIBC - INDICATED VACANCY CREATION FOR INVENTORY
               AND BACKLOG CORRECTION (MEN/YEAR)
    DVAC   - DESIRED VACANCIES  (MEN)
    VAC    - VACANCIES  (MEN)
    DL     - DESIRED LABOR  (MEN)
    L      - LABOR  (MEN)
    TAL    - TIME TO ADJUST LABOR  (YEARS)

DVAC.K=(ANVC.K)(DFV)                                      49, A
    DVAC   - DESIRED VACANCIES  (MEN)
    ANVC   - AVERAGE NEW VACANCY CREATION  (MEN/YEAR)
    DFV    - DELAY IN FILLING VACANCIES  (YEARS)

DL.K=(DPROD.K)(DLI.K)(MGDL.K)                             50, A
    DL     - DESIRED LABOR  (MEN)
    DPROD  - DESIRED PRODUCTION  (UNITS/YEAR)
    DLI    - DESIRED LABOR INTENSITY  (MEN/OUTPUT UNIT/
               YEAR)
    MGDL   - MULTIPLIER FROM GROWTH ON DESIRED LABOR
               (DIMENSIONLESS)

DLI.K=CLIP(LIIFC.K,NLI,SW3,1)                             51, A
SW3=0                                                     51.1, C
NLI=IL/NPROD                                              51.2, N
    DLI    - DESIRED LABOR INTENSITY  (MEN/OUTPUT UNIT/
               YEAR)
    LIIFC  - LABOR INTENSITY INDICATED BY FACTOR COSTS
               (MEN/OUTPUT UNIT/YEAR)
    NLI    - NORMAL LABOR INTENSITY  (MEN/OUTPUT UNIT/
               YEAR)
    SW3    - SWITCH 3  (DIMENSIONLESS)
    IL     - INITIAL LABOR  (MEN)
    NPROD  - NORMAL PRODUCTION (UNITS/YEAR)

LIIFC.K=(ALI.K)(MFCLI.K)                                  52, A
    LIIFC  - LABOR INTENSITY INDICATED BY FACTOR COSTS
               (MEN/OUTPUT UNIT/YEAR)
    ALI    - AVERAGE LABOR INTENSITY  (MEN/OUTPUT UNIT/
               YEAR)
    MFCLI  - MULTIPLIER FROM FACTOR COST ON LABOR
               INTENSITY (DIMENSIONLESS)

ALI.K=ALI.J+(DT/TALI)(LI.J-ALI.J)                         53, L
ALI=LI                                                    53.1, N
TALI=15                                                   53.2, C
    ALI    - AVERAGE LABOR INTENSITY  (MEN/OUTPUT UNIT/
               YEAR)
    TALI   - TIME TO AVERAGE LABOR INTENSITY  (YEARS)
    LI     - LABOR INTENSITY  (MEN/OUTPUT UNIT/YEAR)
```

```
LI.K=L.K/APR.K                                           54, A
    LI      - LABOR INTENSITY  (MEN/OUTPUT UNIT/YEAR)
    L       - LABOR  (MEN)
    APR     - AVERAGE PRODUCTION RATE  (UNITS/YEAR)

MFCLI.K=TABLE(TMFCLI,RRC.K,0,2.5,.5)                     55, A
TMFCLI=3/1.6/1/.6/.3/.15                                 55.1, T
    MFCLI   - MULTIPLIER FROM FACTOR COST ON LABOR
                INTENSITY (DIMENSIONLESS)
    TMFCLI  - TABLE FOR MULTIPLIER FROM FACTOR COST ON
                LABOR INTENSITY
    RRC     - RELATIVE RETURN TO CAPITAL  (DIMENSIONLESS)

RRC.K=RMPC.K/RCC.K                                       56, A
    RRC     - RELATIVE RETURN TO CAPITAL  (DIMENSIONLESS)
    RMPC    - RELATIVE MARGINAL PRODUCT OF CAPITAL (MEN/
                CAPITAL UNIT)
    RCC     - RELATIVE COST OF CAPITAL  (MEN/CAPITAL
                UNIT)

RMPC.K=L.K/CAP.K                                         57, A
    RMPC    - RELATIVE MARGINAL PRODUCT OF CAPITAL (MEN/
                CAPITAL UNIT)
    L       - LABOR  (MEN)
    CAP     - CAPITAL  (CAPITAL UNITS)

RCC.K=ACCU.K/ACLU.K                                      58, A
    RCC     - RELATIVE COST OF CAPITAL  (MEN/CAPITAL
                UNIT)
    ACCU    - ANNUAL COST PER CAPITAL UNIT (DOLLARS/
                CAPITAL UNIT/YEAR)
    ACLU    - ANNUAL COST PER LABOR UNIT  (DOLLARS/MAN/
                YEAR)

ACCU.K=(PC.K)(IR+(1/NLC))                                59, A
    ACCU    - ANNUAL COST PER CAPITAL UNIT (DOLLARS/
                CAPITAL UNIT/YEAR)
    PC      - PRICE OF CAPITAL (DOLLARS/CAPITAL/UNIT)
    IR      - INTEREST RATE  (FRACTION/YEAR)
    NLC     - NORMAL LIFETIME OF CAPITAL  (YEARS)

PC.K=CPC                                                 60, A
CPC=(HW*MHYN)/((ICAP/IL)(IR+(1/NLC)))                    60.1, N
    PC      - PRICE OF CAPITAL (DOLLARS/CAPITAL/UNIT)
    CPC     - CONSTANT PRICE OF CAPITAL  (DOLLARS/CAPITAL
                UNIT)
    HW      - HOURLY WAGE  (DOLLARS/HOUR)
    MHYN    - MAN-HOURS PER YEAR NORMAL  (HOURS/MAN-YEAR)
    ICAP    - INITIAL CAPITAL  (CAPITAL UNITS)
    IL      - INITIAL LABOR  (MEN)
    IR      - INTEREST RATE  (FRACTION/YEAR)
    NLC     - NORMAL LIFETIME OF CAPITAL  (YEARS)

ACLU.K=(HW)(MHYN)                                        61, A
    ACLU    - ANNUAL COST PER LABOR UNIT  (DOLLARS/MAN/
                YEAR)
    HW      - HOURLY WAGE  (DOLLARS/HOUR)
    MHYN    - MAN-HOURS PER YEAR NORMAL  (HOURS/MAN-YEAR)

MGDL.K=1+(EGRP.K)(DFV)                                   62, A
    MGDL    - MULTIPLIER FROM GROWTH ON DESIRED LABOR
                (DIMENSIONLESS)
    EGRP    - EXPECTED GROWTH RATE IN PRODUCTION
                (FRACTION/YEAR)
    DFV     - DELAY IN FILLING VACANCIES  (YEARS)

EGRP.K=(PR.JK-APR.K)/(APR.K*TAPR)                        63, A
    EGRP    - EXPECTED GROWTH RATE IN PRODUCTION
                (FRACTION/YEAR)
    PR      - PRODUCTION RATE  (UNITS/YEAR)
    APR     - AVERAGE PRODUCTION RATE  (UNITS/YEAR)
    TAPR    - TIME TO AVERAGE PRODUCTION RATE  (YEARS)

TR.KL=L.K/ADE.K                                          64, R
    TR      - TERMINATION RATE  (MEN/YEAR)
    L       - LABOR  (MEN)
    ADE     - AVERAGE DURATION OF EMPLOYMENT  (YEARS)
```

```
ADE.K=(NDE)(MLDDE.K)                                      65, A
NDE=2                                                     65.1, C
    ADE    - AVERAGE DURATION OF EMPLOYMENT  (YEARS)
    NDE    - NORMAL DURATION OF EMPLOYMENT  (YEARS)
    MLDDE  - MULTIPLIER FROM LABOR DEMAND ON DURATION OF
               EMPLOYMENT (DIMENSIONLESS)

MLDDE.K=TABLE(TMLDDE,LR.K,0,2,.5)                         66, A
TMLDDE=2.5/1.65/1/.5/.3                                   66.1, T
    MLDDE  - MULTIPLIER FROM LABOR DEMAND ON DURATION OF
               EMPLOYMENT (DIMENSIONLESS)
    TMLDDE - TABLE FOR MULTIPLIER FROM LABOR DEMAND ON
               DURATION ON EMPLOYMENT
    LR     - LABOR RATIO  (DIMENSIONLESS)

LR.K=L.K/DL.K                                             67, A
    LR     - LABOR RATIO  (DIMENSIONLESS)
    L      - LABOR  (MEN)
    DL     - DESIRED LABOR  (MEN)


  ORDERS FOR CAPITAL


CAP.K=CAP.J+(DT)(CA.JK-CD.JK)                             68, L
CAP=ICAP                                                  68.1, N
    CAP    - CAPITAL  (CAPITAL UNITS)
    CA     - CAPITAL ARRIVALS  (CAPITAL UNITS/YEAR)
    CD     - CAPITAL DEPRECIATION  (CAPITAL UNITS/YEAR)
    ICAP   - INITIAL CAPITAL  (CAPITAL UNITS)

CA.KL=CAPO.K/DDC                                          69, R
DDC=2                                                     69.1, C
    CA     - CAPITAL ARRIVALS  (CAPITAL UNITS/YEAR)
    CAPO   - CAPITAL ON ORDER  (CAPITAL UNITS)
    DDC    - DELIVERY DELAY FOR CAPITAL  (YEARS)

CD.KL=CAP.K/ALC.K                                         70, R
    CD     - CAPITAL DEPRECIATION  (CAPITAL UNITS/YEAR)
    CAP    - CAPITAL  (CAPITAL UNITS)
    ALC    - AVERAGE LIFETIME OF CAPITAL  (YEARS)

ALC.K=(NLC)(MCDLC.K)                                      71, A
NLC=15                                                    71.1, C
    ALC    - AVERAGE LIFETIME OF CAPITAL  (YEARS)
    NLC    - NORMAL LIFETIME OF CAPITAL  (YEARS)
    MCDLC  - MULTIPLIER FROM CAPITAL DEMAND ON LIFETIME
               OF CAPITAL (DIMENSIONLESS)

MCDLC.K=TABLE(TMCDLC,CR.K,0,2,.5)                         72, A
TMCDLC=1.4/1.15/1/.85/.75                                 72.1, T
    MCDLC  - MULTIPLIER FROM CAPITAL DEMAND ON LIFETIME
               OF CAPITAL (DIMENSIONLESS)
    TMCDLC - TABLE FOR MULTIPLIER FROM CAPITAL DEMAND ON
               LIFETIME OF CAPITAL
    CR     - CAPITAL RATIO  (DIMENSIONLESS)

CR.K=CAP.K/DCAP.K                                         73, A
    CR     - CAPITAL RATIO  (DIMENSIONLESS)
    CAP    - CAPITAL  (CAPITAL UNITS)
    DCAP   - DESIRED CAPITAL  (CAPITAL UNITS)

CAPO.K=CAPO.J+(DT)(OC.JK-CA.JK)                           74, L
CAPO=(CD)(DDC)                                            74.1, N
    CAPO   - CAPITAL ON ORDER  (CAPITAL UNITS)
    OC     - ORDERS FOR CAPITAL  (CAPITAL UNITS/YEAR)
    CA     - CAPITAL ARRIVALS  (CAPITAL UNITS/YEAR)
    CD     - CAPITAL DEPRECIATION  (CAPITAL UNITS/YEAR)
    DDC    - DELIVERY DELAY FOR CAPITAL  (YEARS)

OC.KL=(AOC.K)(MCDOC.K)                                    75, R
    OC     - ORDERS FOR CAPITAL  (CAPITAL UNITS/YEAR)
    AOC    - AVERAGE ORDERS FOR CAPITAL  (CAPITAL UNITS/
               YEAR)
    MCDOC  - MULTIPLIER FROM CAPITAL DEMAND ON ORDERS
               FOR CAPITAL (DIMENSIONLESS)
```

```
AOC.K=AOC.J+(DT/TAOC)(OC.JK-AOC.J)                          76, L
AOC=CD                                                      76.1, N
TAOC=4                                                      76.2, C
    AOC     - AVERAGE ORDERS FOR CAPITAL  (CAPITAL UNITS/
                YEAR)
    TAOC    - TIME TO AVERAGE ORDERS FOR CAPITAL  (YEARS)
    OC      - ORDERS FOR CAPITAL  (CAPITAL UNITS/YEAR)
    CD      - CAPITAL DEPRECIATION  (CAPITAL UNITS/YEAR)

MCDOC.K=TABLE(TMCDOC,RDOC.K,0,2,.25)                        77, A
TMCDOC=.2/.35/.55/.75/1/1.25/1.45/1.6/1.7                   77.1, T
    MCDOC   - MULTIPLIER FROM CAPITAL DEMAND ON ORDERS
                FOR CAPITAL (DIMENSIONLESS)
    TMCDOC  - TABLE FOR MULTIPLIER FROM CAPITAL DEMAND ON
                ORDERS FOR CAPITAL
    RDOC    - RELATIVE DESIRED ORDERS FOR CAPITAL
                (DIMENSIONLESS)

RDOC.K=(AOC.K+ICOIBC.K)/AOC.K                               78, A
    RDOC    - RELATIVE DESIRED ORDERS FOR CAPITAL
                (DIMENSIONLESS)
    AOC     - AVERAGE ORDERS FOR CAPITAL  (CAPITAL UNITS/
                YEAR)
    ICOIBC  - INDICATED CAPITAL ORDERS FOR INVENTORY AND
                BACKLOG CORRECTION (CAPITAL UNITS/YEAR)

ICOIBC.K=(DCAPO.K-CAPO.K+DCAP.K-CAP.K)/TAC                  79, A
TAC=4                                                       79.1, C
    ICOIBC  - INDICATED CAPITAL ORDERS FOR INVENTORY AND
                BACKLOG CORRECTION (CAPITAL UNITS/YEAR)
    DCAPO   - DESIRED CAPITAL ON ORDER  (CAPITAL UNITS)
    CAPO    - CAPITAL ON ORDER  (CAPITAL UNITS)
    DCAP    - DESIRED CAPITAL  (CAPITAL UNITS)
    CAP     - CAPITAL  (CAPITAL UNITS)
    TAC     - TIME TO ADJUST CAPITAL  (YEARS)

DCAPO.K=(AOC.K)(DDC)                                        80, A
    DCAPO   - DESIRED CAPITAL ON ORDER  (CAPITAL UNITS)
    AOC     - AVERAGE ORDERS FOR CAPITAL  (CAPITAL UNITS/
                YEAR)
    DDC     - DELIVERY DELAY FOR CAPITAL  (YEARS)

DCAP.K=(DPROD.K)(DCI.K)(MGDC.K)                             81, A
    DCAP    - DESIRED CAPITAL  (CAPITAL UNITS)
    DPROD   - DESIRED PRODUCTION  (UNITS/YEAR)
    DCI     - DESIRED CAPITAL INTENSITY (CAPITAL UNITS/
                OUTPUT UNIT/YEAR)
    MGDC    - MULTIPLIER FROM GROWTH ON DESIRED CAPITAL
                (DIMENSIONLESS)

DCI.K=CLIP(CIIFC.K,NCI,SW3,1)                               82, A
NCI=ICAP/NPROD                                              82.1, N
    DCI     - DESIRED CAPITAL INTENSITY (CAPITAL UNITS/
                OUTPUT UNIT/YEAR)
    CIIFC   - CAPITAL INTENSITY INDICATED BY FACTOR COSTS
                (CAPITAL UNITS/OUTPUT UNIT/YEAR)
    NCI     - NORMAL CAPITAL INTENSITY  (CAPITAL UNITS/
                OUTPUT UNIT/YEAR)
    SW3     - SWITCH 3  (DIMENSIONLESS)
    ICAP    - INITIAL CAPITAL  (CAPITAL UNITS)
    NPROD   - NORMAL PRODUCTION (UNITS/YEAR)

CIIFC.K=(ACI.K)(MFCCI.K)                                    83, A
    CIIFC   - CAPITAL INTENSITY INDICATED BY FACTOR COSTS
                (CAPITAL UNITS/OUTPUT UNIT/YEAR)
    ACI     - AVERAGE CAPITAL INTENSITY (CAPITAL UNITS/
                OUTPUT UNIT/YEAR)
    MFCCI   - MULTIPLIER FROM FACTOR COST ON CAPITAL
                INTENSITY (DIMENSIONLESS)

ACI.K=ACI.J+(DT/TACI)(CI.J-ACI.J)                           84, L
ACI=CI                                                      84.1, N
TACI=15                                                     84.2, C
    ACI     - AVERAGE CAPITAL INTENSITY (CAPITAL UNITS/
                OUTPUT UNIT/YEAR)
    TACI    - TIME TO AVERAGE CAPITAL INTENSITY  (YEARS)
    CI      - CAPITAL INTENSITY  (CAPITAL UNITS/OUTPUT
                UNIT/YEAR)
```

```
CI.K=CAP.K/APR.K                                        85, A
    CI      - CAPITAL INTENSITY  (CAPITAL UNITS/OUTPUT
                UNIT/YEAR)
    CAP     - CAPITAL  (CAPITAL UNITS)
    APR     - AVERAGE PRODUCTION RATE  (UNITS/YEAR)

MFCCI.K=TABLE(TMFCCI,RRC.K,0,2.5,.5)                    86, A
TMFCCI=0/.5/1/1.4/1.7/1.9                               86.1, T
    MFCCI   - MULTIPLIER FROM FACTOR COST ON CAPITAL
                INTENSITY (DIMENSIONLESS)
    TMFCCI  - TABLE FOR MULTIPLIER FROM FACTOR COST ON
                CAPITAL INTENSITY
    RRC     - RELATIVE RETURN TO CAPITAL  (DIMENSIONLESS)

MGDC.K=1+(EGRP.K)(DDC)                                  87, A
    MGDC    - MULTIPLIER FROM GROWTH ON DESIRED CAPITAL
                (DIMENSIONLESS)
    EGRP    - EXPECTED GROWTH RATE IN PRODUCTION
                (FRACTION/YEAR)
    DDC     - DELIVERY DELAY FOR CAPITAL  (YEARS)

CONS.K=CLIP(CONSI.K,TCONS.K,SW4,1)                      88, A
SW4=0                                                   88.1, C
    CONS    - CONSUMPTION  (UNITS/YEAR)
    CONSI   - CONSUMPTION FROM INCOME  (UNITS/YEAR)
    TCONS   - TEST CONSUMPTION  (UNITS/YEAR)
    SW4     - SWITCH 4  (DIMENSIONLESS)

TCONS.K=(CCR+STEP(CSH,CST))(NTC.K)+RSW*RAMP(RSLP,       89, A
  RT)
CCR=NPROD                                               89.1, N
CSH=SSC*CCR                                             89.2, N
SSC=0                                                   89.3, C
CST=2                                                   89.4, C
RSW=0                                                   89.5, C
RSLP=20                                                 89.6, C
RT=2                                                    89.7, C
    TCONS   - TEST CONSUMPTION  (UNITS/YEAR)
    CCR     - CONSTANT CONSUMPTION RATE  (UNITS/YEAR)
    CSH     - CONSUMPTION STEP HEIGHT  (UNITS/YEAR)
    CST     - CONSUMPTION STEP TIME  (YEARS)
    NTC     - NOISE IN TEST CONSUMPTION (DIMENSIONLESS)
    RSW     - RAMP SWITCH  (DIMENSIONLESS)
    RSLP    - RAMP SLOPE  (UNITS/YEAR/YEAR)
    RT      - RAMP TIME  (YEARS)
    NPROD   - NORMAL PRODUCTION (UNITS/YEAR)
    SSC     - SWITCH FOR STEP IN CONSUMPTION
                (DIMENSIONLESS)

NTC.K=NTC.J+(DT/TSNTC)(NORMRN(1,SDNTC)-NTC.J)           90, L
NTC=1                                                   90.1, N
TSNTC=1                                                 90.2, C
SDNTC=0                                                 90.3, C
    NTC     - NOISE IN TEST CONSUMPTION (DIMENSIONLESS)
    TSNTC   - TIME TO SMOOTH NOISE IN TEST CONSUMPTION
                (DIMENSIONLESS)
    SDNTC   - STANDARD DEVIATION OF NOISE IN TEST
                CONSUMPTION (DIMENSIONLESS)

CONSI.K=(ARCI.K)(APC)(NCIN.K)                           91, A
APC=.9                                                  91.1, C
    CONSI   - CONSUMPTION FROM INCOME  (UNITS/YEAR)
    ARCI    - AVERAGE REAL CONSUMER INCOME  (UNITS/YEAR)
    APC     - AVERAGE PROPENSITY TO CONSUME
                (DIMENSIONLESS)
    NCIN    - NOISE IN CONSUMPTION FROM INCOME
                (DIMENSIONLESS)

ARCI.K=ARCI.J+(DT/TARCI)(RCI.J-ARCI.J)                  92, L
ARCI=RCI                                                92.1, N
TARCI=2.5                                               92.2, C
    ARCI    - AVERAGE REAL CONSUMER INCOME  (UNITS/YEAR)
    TARCI   - TIME TO AVERAGE REAL CONSUMER INCOME
                (YEARS)
    RCI     - REAL CONSUMER INCOME  (UNITS/YEAR)

RCI.K=(WC.K+EI.K)/P.K                                   93, A
    RCI     - REAL CONSUMER INCOME  (UNITS/YEAR)
    WC      - WAGE COSTS  (DOLLARS/YEAR)
    EI      - EXTERNAL INCOME  (DOLLARS/YEAR)
    P       - PRICE  (DOLLARS/UNIT)
```

```
EI.K=(CEI+STEP(ISH,IST))                                   94, A
CEI=((PR*P)-(WC*APC))/APC                                  94.1, N
ISH=FISH*CEI                                               94.2, N
FISH=0                                                     94.3, C
IST=.2                                                     94.4, C
     EI      - EXTERNAL INCOME  (DOLLARS/YEAR)
     CEI     - CONSTANT EXTERNAL INCOME  (DOLLARS/YEAR)
     ISH     - INCOME STEP HEIGHT  (DOLLARS/YEAR)
     IST     - INCOME STEP TIME  (YEARS)
     PR      - PRODUCTION RATE  (UNITS/YEAR)
     P       - PRICE  (DOLLARS/UNIT)
     WC      - WAGE COSTS  (DOLLARS/YEAR)
     APC     - AVERAGE PROPENSITY TO CONSUME
                 (DIMENSIONLESS)
     FISH    - FRACTION INCOME STEP HEIGHT
                 (DIMENSIONLESS)

NCIN.K=NCIN.J+(DT/TSNCI)(NORMRN(1,SDNCI)-NCIN.J)           95, L
NCIN=1                                                     95.1, N
TSNCI=1                                                    95.2, C
SDNCI=0                                                    95.3, C
     NCIN    - NOISE IN CONSUMPTION FROM INCOME
                 (DIMENSIONLESS)
     TSNCI   - TIME TO SMOOTH NOISE IN CONSUMPTION FROM
                 INCOME (YEARS)
     SDNCI   - STANDARD DEVIATION OF NOISE IN CONSUMPTION
                 FROM INCOME (DIMENSIONLESS)

SCAP.K=SMOOTH(CAP.K,4)                                     96, A
     SCAP    - SMOOTHED CAPITAL (CAPITAL UNITS)
     CAP     - CAPITAL  (CAPITAL UNITS)

FDK.K=CAP.K-SCAP.K                                         97, S
     FDK     - FIRST-DIFFERENCE IN CAPITAL  (CAPITAL
                 UNITS)
     CAP     - CAPITAL  (CAPITAL UNITS)
     SCAP    - SMOOTHED CAPITAL (CAPITAL UNITS)

SPR.K=SMOOTH(PR.JK,.25)                                    98, A
     SPR     - SMOOTHED PRODUCTION RATE  (UNITS/YEAR)
     PR      - PRODUCTION RATE  (UNITS/YEAR)

FDPR.K=PR.JK-SPR.K                                         99, S
     FDPR    - FIRST-DIFFERENCE IN PRODUCTION RATE
                 (UNITS/YEAR)
     PR      - PRODUCTION RATE  (UNITS/YEAR)
     SPR     - SMOOTHED PRODUCTION RATE  (UNITS/YEAR)
```

## A.2 Analyzer Listing

```
NAME     NO    T   DEFINITION

ACCU     59    A   ANNUAL COST PER CAPITAL UNIT (DOLLARS/
                     CAPITAL UNIT/YEAR)
ACI      84    L   AVERAGE CAPITAL INTENSITY (CAPITAL UNITS/
         84.1  N     OUTPUT UNIT/YEAR)
ACLU     61    A   ANNUAL COST PER LABOR UNIT  (DOLLARS/MAN/
                     YEAR)
ADE      65    A   AVERAGE DURATION OF EMPLOYMENT  (YEARS)
ALC      71    A   AVERAGE LIFETIME OF CAPITAL  (YEARS)
ALI      53    L   AVERAGE LABOR INTENSITY  (MEN/OUTPUT UNIT/
         53.1  N     YEAR)
ANVC     45    L   AVERAGE NEW VACANCY CREATION  (MEN/YEAR)
         45.1  N
AOC      76    L   AVERAGE ORDERS FOR CAPITAL  (CAPITAL UNITS/
         76.1  N     YEAR)
AP       15    L   AVERAGE PRICE  (DOLLARS/UNIT)
         15.1  N
APC      91.1  C   AVERAGE PROPENSITY TO CONSUME
                     (DIMENSIONLESS)
```

*The analyzer listing consists of four columns. The first column lists alphabetically all the variable names used in the model. The second column gives the number of the equation in which the variable listed in the first column is defined. Thus, for example, the variable ACCU is defined in equation 59. The third column of the analyzer gives the equation type (see Appendix C for description). Finally, the fourth column gives the definition and units of measure of the variable.

| | | | |
|---|---|---|---|
| APR | 10<br>10.1 | L<br>N | AVERAGE PRODUCTION RATE (UNITS/YEAR) |
| ARCI | 92<br>92.1 | L<br>N | AVERAGE REAL CONSUMER INCOME (UNITS/YEAR) |
| ARLWW | 32<br>32.1 | L<br>N | AVERAGE RELATIVE LENGTH OF WORK WEEK (DIMENSIONLESS) |
| AUCP | 18<br>18.1 | L<br>N | AVERAGE UNIT COSTS OF PRODUCTION (DOLLARS/UNIT) |
| BL | 24<br>24.1 | L<br>N | BACKLOG (UNITS) |
| BLMS | 39 | A | BACKLOG MULTIPLIER FOR SHIPMENTS (DIMENSIONLESS) |
| BLR | 40 | A | BACKLOG RATIO (DIMENSIONLESS) |
| CA | 69 | R | CAPITAL ARRIVALS (CAPITAL UNITS/YEAR) |
| CAP | 68<br>68.1 | L<br>N | CAPITAL (CAPITAL UNITS) |
| CAPO | 74<br>74.1 | L<br>N | CAPITAL ON ORDER (CAPITAL UNITS) |
| CCR | 89.1 | N | CONSTANT CONSUMPTION RATE (UNITS/YEAR) |
| CD | 70 | R | CAPITAL DEPRECIATION (CAPITAL UNITS/YEAR) |
| CEI | 94.1 | N | CONSTANT EXTERNAL INCOME (DOLLARS/YEAR) |
| CEX | 2.4 | N | CAPITAL EXPONENT (DIMENSIONLESS) |
| CI | 85 | A | CAPITAL INTENSITY (CAPITAL UNITS/OUTPUT UNIT/YEAR) |
| CIIFC | 83 | A | CAPITAL INTENSITY INDICATED BY FACTOR COSTS (CAPITAL UNITS/OUTPUT UNIT/YEAR) |
| CONS | 88 | A | CONSUMPTION (UNITS/YEAR) |
| CONSI | 91 | A | CONSUMPTION FROM INCOME (UNITS/YEAR) |
| CPC | 60.1 | N | CONSTANT PRICE OF CAPITAL (DOLLARS/CAPITAL UNIT) |
| CR | 73 | A | CAPITAL RATIO (DIMENSIONLESS) |
| CSH | 89.2 | N | CONSUMPTION STEP HEIGHT (UNITS/YEAR) |
| CST | 89.4 | C | CONSUMPTION STEP TIME (YEARS) |
| CUF | 28<br>28.2 | A<br>N | CAPITAL UTILIZATION FACTOR (DIMENSIONLESS) |
| DBL | 25 | A | DESIRED BACKLOG (UNITS) |
| DCAP | 81 | A | DESIRED CAPITAL (CAPITAL UNITS) |
| DCAPO | 80 | A | DESIRED CAPITAL ON ORDER (CAPITAL UNITS) |
| DCI | 82 | A | DESIRED CAPITAL INTENSITY (CAPITAL UNITS/OUTPUT UNIT/YEAR) |
| DDC | 69.1 | C | DELIVERY DELAY FOR CAPITAL (YEARS) |
| DDG | 35 | A | DELIVERY DELAY FOR GOODS (YEARS) |
| DFV | 42.1 | C | DELAY IN FILLING VACANCIES (YEARS) |
| DINV | 11 | A | DESIRED INVENTORY (UNITS) |
| DL | 50 | A | DESIRED LABOR (MEN) |
| DLI | 51 | A | DESIRED LABOR INTENSITY (MEN/OUTPUT UNIT/YEAR) |
| DPROD | 9 | A | DESIRED PRODUCTION (UNITS/YEAR) |
| DT | 99.4 | C | |
| DVAC | 49 | A | DESIRED VACANCIES (MEN) |
| ECAP | 27 | A | EFFECTIVE CAPITAL (CAPITAL UNITS) |
| EGRP | 63 | A | EXPECTED GROWTH RATE IN PRODUCTION (FRACTION/YEAR) |
| EI | 94 | A | EXTERNAL INCOME (DOLLARS/YEAR) |
| EL | 4 | A | EFFECTIVE LABOR (MEN) |
| FDK | 97 | S | FIRST-DIFFERENCE IN CAPITAL (CAPITAL UNITS) |
| FDPR | 99 | S | FIRST-DIFFERENCE IN PRODUCTION RATE(UNITS/YEAR) |
| FISH | 94.3 | C | FRACTION INCOME STEP HEIGHT(DIMENSIONLESS) |
| HR | 42 | A | HIRING RATE (MEN/YEAR) |
| HW | 20.1 | C | HOURLY WAGE (DOLLARS/HOUR) |
| ICAP | 26.1 | C | INITIAL CAPITAL (CAPITAL UNITS) |
| ICC | 22 | A | INVENTORY CARRYING COSTS (DOLLARS/YEAR) |
| ICOIBC | 79 | A | INDICATED CAPITAL ORDERS FOR INVENTORY AND BACKLOG CORRECTION (CAPITAL UNITS/YEAR) |
| IL | 3.1 | C | INITIAL LABOR (MEN) |
| IMS | 37<br>37.2 | A<br>N | INVENTORY MULTIPLIER FOR SHIPMENTS (DIMENSIONLESS) |
| INV | 1<br>1.1 | L<br>N | INVENTORY (UNITS) |
| INVR | 38 | A | INVENTORY RATIO (DIMENSIONLESS) |
| IR | 22.1 | C | INTEREST RATE (FRACTION/YEAR) |
| ISH | 94.2 | N | INCOME STEP HEIGHT (DOLLARS/YEAR) |
| IST | 94.4 | C | INCOME STEP TIME (YEARS) |
| IVCIBC | 48 | A | INDICATED VACANCY CREATION FOR INVENTORY AND BACKLOG CORRECTION (MEN/YEAR) |

```
L         41    L   LABOR  (MEN)
          41.1 N
LENGTH    99.6 C
LEX        2.3 C   LABOR EXPONENT  (DIMENSIONLESS)
LI        54    A   LABOR INTENSITY  (MEN/OUTPUT UNIT/YEAR)
LIIFC     52    A   LABOR INTENSITY INDICATED BY FACTOR COSTS
                      (MEN/OUTPUT UNIT/YEAR)
LP                  LABOR PRODUCTIVITY  (UNITS/MAN/HOUR)
LR        67    A   LABOR RATIO  (DIMENSIONLESS)
MCDLC     72    A   MULTIPLIER FROM CAPITAL DEMAND ON LIFETIME
                      OF CAPITAL (DIMENSIONLESS)
MCDOC     77    A   MULTIPLIER FROM CAPITAL DEMAND ON ORDERS
                      FOR CAPITAL (DIMENSIONLESS)
MDPP      23    A   MULTIPLIER FROM DESIRED PRODUCTION ON
                      PROFITS  (DIMENSIONLESS)
MFCCI     86    A   MULTIPLIER FROM FACTOR COST ON CAPITAL
                      INTENSITY (DIMENSIONLESS)
MFCLI     55    A   MULTIPLIER FROM FACTOR COST ON LABOR
                      INTENSITY (DIMENSIONLESS)
MGDC      87    A   MULTIPLIER FROM GROWTH ON DESIRED CAPITAL
                      (DIMENSIONLESS)
MGDL      62    A   MULTIPLIER FROM GROWTH ON DESIRED LABOR
                      (DIMENSIONLESS)
MHY        6    A   MAN-HOURS PER YEAR  (HOURS/MAN-YEAR)
           6.1 N
MHYN       5.1 C   MAN-HOURS PER YEAR NORMAL  (HOURS/MAN-YEAR)
MLDDE     66    A   MULTIPLIER FROM LABOR DEMAND ON DURATION OF
                      EMPLOYMENT (DIMENSIONLESS)
MLDO       7    A   MULTIPLIER FROM LABOR DEMAND ON OVERTIME
                      (DIMENSIONLESS)
MLDOL     46    A   MULTIPLIER FROM LABOR DEMAND ON ORDERS FOR
                      LABOR (DIMENSIONLESS)
MLP       30    A   MULTIPLIER ON LABOR PRODUCTIVITY
                      (DIMENSIONLESS)
MOLP      31    A   MULTIPLIER FROM OVERTIME ON LABOR
                      PRODUCTIVITY (DIMENSIONLESS)
MPEDI     12    A   MULTIPLIER FROM PRICE EXPECTATIONS ON
          12.2 N     DESIRED INVENTORY (DIMENSIONLESS)
MPPLP     33    A   MULTIPLIER FROM PRODUCTION PRESSURE ON
                      LABOR PRODUCTIVITY (DIMENSIONLESS)
NBC       25.1 C   NORMAL BACKLOG COVERAGE  (YEARS)
NC                  NOISE IN CONSUMPTION  (DIMENSIONLESS)
NCI       82.1 N   NORMAL CAPITAL INTENSITY  (CAPITAL UNITS/
                      OUTPUT UNIT/YEAR)
NCIN      95    L   NOISE IN CONSUMPTION FROM INCOME
          95.1 N     (DIMENSIONLESS)
NDE       65.1 C   NORMAL DURATION OF EMPLOYMENT  (YEARS)
NECAP     26    A   NORMALIZED EFFECTIVE CAPITAL(DIMENSIONLESS)
NEL        3    A   NORMALIZED EFFECTIVE LABOR (DIMENSIONLESS)
NIC       11.1 C   NORMAL INVENTORY COVERAGE  (YEARS)
NLC       71.1 C   NORMAL LIFETIME OF CAPITAL  (YEARS)
NLI       51.2 N   NORMAL LABOR INTENSITY  (MEN/OUTPUT UNIT/
                      YEAR)
NPM       17.1 C   NORMAL PROFIT MARGIN  (DIMENSIONLESS)
NPR       29    L   NOISE IN PRODUCTION RATE  (DIMENSIONLESS)
          29.1 N
NPROD      2.2 C   NORMAL PRODUCTION (UNITS/YEAR)
NTC       90    L   NOISE IN TEST CONSUMPTION (DIMENSIONLESS)
          90.1 N
NVC       44    R   NEW VACANCY CREATION  (MEN/YEAR)
OC        75    R   ORDERS FOR CAPITAL  (CAPITAL UNITS/YEAR)
OVTP      21.1 C   OVERTIME PREMIUM  (DIMENSIONLESS)
OVTWG     21    A   OVERTIME WAGES  (DOLLARS/YEAR)
P         17    A   PRICE  (DOLLARS/UNIT)
PC        60    A   PRICE OF CAPITAL (DOLLARS/CAPITAL/UNIT)
PLTPER    99.5 C
PR         2    R   PRODUCTION RATE  (UNITS/YEAR)

PRIP      13    L   PERCEIVED RATE OF INCREASE IN PRICE
          13.1 N     (FRACTION/YEAR)
PRR        8    A   PRODUCTION RATIO  (DIMENSIONLESS)
RCC       58    A   RELATIVE COST OF CAPITAL  (MEN/CAPITAL
                      UNIT)
RCI       93    A   REAL CONSUMER INCOME  (UNITS/YEAR)
RDDG      34    A   RELATIVE DELIVERY DELAY FOR GOODS
          34.1 N     (DIMENSIONLESS)
RDOC      78    A   RELATIVE DESIRED ORDERS FOR CAPITAL
                      (DIMENSIONLESS)
```

| | | | |
|---|---|---|---|
| RDOL | 47 | A | RELATIVE DESIRED ORDERS FOR LABOR (DIMENSIONLESS) |
| RIP | 14 | A | RATE OF INCREASE IN PRICE (FRACTION/YEAR) |
| RLWW | 5 | A | RELATIVE LENGTH OF WORK WEEK(DIMENSIONLESS) |
| RMPC | 57 | A | RELATIVE MARGINAL PRODUCT OF CAPITAL (MEN/ CAPITAL UNIT) |
| RRC | 56 | A | RELATIVE RETURN TO CAPITAL (DIMENSIONLESS) |
| RSLP | 89.6 | C | RAMP SLOPE (UNITS/YEAR/YEAR) |
| RSW | 89.5 | C | RAMP SWITCH (DIMENSIONLESS) |
| RT | 89.7 | C | RAMP TIME (YEARS) |
| SAP | 16 | L | SMOOTHED AVERAGE PRICE (DOLLARS/UNIT) |
| | 16.1 | N | |
| SCAP | 96 | A | SMOOTHED CAPITAL (CAPITAL UNITS) |
| SCR | | | STEP IN CONSUMPTION RATE (UNITS/YEAR) |
| SDNCI | 95.3 | C | STANDARD DEVIATION OF NOISE IN CONSUMPTION FROM INCOME (DIMENSIONLESS) |
| SDNPR | 29.3 | C | STANDARD DEVIATION OF NOISE IN PRODUCTION RATE (DIMENSIONLESS) |
| SDNTC | 90.3 | C | STANDARD DEVIATION OF NOISE IN TEST CONSUMPTION (DIMENSIONLESS) |
| SPR | 98 | A | SMOOTHED PRODUCTION RATE (UNITS/YEAR) |
| SR | 36 | A | SHIPMENT RATE (UNITS/YEAR) |
| SSC | 89.3 | C | SWITCH FOR STEP IN CONSUMPTION (DIMENSIONLESS) |
| SW1 | 2.5 | C | SWITCH 1 (DIMENSIONLESS) |
| SW2 | 11.2 | C | SWITCH 2 (DIMENSIONLESS) |
| SW3 | 51.1 | C | SWITCH 3 (DIMENSIONLESS) |
| SW4 | 88.1 | C | SWITCH 4 (DIMENSIONLESS) |
| TAC | 79.1 | C | TIME TO ADJUST CAPITAL (YEARS) |
| TACI | 84.2 | C | TIME TO AVERAGE CAPITAL INTENSITY (YEARS) |
| TAL | 48.1 | C | TIME TO ADJUST LABOR (YEARS) |
| TALI | 53.2 | C | TIME TO AVERAGE LABOR INTENSITY (YEARS) |
| TANVC | 45.2 | C | TIME TO AVERAGE NEW VACANCY CREATION(YEARS) |
| TAOC | 76.2 | C | TIME TO AVERAGE ORDERS FOR CAPITAL (YEARS) |
| TAP | 15.2 | C | TIME TO AVERAGE PRICE (YEARS) |
| TAPR | 10.2 | C | TIME TO AVERAGE PRODUCTION RATE (YEARS) |
| TARCI | 92.2 | C | TIME TO AVERAGE REAL CONSUMER INCOME(YEARS) |
| TARLWW | 32.2 | C | TIME TO AVERAGE RELATIVE LENGTH OF WORK WEEK (YEARS) |
| TAUCP | 18.2 | C | TIME TO AVERAGE UNIT COSTS OF PRODUCTION (YEARS) |
| TBLMS | 39.1 | T | |
| TCIB | 9.1 | C | TIME TO CORRECT INVENTORIES AND BACKLOGS (YEARS) |
| TCONS | 89 | A | TEST CONSUMPTION (UNITS/YEAR) |
| TCUF | 28.1 | T | TABLE FOR CAPITAL UTILIZATION FACTOR |
| TIMS | 37.1 | T | TABLE FOR INVENTORY MULTIPLIER FOR SHIPMENTS |
| TMCDLC | 72.1 | T | TABLE FOR MULTIPLIER FROM CAPITAL DEMAND ON LIFETIME OF CAPITAL |
| TMCDOC | 77.1 | T | TABLE FOR MULTIPLIER FROM CAPITAL DEMAND ON ORDERS -FOR CAPITAL |
| TMDPP | 23.1 | T | TABLE FOR MULTIPLIER FROM DESIRED PRODUCTION ON PROFITS |
| TMFCCI | 86.1 | T | TABLE FOR MULTIPLIER FROM FACTOR COST ON CAPITAL INTENSITY |
| TMFCLI | 55.1 | T | TABLE FOR MULTIPLIER FROM FACTOR COST ON LABOR INTENSITY |
| TMLDDE | 66.1 | T | TABLE FOR MULTIPLIER FROM LABOR DEMAND ON DURATION ON EMPLOYMENT |
| TMLDO | 7.1 | T | TABLE FOR MULTIPLIER FROM LABOR DEMAND ON OVERTIME |
| TMLDOL | 46.1 | T | TABLE FOR MULTIPLIER FROM LABOR DEMAND ON ORDERS FOR LABOR |
| TMOLP | 31.1 | T | TABLE FOR MULTIPLIER FROM OVERTIME ON LABOR PRODUCTIVITY |
| TMPEDI | 12.1 | T | TABLE FOR MULTIPLIER FROM PRICE EXPECTATIONS ON DESIRED INVENTORY |
| TMPPLP | 33.1 | T | TABLE FOR MULTIPLIER FROM PRODUCTION PRESSURE ON LABOR PRODUCTIVITY |
| TPRIP | 13.2 | C | TIME TO PERCEIVE RATE OF INCREASE IN PRICE (YEARS) |
| TR | 64 | R | TERMINATION RATE (MEN/YEAR) |
| TSAP | 16.2 | C | TIME TO SMOOTH AVERAGE PRICE (YEARS) |
| TSNCI | 95.2 | C | TIME TO SMOOTH NOISE IN CONSUMPTION FROM INCOME (YEARS) |

```
TSNPR     29.2 C  TIME TO SMOOTH NOISE IN PRODUCTION RATE
                    (YEARS)
TSNTC     90.2 C  TIME TO SMOOTH NOISE IN TEST CONSUMPTION
                    (DIMENSIONLESS)
UCP       19   A  UNIT COSTS OF PRODUCTION  (DOLLARS/UNIT)
VAC       43   L  VACANCIES  (MEN)
          43.1 N
WC        20   A  WAGE COSTS  (DOLLARS/YEAR)
```

# Appendix B
# Equations Used for the Simulations

```
       * BUSINESS CYCLE MODEL
       NOTE
       NOTE   GOODS SECTOR
       NOTE
       NOTE
       NOTE   BASIC PRODUCTION SECTOR
       NOTE
 1     L      INV.K=INV.J+(DT)(PR.JK-SR.J)
       N      INV=DINV
 2     R      PR.KL=(NPROD)(EXP(LEX*LOGN(NEL.K)))(EXP(CEX*LOGN(NECAP.K)))
       X   (NPR.K)(CLIP(MLP.K,1,SW1,1))
       C      NPROD=3E6
       C      LEX=1
       N      CEX=1-LEX
       C      SW1=Ø
 3     A      NEL.K=EL.K/IL
       C      IL=15ØØ
 4     A      EL.K=(L.K)(RLWW.K)
 5     A      RLWW.K=MHY.K/MHYN
       C      MHYN=2Ø8Ø
 6     A      MHY.K=(MHYN)(MLDO.K)
       N      MHY=MHYN
 7     A      MLDO.K=TABHL(TMLDO,PRR.K,.6,1.4,.1)
       T      TMLDO=.85/.87/.9/.94/1/1.Ø7/1.14/1.18/1.2
 8     A      PRR.K=DPROD.K/APR.K
 9     A      DPROD.K=APR.K+(DINV.K-INV.K+BL.K-DBL.K)/TCIB
       C      TCIB=.8
 1Ø    L      APR.K=APR.J+(DT/TAPR)(PR.JK-APR.K)
       N      APR=PR
       C      TAPR=1
 11    A      DINV.K=(APR.K)(NIC)(CLIP(MPEDI.K,1,SW2,1))
       C      NIC=.5
       C      SW2=Ø
 12    A      MPEDI.K=TABLE(TMPEDI,PRIP.K,-.12,.12,.Ø6)
       T      TMPEDI=.9/.93/1/1.Ø7/1.1
       N      MPEDI=1
 13    L      PRIP.K=PRIP.J+(DT/TPRIP)(RIP.J-PRIP.J)
       N      PRIP=RIP
       C      TPRIP=1.5
 14    A      RIP.K=(AP.K-SAP.K)/(SAP.K*TSAP)
 15    L      AP.K=AP.J+(DT/TAP)(P.J-AP.J)
       N      AP=P
       C      TAP=.33
 16    L      SAP.K=SAP.J+(DT/TSAP)(AP.J-SAP.J)
       N      SAP=AP
       C      TSAP=.33
 17    A      P.K=(AUCP.K)(1+NPM)(MDPP.K)
       C      NPM=.1
 18    L      AUCP.K=AUCP.J+(DT/TAUCP)(UCP.J-AUCP.J)
       N      AUCP=WC/(APR-(INV)(IR))
       C      TAUCP=1
 19    A      UCP.K=(WC.K+ICC.K)/APR.K
```

```
20    A     WC.K=(L.K)(MHY.K)(HW)+OVTWG.K
      C     HW=4
21    A     OVTWG.K=MAX(Ø,(L.K)(HW)(OVTP)(MHY.K-MHYN))
      C     OVTP=.3
22    A     ICC.K=(INV.K)(AUCP.K)(IR)
      C     IR=.Ø6
23    A     MDPP.K=TABLE(TMDPP,PRR.K,Ø,2,.5)
      T     TMDPP=.75/.85/1/1.15/1.4
24    L     BL.K=BL.J+(DT)(CONS.J-SR.J)
      N     BL=DBL
25    A     DBL.K=(APR.K)(NBC)
      C     NBC=.2
26    A     NECAP.K=ECAP.K/ICAP
      C     ICAP=7.5E6
27    A     ECAP.K=(CAP.K)(CUF.K)
28    A     CUF.K=TABHL(TCUF,PRR.K,.6,1.4,.1)
      T     TCUF=.8/.83/.87/.92/1/1.05/1.08/1.1/1.11
      N     CUF=1
29    L     NPR.K=NPR.J+(DT/TSNPR)(NORMRN(1,SDNPR)-NPR.J)
      N     NPR=1
      C     TSNPR=1
      C     SDNPR=Ø
30    A     MLP.K=(MOLP.K)(MPPLP.K)
31    A     MOLP.K=TABLE(TMOLP,ARLWW.K,.8,1.2,.1)
      T     TMOLP=1.Ø6/1.Ø4/1/.95/.9
32    L     ARLWW.K=ARLWW.K+(DT/TARLWW)(RLWW.J-ARLWW.J)
      N     ARLWW=1
      C     TARLWW=.33
33    A     MPPLP.K=TABLE(TMPPLP,RDDG.K,Ø,2,.5)
      T     TMPPLP=1.1/1.Ø7/1/.8/.7
34    A     RDDG.K=DDG.K/NBC
      N     RDDG=1
35    A     DDG.K=BL.K/SR.K
36    A     SR.K=(APR.K)(IMS.K)(BLMS.K)
37    A     IMS.K=TABHL(TIMS,INVR.K,Ø,2,.5)
      T     TIMS=Ø/.6/1/1.4/1.6
      N     IMS=1
38    A     INVR.K=INV.K/DINV.K
39    A     BLMS.K=TABHL(TBLMS,BLR.K,Ø,2,.5)
      T     TBLMS=Ø/.6/1/1.4/1.6
4Ø    A     BLR.K=BL.K/DBL.K
      NOTE
      NOTE  ORDERS FOR LABOR
41    L     L.K=L.J+(DT)(HR.J-TR.JK)
      N     L=IL
42    A     HR.K=VAC.K/DFV
      C     DFV=.25
43    L     VAC.K=VAC.J+(DT)(NVC.JK-HR.J)
      N     VAC=(L/NDE)(DFV)
44    R     NVC.KL=(ANVC.K)(MLDOL.K)
45    L     ANVC.K=ANVC.J+(DT/TANVC)(NVC.JK-ANVC.J)
      N     ANVC=L/NDE
      C     TANVC=.5
46    A     MLDOL.K=TABLE(TMLDOL,RDOL.K,Ø,2,.25)
      T     TMLDOL=.2/.35/.55/.75/1/1.25/1.45/1.6/1.7
47    A     RDOL.K=(ANVC.K+IVCIBC.K)/ANVC.K
48    A     IVCIBC.K=(DVAC.K-VAC.K+DL.K-L.K)/TAL
      C     TAL=.5
49    A     DVAC.K=(ANVC.K)(DFV)
5Ø    A     DL.K=(DPROD.K)(DLI.K)(MGDL.K)
51    A     DLI.K=CLIP(LIIFC.K,NLI,SW3,1)
      C     SW3=Ø
      N     NLI=IL/NPROD
52    A     LIIFC.K=(ALI.K)(MFCLI.K)
53    L     ALI.K=ALI.J+(DT/TALI)(LI.J-ALI.J)
      N     ALI=LI
      C     TALI=15
54    A     LI.K=L.K/APR.K
55    A     MFCLI.K=TABLE(TMFCLI,RRC.K,Ø,2.5,.5)
      T     TMFCLI=3/1.6/1/.6/.3/.15
56    A     RRC.K=RMPC.K/RCC.K
57    A     RMPC.K=L.K/CAP.K
58    A     RCC.K=ACCU.K/ACLU.K
59    A     ACCU.K=(PC.K)(IR+(1/NLC))
6Ø    A     PC.K=CPC
      N     CPC=(HW*MHYN)/((ICAP/IL)(IR+(1/NLC)))
61    A     ACLU.K=(HW)(MHYN)
62    A     MGDL.K=1+(EGRP.K)(DFV)
```

```
63    A     EGRP.K=(PR.JK-APR.K)/(APR.K*TAPR)
64    R     TR.KL=L.K/ADE.K
65    A     ADE.K=(NDE)(MLDDE.K)
      C     NDE=2
66    A     MLDDE.K=TABLE(TMLDDE,LR.K,0,2,.5)
      T     TMLDDE=2.5/1.65/1/.5/.3
67    A     LR.K=L.K/DL.K
      NOTE
      NOTE  ORDERS FOR CAPITAL
68    L     CAP.K=CAP.J+(DT)(CA.JK-CD.JK)
      N     CAP=ICAP
69    R     CA.KL=CAPO.K/DDC
      C     DDC=2
70    R     CD.KL=CAP.K/ALC.K
71    A     ALC.K=(NLC)(MCDLC.K)
      C     NLC=15
72    A     MCDLC.K=TABLE(TMCDLC,CR.K,0,2,.5)
      T     TMCDLC=1.4/1.15/1/.85/.75
73    A     CR.K=CAP.K/DCAP.K
74    L     CAPO.K=CAPO.J+(DT)(OC.JK-CA.JK)
      N     CAPO=(CD)(DDC)
75    R     OC.KL=(AOC.K)(MCDOC.K)
76    L     AOC.K=AOC.J+(DT/TAOC)(OC.JK-AOC.J)
      N     AOC=CD
      C     TAOC=4
77    A     MCDOC.K=TABLE(TMCDOC,RDOC.K,0,2,.25)
      T     TMCDOC=.2/.35/.55/.75/1/1.25/1.45/1.6/1.7
78    A     RDOC.K=(AOC.K+ICOIBC.K)/AOC.K
79    A     ICOIBC.K=(DCAPO.K-CAPO.K+DCAP.K-CAP.K)/TAC
      C     TAC=4
80    A     DCAPO.K=(AOC.K)(DDC)
81    A     DCAP.K=(DPROD.K)(DCI.K)(MGDC.K)
82    A     DCI.K=CLIP(CIIFC.K,NCI,SW3,1)
      N     NCI=ICAP/NPROD
83    A     CIIFC.K=(ACI.K)(MFCCI.K)
84    L     ACI.K=ACI.J+(DT/TACI)(CI.J-ACI.J)
      N     ACI=CI
      C     TACI=15
85    A     CI.K=CAP.K/APR.K
86    A     MFCCI.K=TABLE(TMFCCI,RRC.K,0,2.5,.5)
      T     TMFCCI=0/.5/1/1.4/1.7/1.9
87    A     MGDC.K=1+(EGRP.K)(DDC)
      NOTE
      NOTE  TEST EQUATIONS
      NOTE
88    A     CONS.K=CLIP(CONSI.K,TCONS.K,SW4,1)
      C     SW4=0
89    A     TCONS.K=(CCR+STEP(CSH,CST))(NTC.K)+RSW*RAMP(RSLP,RT)
      N     CCR=NPROD
      N     CSH=SSC*CCR
      C     SSC=0
      C     CST=2
      C     RSW=0
      C     RSLP=20
      C     RT=2
90    L     NTC.K=NTC.J+(DT/TSNTC)(NORMRN(1,SDNTC)-NTC.J)
      N     NTC=1
      C     TSNTC=1
      C     SDNTC=0
91    A     CONSI.K=(ARCI.K)(APC)(NCIN.K)
      C     APC=.9
92    L     ARCI.K=ARCI.J+(DT/TARCI)(RCI.J-ARCI.J)
      N     ARCI=RCI
      C     TARCI=2.5
93    A     RCI.K=(WC.K+EI.K)/P.K
94    A     EI.K=(CEI+STEP(ISH,IST))
      N     CEI=((PR*P)-(WC*APC))/APC
      N     ISH=FISH*CEI
      C     FISH=0
      C     IST=.2
95    L     NCIN.K=NCIN.J+(DT/TSNCI)(NORMRN(1,SDNCI)-NCIN.J)
      N     NCIN=1
      C     TSNCI=1
      C     SDNCI=0
96    A     SCAP.K=SMOOTH(CAP.K,4)
97    S     FDK.K=CAP.K-SCAP.K
98    A     SPR.K=SMOOTH(PR.JK,.25)
99    S     FDPR.K=PR.JK-SPR.K
```

```
NOTE
NOTE  CONTROL CARDS
NOTE
C      DT=.0625
C      PLTPER=1
C      LENGTH=0
RUN
NOTE
NOTE  CONTROL CARDS
NOTE
CP DT=.0078125
CP LENGTH=10
CP PLTPER=.25
CP CST=.5
C SSC=.15
PLOT INV=I,DINV=D(1.3E6,2.1E6)/PR=P,SR=S,CONS=C(3E6,4E6)/BL=B,DBL=G(5E5,
X  9E5)
PLOT DPROD=D(3E6,3.8E6)/L=L,DL=F(1400,2200)/RLWW=R(.8,1.2)/HR=H
RUN  FIGURE 3-17
C SSC=.15
T TMLDO=.92/.93/.95/.97/1/1.04/1.07/1.09/1.1
RUN  FIGURE 3-22
C SSC=.15
C TCIB=.4
RUN  FIGURE 3-24
C SSC=.15
C TCIB=1.6
RUN  FIGURE 3-25
C LENGTH=20
C PLTPER=.5
C SDNTC=.1
PLOT INV=I/L=L/PR=P/CONS=C
RUN  FIGURE 3-21
C LENGTH=10
C PLTPER=.25
C SW1=1
C SSC=.15
PLOT INV=I,DINV=D(1.3E6,2.1E6)/PR=P,CONS=C(3E6,4E6)/BL=B,DBL=G(5E5,9E5)
PLOT DPROD=D(3E6,3.8E6)/L=L,DL=F(1400,2200)/RLWW=R(.8,1.2)/MOLP=O/MPPLP=
X  P/RDDG=G
RUN  FIGURE 3-31
C LENGTH=10
C PLTPER=.25
C SW2=1
C SSC=.15
PLOT INV=I,DINV=D/PR=P,CONS=C/BL=B,DBL=G
PLOT DPROD=D/L=L,DL=F/P=$/MDPP=P/MPEDI=M
RUN  FIGURE 3-38
C LENGTH=20
C PLTPER=.5
C SW4=1
C FISH=.05
PLOT INV=I,DINV=D/BL=B/PR=P/CONS=C/P=$
PLOT MDPP=M/L=L/RCI=R
PLOT FDPR=F
RUN  FIGURES 3-41 AND 3-42
C LENGTH=25
C PLTPER=.5
C SW4=1
C SDNCI=.1
PLOT INV=I,DINV=D/PR=P,CONS=C
PLOT BL=B,DBL=G/P=$
PLOT MDPP=M/L=L,DL=F/RCI=R/DPROD=D
RUN  FIGURE 3-40
C LENGTH=40
C DT=.0625
C SSC=.15
C LEX=0
C CST=2
PLOT INV=I,DINV=D/PR=P,CONS=C/BL=B,DBL=G
PLOT DPROD=D/CAP=K,DCAP=A/OC=O
RUN  FIGURE 4-8
C LENGTH=40
C PLTPER=1
C RSW=1
PLOT INV=I/BL=B/PR=P/CAP=C
PLOT FDK=F
C LEX=0
```

```
RUN  FIGURES 4-10 AND 4-11
C LENGTH=40
C LEX=0
C TAPR=5
C TCIB=2.5
C SSC=.15
C NBC=2
RUN  FIGURE 4-12
C LEX=.5
C SW3=1
C LENGTH=40
C SDNPR=.1
PLOT PR=P/CAP=C
PLOT INV=I/L=L
RUN  FIGURE 5-5
C LEX=.5
C SW3=1
C LENGTH=100
C SDNPR=.1
PLOT L=L/PR=P/CAP=C
RUN  FIGURE 5-6
C LEX=.5
C SW3=1
C LENGTH=100
C SDNTC=.1
RUN  FIGURE 5-7
```

# Appendix C
# Equation Structure of System Dynamics Models

This appendix briefly outlines the equation format used in system dynamics modeling. The focus here is on explaining the mechanics of constructing a system dynamics model as a minimum basis for understanding the equations given in the text. The conceptual and theoretical foundations of system dynamics are presented in Forrester (1961, 1968) and Goodman (1974).

In formal mathematical terms, system dynamics models are systems of discrete difference equations. Such systems have the general form:

$$L_t = L_{t-\Delta t} + \Delta(L_{t-\Delta t}) \tag{C.1}$$

$$\Delta(L_{t-\Delta t}) = f(L_{t-\Delta t}) \tag{C.2}$$

In Equation (C.1), $L_t$ is the value of variable L at time t.[1] Equation (C.1), then, indicates that the present value of L, denoted $L_t$, equals the previous value of the variable $\Delta$t time units ago, $L_{t-\Delta t}$, plus the change in L occurring over the interval (t − $\Delta$t) to t. Equation (C.2) states that the change in L, denoted $\Delta(L_{t-\Delta t})$, is some function f of $L_{t-\Delta t}$. As discussed below, the time interval between computations, $\Delta$t, is chosen sufficiently small so that the behavior of L over time approximates that of a continuous system.

## C.1 Computation Sequence

The following section outlines the principal features of the DYNAMO computer language and the computation scheme used to trace the behavior of a system dynamics model.[2] The computation progresses in time steps as in Figure C-1. The figure assumes that the computations at time 5 have been completed, ready to begin computing the condition of the system at the next solution period, 5 + DT. The symbol DT, difference in time, is used for the length of the time interval between computations. The 5 and the 6 in the figure represent the units of time used in defining the system, for example, weeks or months, but the appropriate solution interval need not be the same

[1]For readers with a background in matrix algebra, the variable L may be thought of as a vector of variables $L_1$ through $L_n$, with equations (C.1) and (C.2) describing the behavior of the entire vector defined by L.

[2]Most of the succeeding material is drawn from Forrester (1968), with permission of the author and publisher.

as the unit of time measurement. The figure illustrates a situation where there are four computations of system condition in each unit of time.

As shown in Figure C-1, the arbitrary convention has been adopted of using K to designate the point in time to which the current computation applies. The time 5 + DT is designated by the K as being the point in the time sequence now being evaluated. Correspondingly, J is used to designate the time at which the preceding computation was made, and L to designate the next point in time. The equations are so structured that no other points in time need enter into the computation process. The computation is confined completely to the time J, the interval JK from J to K, the time K, and the interval KL.

At the start of the computations at time K, there are available from the previous computations the levels at time J and the rates of flow that existed over the interval JK. In Figure C-1 the levels L1.J and L2.J designate two values of levels (system states) at time J.[3] Also illustrated are three rates that existed over the time interval JK: the rate R1.JK flowed into level L1 and is the only rate that affected level L1; the rate R2I.JK flowed into level L2; and the rate R20.JK flowed out of level L2.

The rates of flow are expressed in the time units of the system, such as dollars per week (in Figure C-1, the time unit is from 5 to 6), not in terms of the solution interval DT. The selection of a solution interval DT is a technical matter to be discussed later and usually can be specified only after the model has already been constructed in terms of the time unit that is customarily used in the real system being represented.

In Figure C-1, all the information is available that is needed to compute the new values of levels at time K. But the new values of rates for the KL interval cannot yet be computed because they depend on the not-yet-available levels at time K. The constant rates of flow during the JK interval acted on the levels beginning at time J and caused the levels to change at a uniform slope over the interval. The new values of levels are found by adding and subtracting the changes represented by the rates. The changes are found by multiplying the rates by the solution time interval. For example, the change in inventory in a one-quarter-month solution interval caused by a production rate of 800

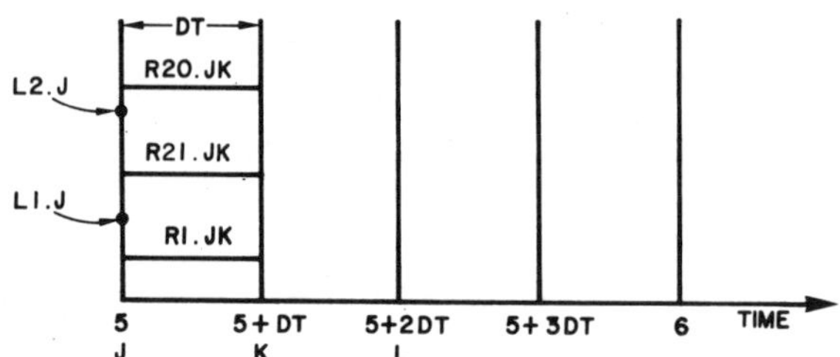


**Figure C-1** Start of new computation sequence
Source: Adapted from Forrester (1968).

[3]As discussed in section C.2, a "level" or a "stock" variable is an accumulation, such as a bank balance, an inventory of goods, or a level of employment. A "rate" is a flow that either increases or decreases a level. For example, a bank balance (a level) is increased by the rate of deposit of money (measured in dollars per unit time) and by the rate of accrual of interest. The bank balance is decreased through the withdrawal rate of money.

cartons per month would be 200 cartons added to inventory. All the levels can be computed. The sequence of computation does not matter because each level depends only on its own old value and on rates in the JK interval. No level depends directly on any other level. Finishing the computation of levels creates the situation in Figure C-2, where the new levels for time K are now available. Although no values are actually computed except at the discrete solution intervals separated by DT, the nature of the rate and level equations implies that the constant rates have caused continuously changing levels as shown by the dashed lines. Levels are continuous curves in the form of connected straight-line sections that can change slope at the solution times.

Only the present values of levels at time K are needed to compute the forthcoming rates that represent the action during the KL interval, for the forthcoming action is based only on the currently available information at time K. Once all levels are computed, the rates can be computed. The order in which the rates are computed does not matter because they do not depend on one another. All the information needed for all the rates is available in the levels at time K.

The computation of the new rates brings the situation to that in Figure C-3. The rates of flow are thought of as constant over a solution interval and change discontinuously to a new value at the solution time. The solution intervals are taken short enough that the stepwise discontinuities in rates are of no significance. Figure C-3 shows the completion of the computations at time K. The entire process is now repeated for the next point in time. To do this, the first step is to advance the time designators, J, K, and L, by one solution interval as shown in Figure C-4. Relative to the new position of K, the conditions are the same as in Figure C-1. The K levels have become the J levels,

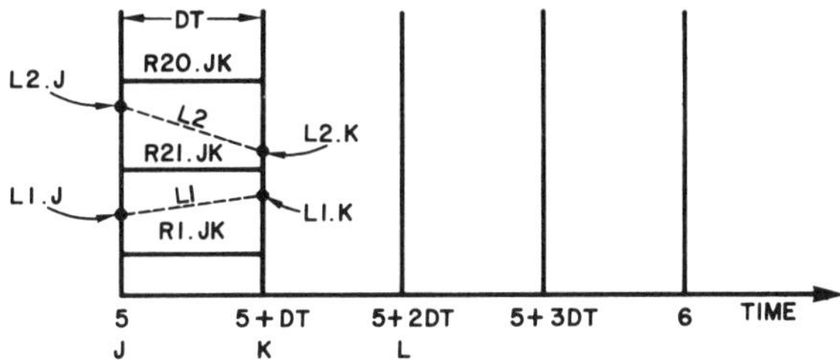


**Figure C-2** After computation of levels

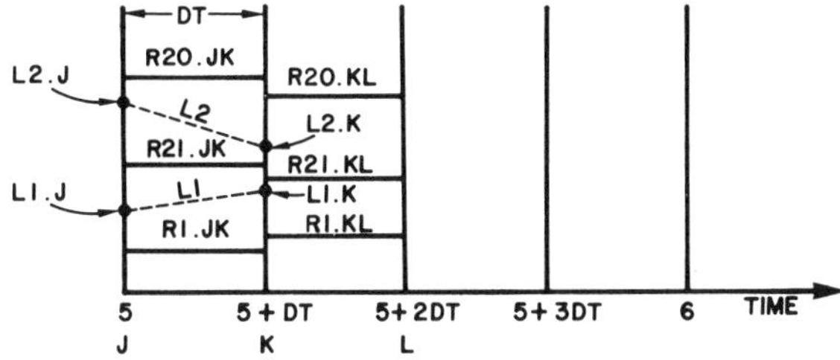


**Figure C-3** After computation of rates

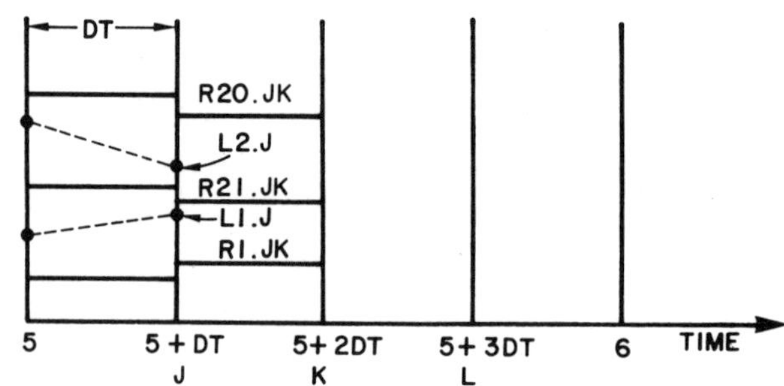


**Figure C-4** Time designators advanced to next solution interval

and the KL rates have become the JK rates. The levels at time J and the rates for the interval JK are available, and the new values of levels can be computed.

A variation from the level-rate sequence of computation occurs at the beginning time, t = 0, for a simulation series. The initial values of all levels must be given. The rates before time = 0 are immaterial. With the levels already available, the computation begins by computing the rates for the interval from time = 0 to time = 0 + DT. Thereafter, the full cycle of computing first the levels and then the rates is followed.

## C.2 Level Equations

A level equation represents a reservoir to accumulate the rates of flow that increase and decrease the content of the reservoir. The new value of a level is calculated by adding to or subtracting from the previous value the change that has occurred during the intervening time interval. The following format is used for a level equation:[4]

L.K = L.J. + (DT)(RA.JK – RS.JK) L

L = level (units)
L.K = new value of level being computed at time K (units)
L.J = value of level from previous time J (units)
DT = the length of the solution interval between time J and time K (time measure)
RA = rate being added to level L (units/time measure)
RA.JK = the value of the rate added during the JK time interval (units per time measure)
RS = rate being subtracted from level L (units per time measure)
RS.JK = the value of the rate subtracted during the JK time interval (units per time measure)

A flow diagram of the level L and rates RA and RS is shown in Figure C-5. The level is represented as a rectangle, and the rates of flow as valves. The solid line through RA into L indicates that RA is an inflow rate to L. The flow originates in a cloud. Such a cloud symbol represents a source. The designation of the source of the

[4]Recall from Chapter 3 that an L at the right side of an equation denotes an equation defining a level variable.

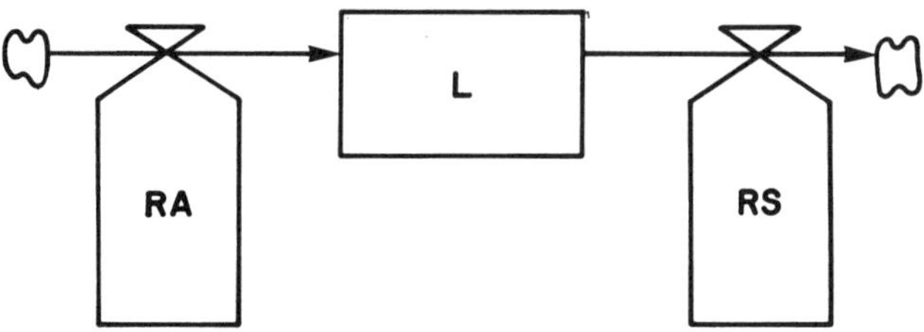


**Figure C-5** A level variable with a single inflow and a single outflow

flow with a cloud indicates that the flow originates outside the boundary of the system being studied.[5] Analogously, the flow into the cloud at the right of Figure C-5 represents a destination or ''sink'' lying outside the system boundary.[6]

Any number of rates, one or more, can be added to or subtracted from a level. This is the only flexibility permissible in the standard level equation. The right-hand side of the equation must contain the previous value of the level being computed. It must also contain the solution interval DT as a multiplier of the flow rates. The level equation is the only equation type that properly contains the solution interval DT.

The solution interval DT is a parameter of the computing process, not a parameter of the real system that the model represents. The flow rates of the system, measured in units per time (for example, dollars per year, or men per month) are accumulated in steps or batches over the successive time intervals of DT in length. The solution interval DT, measured in units of time, converts the flow rates to a quantity of the item flowing. It is this product of flow rate multiplied by time that creates the correct units of measure for adding to the value of the level. The solution interval can be arbitrarily changed (if it does not become too long) without affecting the validity of the model.[7] All other equations in the model are formulated in terms of the basic unit of time used in the real system. The solution interval DT should not appear in any equation other than a level equation.

The level equation performs the process of integration. In the notation of calculus and differential equations, the preceding level equation would be written as follows:

$$L_t = L_0 + \int_0^t (RA - RS)dt,$$

where

$L_t$ = the value of the level at any time t (units)

$L_0$ = the initial value of the level at t = 0

$\int_0^t$ = the operator indicating integration or accumulation from time = 0 until time = t of the difference in flow rates (RA − RS)

[5]See Forrester (1961) for a discussion of the criteria for selecting a model boundary.

[6]A flow between two levels within the system boundary would be represented by a solid line from the source level to the destination level.

[7]See Forrester (1961), sec. 7.5 and app. D, for a discussion of the criteria for selecting DT.

RA = the flow rate being added
RS = the flow rate being subtracted
dt = the differential operator representing the infinitesimally small difference in time that multiplies the flow rates (corresponds to the coarser time steps represented by DT)

As described at the beginning of Appendix C, a level equation is also known as a first-order difference equation in the branch of mathematics dealing with step-by-step integration.

## C.3 Rate Equations

Rate equations state how the flows within a system are controlled. The inputs to a rate equation are system levels and constants. The output of a rate equation controls a flow to, from, or between levels.

Following the time notation of Section C.2, the rate equation is computed at time K, using the information from levels at time K, to find the forthcoming flow rates for the KL interval.

The form of a rate equation is:

$$R.KL = f(\text{levels and constants}),$$

where the right-hand side implies any function, or relationship, of levels and constants that describes the policy controlling the rate.

The rate equations are policy statements that tell how decisions are made. The policy (rate equation) is the general statement of how the pertinent information is to be converted into a decision (or flow or present action stream, all being synonymous terms). The rate equations tell how the system controls itself.

The words *policy* and *decision* have broader meanings here than in common usage. They go beyond the usual human decisions and include the control processes that are implicit in system structure and in habit and tradition. A rate equation (or policy statement) might describe how the hiring rate in a firm depends on the level of vacancies and the level of available unemployed. A rate equation could also represent the subjective and intuitive responses of people to the social pressures within an organization; or a rate equation might represent the explicit policies that control inventory ordering on the basis of current inventory and the average sales rate.

The rate equations are more subtle than the level equations. The rate equations state our perception of how the real-system decisions respond to the circumstances surrounding the decision point.

## C.4 Auxiliary Equations

Very often the clarity and meaning of a rate equation can be enhanced by dividing it into parts that are written as separate equations. These parts, called *auxiliary equations*, are algebraic subdivisions of the rates.

Suppose that desired inventory in an inventory ordering equation is a variable that depends on the average sales rate. A flow diagram of the system appears in Figure

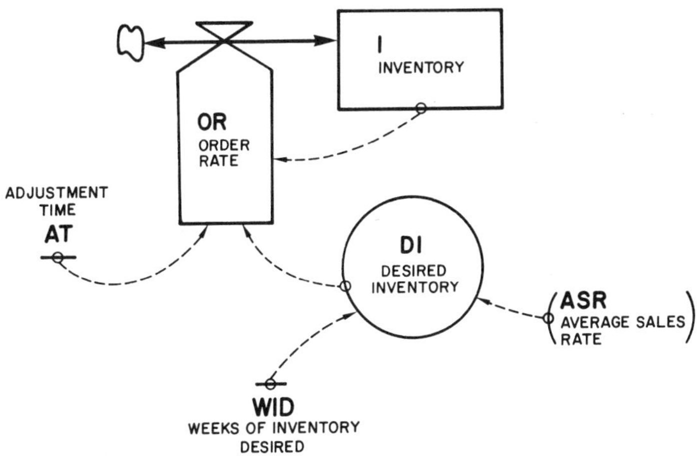


**Figure C-6** A simple inventory-control model

C-6.[8] The rate equation for ordering and the accompanying auxiliary equation for desired inventory could then be:

$$OR.KL = \frac{1}{AT}(DI.K - I.K)$$

$$DI.K = (WID)(ASR.K),$$

OR =order rate (units per week)
AT =adjustment time (weeks)
DI =desired inventory (units)
I =inventory (units)
WID =weeks of inventory desired (weeks)
ASR =average sales rate (units per week)

In the preceding equation, WID is a constant, the value of which states the desired inventory in terms of weeks of average sales. The expression for DI can be substituted into the rate equation to create the following rate equation that depends only on levels and constants:[9]

$$OR.KL = \frac{1}{AT}\Big[(WID)\ (ASR.K) - I.K\Big] \qquad R$$

[8]In the flow diagram, circles represent auxiliary variables. Information links, shown as dashed lines, are drawn from any level or auxiliary variable to each auxiliary and rate variable it affects. Thus, for example, in Figure C-6, an information link is drawn from inventory I to order rate OR. Constants are shown in flow diagrams by short solid lines above or beneath the name; the lines are connected by information links to all rates or auxiliary variables that depend on the particular constant. Thus, for example, Figure C-6 shows that desired inventory DI depends on the constant WID. Finally, in Figure C-6, the average sales rate ASR is shown enclosed in parentheses with an information link to DI. The parentheses indicate that the determinants of ASR lie outside the flow diagram being considered.

[9]An *average* sales rate is a level variable. A simple test to distinguish levels and rates is the following. Suppose all action in the system halted. Then all rates of flow would be zero, but all level variables would continue to exist. Thus, for example, if all activity in a firm stopped, there would be no sales rate, but the average sales rate over the previous year or month would still exist. See Forrester (1961, 1968) for a further discussion of level and rate variables.

In this form, the auxiliary equation has disappeared.

Auxiliary equations must be evaluated after the level equations on which they depend, and before the rate equations of which they are a part. When auxiliary equations exist—and they ordinarily will be numerous—the computation is in the sequence of levels, auxiliaries, and rates.

Unlike the levels and rates, auxiliary equations can depend on other auxiliary equations in a chain, so some groups of equations may have to be evaluated in a particular order. When there are interlinked chains of auxiliary equations, they must be evaluated in the sequence that permits successive substitution. Such a sequence will always exist in a properly formulated system.

## C.5 Constant and Initial Value Equations

*Constants.* A constant, represented by a symbolic name, is given a numerical value in a constant equation. It carries the type designator C after the equation number. A constant has no time postscript because it does not change through time.

$$\text{XY.K} = (\text{AB})\,(\text{Z.K}) \qquad \text{A}$$
$$\text{AB} = 15 \qquad \text{C}$$

The value of the constant AB is given in the preceding constant equation. In model listings, the equation number of a constant will be given as a decimal subdivision of the primary equation number in which the constant first appears.

*Initially Computed Constants.* It is often convenient to specify one constant in terms of another constant when the two constants always bear a fixed relationship to each other. Suppose the constant CD is always to be 14 times the value of AB. CD would then be written as

$$\text{CD} = (14)\,(\text{AB}) \qquad \text{N}$$

The type designator N (the same as for the initial value equations that give the initial values of levels) indicates that this equation need be evaluated only once at the beginning of the simulation computation, because the constants, by their very nature and definition, are values that are not to vary during any one simulation run.

*Initial Value Equations.* All level equations must be given initial values at the start of the simulation computation. These level variables represent the complete condition of the system necessary for determining the forthcoming flow rates. All system history that influences present action is represented by *present* values of appropriate level variables. It is the present version of history represented in the present values of system levels that governs present action. Initial values for rate variables need not and should not be given because they are fully determined by the initial values of the level variables.

From the initial values of level variables, the rates of flow immediately following time zero can be computed and, with the initial values and the rates, the new values of levels at the end of the first time step can be computed. The initial value equation will carry the type designator N after the equation number. No time postscripts are used. The right side of the initial value equation is written in terms of numerical values, symbolically indicated constants, and the initial values of other levels. An initial value equation is customarily written immediately following the corresponding level equation:

$$PT.K = PT.J + (DT)(M.JK - N.JK) \qquad L$$
$$PT = 8 \qquad N$$

The initial value equation above could also have been written in terms of constants as

$$PT = (3)(CD) \qquad N$$

or

$$PT = AB \qquad N$$

It is unambiguous and permissible to state an initial value of one level equation in terms of the initial value of some other level as long as the latter is independent of the first. For example, the following initial value depends on the initial value of the variable PT:

$$RS.K = RS.J + (DT)(ML.JK - NL.JK) \qquad L$$
$$RS = PT \qquad N$$

## C.6 Table Equations

A table equation (table function) gives the numerical values of a dependent variable as a function of an independent variable over a specified range. Such equations represent a simple way of expressing relationships, particularly nonlinear relations, between variables. For example, suppose that the average lifetime of capital equipment in a firm is a function of the need for capital as measured by a variable called the capital ratio CR. A simple model of this process is given in the equations:[10]

```
ALC.K=(NLC)(MCDLC.K)                                    71, A
NLC=15                                                  71.1, C
    ALC    - AVERAGE LIFETIME OF CAPITAL   (YEARS)
    NLC    - NORMAL LIFETIME OF CAPITAL   (YEARS)
    MCDLC  - MULTIPLIER FROM CAPITAL DEMAND ON LIFETIME
               OF CAPITAL (DIMENSIONLESS)

MCDLC.K=TABLE(TMCDLC,CR.K,0,2,.5)                       72, A
TMCDLC=1.4/1.15/1/.85/.75                               72.1, T
    MCDLC  - MULTIPLIER FROM CAPITAL DEMAND ON LIFETIME
               OF CAPITAL (DIMENSIONLESS)
    TMCDLC - TABLE FOR MULTIPLIER FROM CAPITAL DEMAND ON
               LIFETIME OF CAPITAL
    CR     - CAPITAL RATIO   (DIMENSIONLESS)
```

In these equations, the average lifetime of capital ALC equals a normal lifetime times a multiplier from capital demand on the lifetime of capital MCDLC. MCDLC, in turn, is specified as a table (TABLE) function of the capital ratio (Figure C-7). The table TMCDLC gives the values of MCDLC for corresponding values of CR between 0 and 2 at intervals of 0.5. Thus, for example, if CR is 0, MCDLC has a value of 1.4;

[10]See Chapter 4, section 4.2, for a discussion of this example.

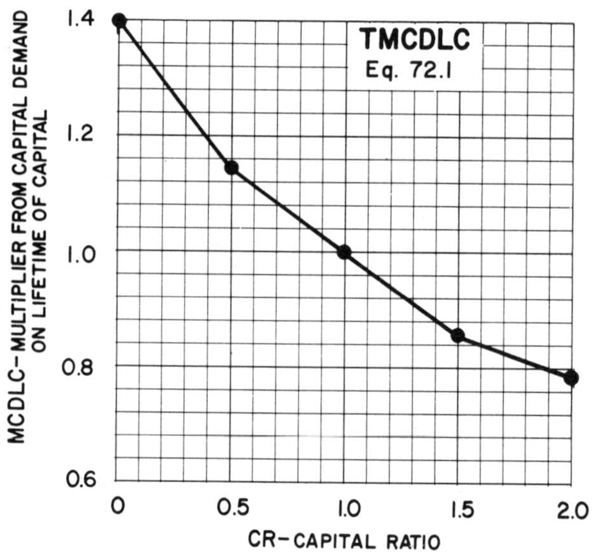


**Figure C-7** The influence of capital demand on average lifetime of capital

when CR is 0.5, MCDLC equals 1.15, and so on. If CR takes on a value intermediate between two points, say 0.2, a corresponding value of MCDLC is obtained by extrapolating linearly between the two values in the table function, here yielding a value of 1.3 [ = 1.15 + (1.4 − 1.15) (0.2/0.5)]. If CR exceeds the specification range (say, it equals 4), MCDLC will assume the corresponding extreme value of the table function (here 0.75, meaning that the average lifetime of capital is never below 75 percent of its normal life).

## C.7 Specification Cards

To simulate a model and plot the resulting output, several constants must be specified: the solution interval for the simulation (the DT), the total length of the simulation (denoted LENGTH), and the interval between successive plot-outs of a variable (denoted plot-period or PLTPER); in addition, the variables to be plotted must be listed on plot cards. A sample set of specification cards could appear as:

```
DT = .1                       C
LENGTH = 40                   C
PLTPER = 1                    C
PLOT HR = H (400,1200)
```

In these equations, DT, LENGTH, and PLTPER are all defined as constants. The LENGTH of the simulation is 40 years and PLTPER is 1 year, so 40 values of each variable will be plotted. In the simple example above, only one variable, hiring rate HR, is plotted. The PLOT statement designates that HR should be plotted with the symbol H on a scale of 400 to 1,200 men per year. If no range for a particular output variable is specified, the DYNAMO compiler will automatically set the vertical plot scales.

# Appendix D
# Delays

This appendix provides a brief introduction to the formulation and behavior of delays. A delay, as described by Forrester,

> is essentially a conversion process that accepts a given inflow rate and delivers a resulting flow rate at the output. The outflow may differ instant by instant from the inflow rate under dynamic circumstances where the rates are changing in value. This necessarily implies that the delay contains a variable amount of the quantity in transit. The content of the delay increases whenever the inflow exceeds the outflow, and vice versa.
>
> A delay is a special, simplified category of the general concept of inventories or levels. All levels exist to permit the inflow rates to differ, over limited intervals, from the outflow rates.[1]

The delays typically used in system dynamics modeling belong to the class of exponential delays. These delays are simple in form and simulate real-world delay processes in a fairly realistic manner.[2] Section D.1 discusses the formulation of material delays. Section D.2 discusses information delays (exponential averages) and describes the basic relationships between information and material delays.

## D.1 Material Delays

A first-order material delay consists simply of a level (which absorbs the difference between the inflow and outflow rates) and an outflow rate that depends on the level and on an average delay time. The outflow rate of a material delay equals the level divided by the average delay time (which may in principle be either a constant or a variable):

OUT.KL = LEV.K/DEL R

where

OUT = outflow from delay

[1]Forrester (1961), p. 86.

[2]This appendix discusses only the simplest form of exponential delays, termed first-order delays. (See ibid., chap. 9 and app. H for a discussion.) In the economic and econometric literature, first-order exponential-delay formulations are frequently called Koyck transformations.

LEV = level measuring contents of delay
DEL = average delay time

The representation of a material delay also includes an equation to generate the level representing the total amount of goods, money, or people in transit. Taken together, the level and overflow rate equations serve to convert an inflow rate IN into a delayed outflow OUT, as follows:

LEV.K = LEV.J + (DT) (IN.JK − OUT.JK)  L

where

LEV = level measuring contents of delay
IN = inflow to delay
OUT = outflow from delay

As an example of a material delay, we might consider the response of the hiring rate in a firm to the rate of new vacancy creation. In Figure D-1, the rate of new vacancy creation NVC augments the level of vacancies VAC. The hiring rate HR is an outflow from the vacancy level and equals the level of vacancies VAC divided by the delay in filling vacancies DFV. Thus, for example, if DFV is 4 weeks, then one-quarter of all vacancies would be filled, on average, each week. The level of vacancies therefore represents a delay between new-vacancy creation (representing the decision to hire people) and the actual hiring rate.

A first-order delay, as in Figure D-1, responds to a step increase in the inflow rate as shown in Figure D-2. In Figure D-2, the output of the delay gradually rises toward the input rate and eventually equals it. The delay characteristics of the system are represented by the interval during which the output variable lags behind the input.

## D.2 Information Delays

Information delays, also called exponential averages, arise in any channel when data are smoothed or averaged in an effort to detect underlying trends. Smoothing or

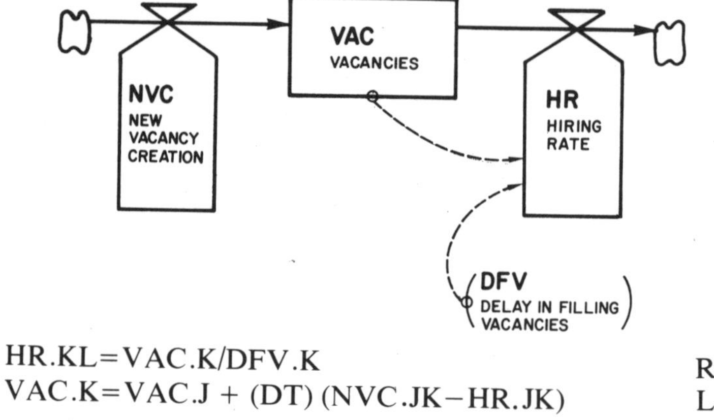


HR.KL=VAC.K/DFV.K  R
VAC.K=VAC.J + (DT) (NVC.JK−HR.JK)  L

**Figure D-1** The hiring rate as a delayed version of vacancy creation

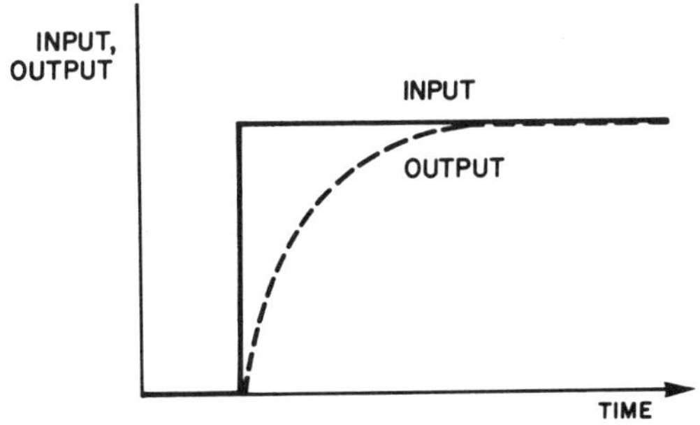


**Figure D-2** Step response of a first-day order material delay

averaging necessarily introduces some delay in decision making, as decisions are normally deferred until persistent or stable patterns are detected; for example, increased orders for a firm's product may only lead to an expansion of output if the higher order rate persists for several weeks or months.

Information delays are represented in system dynamics models in the following manner:

$$\text{OUT.K} = \text{OUT.J} + (\text{DT/DEL})\,(\text{IN.JK} - \text{OUT.J}) \qquad \text{L}$$

where

OUT = output of delay
DEL = average delay time
IN = input to the delay

In the preceding equations, IN is the variable being smoothed, and OUT is the smoothed value of IN. OUT equals its previous value (OUT.J) plus a correction term that is proportional to the difference between the input and output. Thus, if the input IN exceeds the output, OUT will gradually increase toward it over time. Analogously, if IN exceeds OUT, OUT will decline toward it. The delay time DEL measures the interval over which the adjustment takes place. A long delay time will produce a gradual adjustment, thereby heavily smoothing the data to filter out random noise from the observations of IN; analogously, a short delay time will produce rapid adjustment and, consequently, low smoothing.[3]

The first-order information delay has the same time response as a first-order material delay with the same delay time. In fact, the information and material delays are identical if the delay time DEL is constant over time. This equivalence can be seen by rewriting the equations in section D.1 to "solve" for the output OUT in terms of the input IN. Rewriting the output equation one time-period earlier:

$$\text{OUT.JK} = \text{LEV.J/DEL}.$$

Solving for LEV.J now yields

[3]The information delay can also be written in a simpler form:

$$\text{OUT.K} = \text{SMOOTH(IN.JK,DEL)}. \qquad \text{A}$$

The DYNAMO compiler will automatically convert this notation into the equations given in the text.

$$\text{LEV.J} = (\text{OUT.JK})(\text{DEL}).$$

Substituting into the level equation,

$$\text{LEV.K} = (\text{OUT.JK})(\text{DEL}) + (\text{DT})(\text{IN.JK} - \text{OUT.JK}).$$

Finally, substituting for LEV.K and dividing by DEL yields

$$\text{OUT.KL} = \text{OUT.JK} + (\text{DT}/\text{DEL})(\text{IN.JK} - \text{OUT.JK}).$$

The last equation is of the same form as the first-order information delay. The information and material delays differ only when the delay time DEL is in itself a variable. By analyzing the respective equations for information and material delays, the reader can verify that the output of an information delay is unaffected if its delay time is altered, while the output of a material delay is changed if its delay time changes.[4] The explanation for these results is stated by Forrester:

> A material delay should not lose or create any units in the flow that is traveling through it. This means that in a material delay with a constant inflow rate the outflow will exhibit a transient change if the delay constant is changed. It is necessary that the output should differ from the input for a time long enough for the internal level stored in the delay to be adjusted. . . .
>
> On the other hand, in delaying the flow of a constantly repeated value of information, this value should not change merely because the transmission delay is changed.[5]

[4] See Forrester (1961), app. H, for a detailed discussion.
[5] Ibid., p. 418.

# Bibliography


Abramovitz (1950) — Abramovitz, Moses. *Inventories and Business Cycles* (New York: National Bureau of Economic Research, 1950).

Abramovitz (1961) — Abramovitz, Moses. "The Nature and Significance of Kuznets Cycles," *Economic Development and Cultural Change*, vol. 9 (April 1961).

Adelman and Adelman (1959) — Adelman, I., and F. L. Adelman. "The Dynamic Properties of the Klein-Goldberger Model," *Econometrica*, vol. 27, no. 4 (October 1959), pp. 596–625.

Aftalion (1909) — Aftalion, Albert. "La réalité des sur productions générals: essai d'une théorie des crises générals et périodiques," *Révue d'économie politique*, 1909.

Aftalion (1927) — Aftalion, Albert. "The Theory of Economic Cycles Based on the Capitalistic Technique of Production," *Review of Economic Statistics*, October 1927.

Alexander (1958) — Alexander, Sidney S. "Rate of Change Approaches to Forecasting—Diffusion Indexes, and First Differences," *Economic Journal*, vol. 68 (June 1958).

Allen (1959) — Allen, R. G. D. *Mathematical Economics* (London: Macmillan & Co., 1959).

American Economics Association (1944) — American Economics Association. *Readings in Business Cycle Theory* (Philadelphia, Pa.: The Blakeston Company, 1944).

Ando et al. (1973) — Ando, Albert, Franco Modigliani, Robert Rasche, and Stephen J. Turnovsky. "On the Role of Expectations of Price and Technological Change in an Investment Function," mimeographed (Cambridge, Mass., 1973).

Bain (1939) — Bain, J. S. "The Relation of the Economic Life of Equipment to Reinvestment Cycles," *Review of Economic Statistics*, vol. 21 (May 1939), pp. 79–88.

Bergmann (1974) — Bergmann, Barbara R. "A Microsimulation of the Macroeconomy with Explicitly Represented Money Flows," *Annals of Social and Economic Measurement*, vol. 3, no. 3 (July 1974), pp. 475–493.

Bischoff (1971) — Bischoff, Charles W. "Business Investment in the 1970s: A Comparison of Models," *Brookings Papers on Economic Activity* (1971:1), pp. 13–64.

Bouniatian (1924) — Bouniatian, M. "Ma théorie des crises et les critiques de M. Aftalion," *Revue d'economie politique*, 1924.

Bower (1972) — Bower, Joseph. *Managing the Resource Allocation Process* (Homewood, Ill.: Richard D. Irwin, 1972).

Bronfenbrenner (1969) — Bronfenbrenner, Martin, ed. *Is the Business Cycle Obsolete?* (New York: John Wiley & Sons, 1969).

Burns (1934) — Burns, Arthur F. *Production Trends in the United States since 1870* (New York: National Bureau of Economic Research, 1934).

Burns (1969) — Burns, Arthur F. *The Business Cycle in a Changing World* (New York: National Bureau of Economic Research, 1969).

Burns and Mitchell (1946) — Burns, Arthur F., and Wesley C. Mitchell. *Measuring Business Cycles* (New York: National Bureau of Economic Research, 1946).

Chenery (1952) — Chenery, Hollis B. "Overcapacity and the Acceleration Principle," *Econometrica*, vol. 20 (January 1952), pp. 1–28.

Clark and Cohen (1963) — Clark, John J., and Morris Cohen, eds. *Business Fluctuations, Growth, and Economic Stabilization* (New York: Random House, 1963).

Clark (1917) — Clark, John M. "Business Acceleration and the Law of Demand: A Technical Factor in Economic Cycles," *Journal of Political Economy*, vol. 25, no. 3 (March 1917), pp. 217–235.

Cobb and Douglas (1928) — Cobb, C. W., and P. H. Douglas. "A Theory of Production," *American Economic Review*, vol. 18, no. 1 (March 1928), pp. 139–165.

Creamer (1964) — Creamer, Daniel. "Estimates of Capacity Utilization in Manufacturing: A Description and Appraisal," in *Inflation, Growth, and Employment*, edited by Joseph W. Conard (New York: Prentice-Hall, 1964).

Daly (1969) — Daly, Donald J. "Business Cycles in Canada: Their Persistence," in Bronfenbrenner (1969), chap. 2.

Darling (1959) — Darling, Paul G. "Manufacturer's Inventory Investment, 1947–1958," *American Economic Review*, vol. 49, no. 4 (December 1959), pp. 950–962.

Dennison (1922) — Dennison, Henry S. "Management and Business Cycles," *Journal of the American Statistical Association*, vol. 18 (March 1922), pp. 20–31.

Douglas (1948) — Douglas, Paul H. "Are There Laws of Production?" *American Economic Review*, vol. 38, no. 1 (March 1948), pp. 1–41.

Duesenberry (1958) — Duesenberry, James S. *Business Cycles and Economic Growth* (New York: McGraw-Hill, 1958).

Eisner (1957) — Eisner, Robert. "Interview and Other Survey Techniques and the Study of Investment," in National Bureau of Economic Research (1957).

Eisner (1963) — Eisner, Robert. "Investment Plans and Realizations," *American Economic Review*, vol. 53 (May 1963), pp. 237–246.

Evans (1969) — Evans, Michael K. *Macroeconomic Activity* (New York: Harper & Row, 1969).

Forrester (1961) — Forrester, Jay W. *Industrial Dynamics* (Cambridge, Mass.: The MIT Press, 1961).

Forrester (1968) — Forrester, Jay W. *Principles of Systems* (Cambridge, Mass.: Wright-Allen Press, 1968).

Forrester (1973) — Forrester, Jay W. "Inflation—Comments on the Speech of December 29, 1972, by Arthur F. Burns," System Dynamics Group Memorandum D-1771-1 (Cambridge, Mass.: M.I.T., February 1973).

| | |
|---|---|
| Forrester (1975) | Forrester, Jay W. "Understanding Social and Economic Change in the United States," *Proceedings of the 1975 Computer Simulation Conference*, San Francisco, July 1975. |
| Forrester, Low, and Mass (1974) | Forrester, Jay W., Gilbert W. Low, and Nathaniel J. Mass. "The Debate on *World Dynamics*: A Response to Nordhaus," *Policy Sciences*, June 1974. |
| Frank (1923) | Frank, Lawrence K. "A Theory of Business Cycles," *Quarterly Journal of Economics*, vol. 37 (August 1923), pp. 625–642. |
| Friedman (1957) | Friedman, Milton. *A Theory of the Consumption Function* (Princeton, N.J.: Princeton University Press, 1957). |
| Friedman and Schwartz (1963) | Friedman, Milton, and Anna J. Schwartz. "Money and Business Cycles," *Review of Economics and Statistics*, vol. 45 (February 1963), pp. 32–78. |
| Frisch (1933) | Frisch, Ragnar. "Propagation Problems and Impulse Problems in Dynamic Economics," in *Economic Essays in Honor of Gustav Cassel* (London: George Allen & Unwin, 1933); reprinted in Gordon and Klein (1965), pp. 155–185. |
| Fromm (1961) | Fromm, Gary. "Inventories, Business Cycles, and Economic Stabilization," in Joint Economic Committee (1961), pt. 4, pp. 37–91. |
| Garvy (1943) | Garvy, George. "Kondratieff's Theory of Long Cycles," *Review of Economic Statistics*, vol. 25 (November 1943), pp. 203–220. |
| Goodman (1974) | Goodman, Michael R. *Study Notes in System Dynamics* (Cambridge, Mass.: Wright-Allen Press, 1974). |
| Goodwin (1948) | Goodwin, R. M. "Secular and Cyclical Aspects of the Multiplier and the Accelerator," in *Income, Employment and Public Policy: Essays in Honor of Alvin H. Hansen*, edited by Lloyd A. Metzler (New York: Norton, 1948), pp. 108–132. |
| Goodwin (1951) | Goodwin, R. M. "The Non-Linear Accelerator and the Persistence of Business Cycles," *Econometrica*, vol. 19, no. 1 (January 1951), pp. 1–17. |
| Goodwin (1955) | Goodwin, R. M. "A Model of Cyclical Growth," in *The Business Cycle in the Postwar World*, edited by E. Lundberg (London: Macmillan & Co., 1955). |
| Gordon (1961) | Gordon, Robert A. *Business Fluctuations* (New York: Harper & Row, 1961). |
| Gordon and Klein (1965) | Gordon, Robert A., and Lawrence R. Klein, eds. *Readings in Business Cycle Theory* (Homewood, Ill.: Richard D. Irwin, 1965). |
| Haberler (1964) | Haberler, Gottfried. *Prosperity and Depression* (London: George Allen & Unwin, 1964). |
| Hansen (1951) | Hansen, Alvin H. *Business Cycles and National Income* (New York: W. W. Norton, 1951). |
| Hawtrey (1926) | Hawtrey, Ralph G. "The Trade Cycle," *De Economist* (Amsterdam), 1926; reprinted in American Economics Association (1944), pp. 330–349. |
| Hawtrey (1928) | Hawtrey, Ralph G. *Trade and Credit* (London: Longmans, Green and Company, 1928). |
| Hayek (1935) | Hayek, F. A. *Prices and Production* (London: George Routledge, 1935). |
| Henize (1974) | Henize, John. "Job Vacancies and the Money Wage Rate in U. S. Manufacturing," System Dynamics Group Memorandum D-1972 (Cambridge, Mass.: M.I.T., January 1974). |

| | |
|---|---|
| Hickman (1963) | Hickman, Bert G. "The Postwar Retardation: Another Long Swing in the Rate of Growth?" *American Economic Review*, vol. 53 (May 1963), pp. 490–507. |
| Hickman (1972) | Hickman, Bert G., ed. *Econometric Models of Cyclical Behavior* (New York: Columbia University Press, 1972). |
| Hicks (1949) | Hicks, John R. "Mr. Harrod's Dynamic Theory," *Economica*, vol. 16 (May 1949), pp. 106–121. |
| Hicks (1950) | Hicks, John R. *A Contribution to the Theory of the Trade Cycle* (London: Clarendon Press, 1950). |
| Holt and Modigliani (1961) | Holt, Charles C., and Franco Modigliani. "Firm Cost Structures and the Dynamic Responses of Inventories, Production, Work Force, and Orders to Sales Fluctuations," in Joint Economic Committee (1961), pt. 2, pp. 1–55. |
| Hultgren (1960) | Hultgren, Thor. *Changes in Labor Cost During Cycles in Production and Business*, National Bureau of Economic Research Occasional Paper 74, 1960. |
| Joint Economic Committee (1961) | Joint Economic Committee. *Inventory Fluctuations and Economic Stabilization* (Washington, D.C., 1961). |
| Jorgensen, Hunter, and Nadiri (1970) | Jorgensen, Dale W., Jerald Hunter, and M. Ishag Nadiri. "A Comparison of Alternative Econometric Models of Quarterly Investment Behavior," *Econometrica*, vol. 38, no. 2 (March 1970), pp. 187–212. |
| Jorgensen and Siebert (1968) | Jorgensen, Dale W., and Calvin Siebert. "A Comparison of Alternative Theories of Corporate Investment Behavior," *American Economic Review*, September 1968, pp. 681–712. |
| Kaldor (1940) | Kaldor, Nicholas. "A Model of the Trade Cycle," *Economic Journal*, vol. 50 (March 1940), pp. 78–92. |
| Kalecki (1935) | Kalecki, M. "A Macro-dynamic Theory of Business Cycles," *Econometrica*, vol. 3 (1935), pp. 327–344. |
| Keynes (1936) | Keynes, John M. *The General Theory of Employment, Interest and Money* (New York: Harcourt, Brace, 1936). |
| Klein (1964) | Klein, Lawrence R. "A Postwar Quarterly Model: Descriptions and Applications," in National Bureau of Economic Research, *Models of Income Determination*, Studies in Income and Wealth, vol. 28 (Princeton, N.J.: Princeton University Press, 1964). |
| Klein (1966) | Klein, Lawrence R. *The Keynesian Revolution* (New York: Macmillan Co., 1966). |
| Klein and Popkin (1961) | Klein, Lawrence R., and Joel Popkin. "An Econometric Analysis of the Postwar Relationship between Inventory Fluctuation and Change in Aggregate Economic Activity," in Joint Economic Committee (1961), pt. 3, pp. 71–86. |
| Klein and Preston (1967) | Klein, Lawrence R., and R. S. Preston. "The Measurement of Capacity Utilization," *American Economic Review*, vol. 57, no. 1 (March 1967), pp. 34–58. |
| Kondratieff (1935) | Kondratieff, N. D. "The Long Waves in Economic Life," *Review of Economic Statistics*, vol. 17 (November 1935), pp. 105–115. |
| Koyck (1954) | Koyck, L. M. *Distributed Lags and Investment Analysis* (Amsterdam: North-Holland Publishing Co., 1954). |
| Kuh (1965) | Kuh, Edwin. "Cyclical and Secular Labor Productivity in United States Manufacturing," *Review of Economics and Statistics*, vol. 47, no. 1 (February 1965), pp. 1–13. |

Kuh and Meyer (1957) — Kuh, Edwin, and J. R. Meyer. *The Investment Decision* (Cambridge, Mass.: Harvard University Press, 1957).

Kuznets (1926) — Kuznets, Simon. *Cyclical Fluctuations, Retail and Wholesale Trade, United States, 1919–1925* (New York: National Bureau of Economic Research, 1926).

Kuznets (1930) — Kuznets, Simon. *Secular Movements in Production and Prices* (New York: Houghton Mifflin, 1930).

Lee (1963) — Lee, Maurice W. *Macroeconomic Fluctuations, Growth, and Stability* (Homewood, Ill.: Richard D. Irwin, 1963).

Lewis and O'Leary (1955) — Lewis, W. A., and P. J. O'Leary. "Secular Swings in Production and Trade, 1870–1913," *Manchester School of Economics and Social Studies*, vol. 23, no. 2 (May 1955), pp. 113–152.

Lovell (1961*a*) — Lovell, Michael C. "Factors Determining Manufacturing Inventory Investment," in Joint Economic Committee (1961), pt. 2, pp. 119–158.

Lovell (1961*b*) — Lovell, Michael C. "Manufacturer's Inventories, Sales Expectations, and the Accelerator Principle," *Econometrica*, vol. 29, no. 3 (July 1961), pp. 293–314.

Lovell (1967) — Lovell, Michael C. "Sales Anticipations," Planned Inventory Investment, and Realizations," in *Determinants of Investment Behavior*, edited by Robert Ferber (New York: Columbia University Press, 1967), pp. 537–580.

Mack (1967) — Mack, Ruth P. *Information, Expectation, and Inventory Fluctuation* (New York: National Bureau of Economic Research, 1967).

Mass (1974*a*) — Mass, Nathaniel J. "A Dynamic Model of Managerial Recruitment and Attrition," System Dynamics Group Memorandum D-1975-1 (Cambridge, Mass.: M.I.T., January 1974).

Mass (1974*b*) — Mass, Nathaniel J. "Self-Learning Revival Policies in Urban Dynamics," in *Readings in Urban Dynamics*, vol. 1, edited by Nathaniel J. Mass (Cambridge, Mass.: Wright-Allen Press, 1974), pp. 227–243.

Mass and Senge (1974) — Mass, Nathaniel J., and Peter M. Senge. "Understanding Oscillations in Simple Systems," System Dynamics Group Memorandum D-2045-1 (Cambridge, Mass.: M.I.T., July 1974).

Mayer and Soneblum (1955) — Mayer, T., and S. Soneblum. "Lead Times for Fixed Investment," *Review of Economics and Statistics*, vol. 37, no. 1 (August 1955), pp. 300–304.

Mayer (1958) — Mayer T. "The Inflexibility of Monetary Policy," *Review of Economics and Statistics*, vol. 40, no. 4 (November 1958), pp. 358–374.

Mayer (1960) — Mayer T. "Plant and Equipment Lead Times," *Journal of Business*, vol. 33, no. 2 (April 1960), pp. 127–132.

Metzler (1941) — Metzler, Lloyd A. "The Nature and Stability of Inventory Cycles," *Review of Economic Statistics*, vol. 23, no. 3 (August 1941), pp. 113–129.

Metzler (1946) — Metzler, Lloyd A. "Business Cycles and the Modern Theory of Employment," *American Economic Review*," vol. 36 (June 1946), pp. 278–291.

Metzler (1947) — Metzler, Lloyd A. "Factors Governing the Length of Inventory Cycles," *Review of Economic Statistics*, vol. 29 (February 1947), pp. 1–15.

Mills (1957) — Mills, Edwin S. "The Theory of Inventory Decisions," *Econometrica*, vol. 25 (April 1957), pp. 222–239.

Mitchell, Thomas W. (1923) — Mitchell, Thomas W. "Competitive Illusion as a Cause of Business Cycles," *Quarterly Journal of Economics*, vol. 38 (August 1923), pp. 631–652.

Mitchell, Wesley C. (1927) — Mitchell, Wesley C. *Business Cycles—The Problem and Its Setting* (New York: National Bureau of Economic Research, 1927).

Mitchell, Wesley C. (1941) — Mitchell, Wesley C. *Business Cycles and Their Causes* (Berkeley: University of California Press, 1941).

Mitchell, Wesley C. (1951) — Mitchell, Wesley C. *What Happens during Business Cycles* (New York: National Bureau of Economic Research, 1951).

Modigliani (1973) — Modigliani, Franco. "The Channels of Monetary Policy in the FMP Econometric Model of the U.S.," Alfred P. Sloan School of Management working paper (Cambridge, Mass.: M.I.T., 1973).

National Bureau of Economic Research (1951) — National Bureau of Economic Research. *Conference on Business Cycles* (New York, 1951).

National Bureau of Economic Research (1957) — National Bureau of Economic Research. *Problems of Capital Formation: Concepts, Measurement, and Controlling Factors* (Princeton, N.J.: Princeton University Press, 1957).

Nurkse (1952) — Nurkse, Ragnar. "The Cyclical Pattern of Inventory Investment," *Quarterly Journal of Economics*, vol. 66 (August 1952).

Nurkse (1954) — Nurkse, Ragnar. "Period Analysis and Inventory Cycles," *Oxford Economic Papers*, vol. 6 (September 1954), pp. 203–225.

Okun (1962) — Okun, Arthur M. "Potential GNP: Its Measurement and Significance," *Proceedings of the Business and Economic Statistics Section of the American Statistical Association*, 1962.

Phillips (1963) — Phillips, A. "An Appraisal of Measures of Capacity," *American Economic Review Papers and Proceedings*, vol. 53, no. 2 (May 1963), pp. 275–292.

Pigou (1920) — Pigou, A. C. *Economics of Welfare* (London: Macmillan & Co., 1920).

Pigou (1927) — Pigou, A. C. *Industrial Fluctuations* (London: Macmillan & Co., 1927).

Robertson (1915) — Robertson, D. H. *A Study of Industrial Fluctuations* (Westminster: P. S. King & Son, 1915).

Robertson (1926) — Robertson, D. H. *Banking Policy and the Price Level* (Westminster: P. S. King & Son, 1926).

Samuelson (1939) — Samuelson, Paul A. "Interactions between the Multiplier Analysis and the Principle of Acceleration," *Review of Economics and Statistics*, vol. 21, no. 2 (May 1939), pp. 75–78.

Samuelson (1973) — Samuelson, Paul A. *Economics* (New York: McGraw-Hill, 1973).

Smith (1970) — Smith, Warren L. *Macroeconomics* (Homewood, Ill.: Richard D. Irwin, 1970).

Smithies (1957) — Smithies, Arthur. "Economic Fluctuations and Growth," *Econometrica*, vol. 25, no. 1 (January 1957), pp. 1–52.

Solow (1962) — Solow, Robert M. "Technical Progress, Capital Formation, and Economic Growth," *American Economic Review*, vol. 52 (May 1962), pp. 76–78.

Sowell (1972) — Sowell, Thomas. *Say's Law* (Princeton University Press, 1972).

Stanback (1961) — Stanback, Thomas M., Jr. *Postwar Cycles in Manufacturers' Inventories* (Princeton, N.J.: Princeton University Press, 1961);

portions reproduced in Joint Economic Committee (1961), pt. 2, pp. 1–143.

Tinbergen (1938) — Tinbergen, Jan. "Statistical Evidence on the Acceleration Principle," *Economica*, May 1938, pp. 164–176.

Tinbergen (1939) — Tinbergen, Jan. *Statistical Testing of Business-Cycle Theories* (Geneva: League of Nations, 1939).

Wardwell (1927) — Wardwell, C. A. *An Investigation of Economic Data for Major Cycles* (Philadelphia, 1927).

Wicksell (1907) — Wicksell, Knut. "The Influence of the Rate of Interest on Prices," *Economic Journal*, vol. 17 (1907), pp. 213–220.

Wicksell (1935) — Wicksell, Knut. *Lectures on Political Economy* (London: Macmillan & Co., 1935).

Zarnowitz (1961) — Zarnowitz, Victor. "The Timing of Manufacturer's Orders during Business Cycles," in *Business Cycle Indicators*, edited by Geoffrey H. Moore (Princeton, N.J.: Princeton University Press, 1961).

Zarnowitz (1972) — Zarnowitz, Victor, ed. *The Business Cycle Today* (New York: National Bureau of Economic Research, 1972).

# List of Figures

# Index

*Notes*

*Notes*

*Notes*

*Notes*

*Notes*

**THE LIFE CYCLE OF ECONOMIC DEVELOPMENT**

by Nathan B. Forrester

Describes a system dynamics model of national economic development for an industrial economy. It interrelates the five production sectors of a national economy to examine the shifting allocation of labor and capital between these sectors as development progresses. The model deals with a 250-year period of economic development and focuses on changes during the 100 year transition phase between growth and equilibrium.

1973, second edition, 194 pages, illustrated

**STUDY NOTES IN SYSTEM DYNAMICS**

by Michael R. Goodman

Collects supplementary material for teaching or self-study in system dynamics. It focuses on simple structures and describes elements of positive, negative, and combined positive and negative feedback loops. A large number of practice exercises with accompanying solutions are included.

1974, paperback, 388 pages, illustrated

**READINGS IN URBAN DYNAMICS: VOLUME 1**

edited by Nathaniel J. Mass

Explores and extends concepts introduced by Jay W. Forrester's *Urban Dynamics*. This collection of papers addresses many of the basic issues raised by reviewers of *Urban Dynamics* and discusses applications of system dynamics to urban policy design.

1974, 303 pages, illustrated

**DYNAMICS OF COMMODITY PRODUCTION CYCLES**

by Dennis L. Meadows

Develops a general model of the economic, biological, technological, and psychological factors which lead to instability in commodity systems. With appropriate parameter values, the model explains the hog, cattle and chicken cycles observed in the real world.

1970, 104 pages, illustrated

**DYNAMICS OF GROWTH IN A FINITE WORLD**

by Dennis L. Meadows, William W. Behrens III, Donella H. Meadows, Roger F. Naill, Jørgen Randers, and Erich K. O. Zahn

Details the research on which the Club of Rome's first report *The Limits To Growth* is based. This technical report describes the purpose and methodology of the global modeling effort and presents the World 3 model equation by equation.

1974, 637 pages, illustrated

**TOWARD GLOBAL EQUILIBRIUM: COLLECTED PAPERS**

edited by Dennis L. Meadows and Donella H. Meadows

Contains 13 papers which describe individual research on dynamic issues evolving from the Club of Rome project. It presents detailed analyses of several important global problems, e.g. DDT and mercury pollution, natural resource depletion, solid waste disposal, etc., and provides policy suggestions which may alleviate these problems. It also examines the economic, political, and ethical implications of growth and the transition to equilibrium.

1973, 358 pages, illustrated

**READINGS IN URBAN DYNAMICS: VOLUME 2**

edited by Schroeder, Alfeld, and Sweeney

Addresses both practical and methodological issues in the field of urban dynamics modeling. The book describes model extensions that permit explicit analysis of land rezoning decisions and the problem of housing abandonment. Includes a full technical report on the application of urban dynamics modeling to Lowell, Massachusetts.

Forthcoming Fall 1975, approximately 400 pages, illustrated

All Wright-Allen Press titles are distributed outside of the United States and Canada exclusively by John Wiley & Sons:

John Wiley & Sons, Inc.
605 Third Avenue
New York, New York 10016
U.S.A.

Orders should be placed with John Wiley & Sons through a local bookseller.